# INTEGRAL EUROPE

# INTEGRAL EUROPE

FAST-CAPITALISM,
MULTICULTURALISM,
NEOFASCISM

*DOUGLAS R. HOLMES*

PRINCETON UNIVERSITY PRESS

PRINCETON AND OXFORD

*Library of Congress Cataloging-in-Publication Data*

Holmes, Douglas R., 1949–
Integral Europe : fast-capitalism, multiculturalism, neofasicsm / Douglas R. Holmes.
p.  cm.
Includes bibliographical references and index.
ISBN 0-691-03388-9 (alk. paper) — ISBN 0-691-05089-9 (pbk. : alk. paper)
1. Political culture—Europe—History—20th century. 2. Political anthropology—
Europe. 3. Political socialization—Europe—History—20th century. 4. Europe—
Economic conditions—1945– 5. Fascism—Europe. 6. Multiculturalism—Europe—
History—20th century. I. Title.

D2009 .H65 2000
940.55—dc21      00-036686

This book has been composed in Sabon

www.pup.princeton.edu

Printed in the United States of America

10  9  8  7  6  5  4  3  2  1

*For Pam and Eli*

# CONTENTS

THIS TEXT EXAMINES how a group of committed partisans sought during the last decade of the twentieth century to recast European society as a moral framework, analytical construct, and empirical fact. The study focuses on their alternative depiction of society, a view of collectivity with deep roots in European romantic tradition and, more broadly, in what Isaiah Berlin calls the "Counter-Enlightenment." In fundamental ways this type of societal framework—which I describe as integralist in nature—is opposed to modernist conceptions of society as embodied, most notably, in the contemporary project of advanced European integration. Integralism is premised on a distinctive orientation to collective experience with unusual intellectual resonances: Johann Herder's populism, expressionism, and pluralism; Emile Durkheim's mechanical solidarity; and Georges Sorel's synthesis of nationalism and socialism. I demonstrate in this text how these elements can be cast as a volatile theory of society.

There are many ways I could have studied the general phenomenon of integralism ethnographically. I initially encountered it in rural districts of Italy, manifest as intimate forms of social practice and as shared idioms of cultural expression, as a style of life. I chose, however, to reorient the research by focusing on politicians who were articulating radical agendas that drew directly on integralist ideals and who sought to exploit the distinctive contemporary struggles they encompassed for individuals and groups. I found these political figures capable of endowing these changes with not just a distinctive narration but also a critical language, a language that drew on what they understood as "inner truths" for its legitimacy and power.

In pursuing this research I have navigated a broad range of scholarship outside of anthropology from the political science of European integration to the history of European fascism. The reader will note that I employ this other scholarship in a double fashion—on the one hand, to further directly my own argumentation and, on the other, to establish an alternative or complementary anthropological perspective on these same issues. My purpose is to contribute to the delineation of a distinctive purview for an anthropology of Europe. I am by no means alone in this project. This preoccupation has been at the center of Michael Herzfeld's work as well as the work of John Borneman.

Although my research is, I believe, fundamentally consistent with the tradition of anthropological work in Europe, it also involves a series of experiments. The most obvious of these is the movement of the analysis across a series of different sites. The major circuit traced in this text is from northern Italy to Strasbourg and Brussels, the two venues of the European Parliament, and finally to the East End of London. I have avoided making broad methodological claims for this kind of multisited maneuver, because I think the reader will see why these moves were necessary given the specific issues I was pursuing and the circumstances that presented themselves during the course of the research.

One final point. I have been tempted to apply the notion of integralism to other very pressing political problems in Europe, problems that were unfolding at some distance from the sites I explored ethnographically. I have resisted this temptation because I did not want to extend the project into areas where I had limited or no expertise. Thus the ghastly formations of integralism that emerged in Serbia, Croatia, Bosnia, and Kosovo in the 1990s have not been included in the analysis. That said, I believe the general framework presented in this book can be applied productively to the fundamental nature of these searing mutations of *European* integralism.

# ACKNOWLEDGMENTS

I BEGAN WRITING this text while teaching at the Graduate Institute of the Liberal Arts at Emory University in the spring of 1996. Ivan Karp and Cory Kratz made my stay at Atlanta productive and enjoyable. They kept me well fed with rich social, intellectual, and culinary fare. I presented the first draft of the introduction at a faculty seminar in the anthropology department at Emory. The responses of faculty and students were helpful in clarifying the peculiar problems of reception this text poses. My graduate students in the ILA, particularly Michael McGovern, made acute observations that stimulated my thinking on the contemporary character of the ethnographic project.

I met with George Marcus on a more or less weekly basis during the writing of this book. We talked about family, children, and academic politics. But our conversation continually returned to a series of recurrent questions: What kind of new domains could be explored ethnographically? How could the ethnographic encounter be staged in new ways? More than anything else, I value these conversations with George as a basis of friendship, but they also clarified my own restlessness about ethnography. This text is very much a product of those interchanges. I am also grateful to the other members of the Rice anthropology department, former and present graduate students, and, especially, Carol Speranza who made my regular visits to the department a particular pleasure.

I am very grateful to my editor, Mary Murrell, who guided the review process through many twists and turns. Michael Herzfeld and the anonymous readers for the press provided critical commentaries that became the basis for very important revisions of the manuscript. I also benefited from critical readings of earlier versions of the manuscript by three Europeanists: Sue Carol Rogers, Gavin Smith, and Thomas Wilson.

Robert Reichlin has been a devoted friend and an intellectual companion for almost two decades, and his insights and reflections have shaped my thinking on many of the issues examined in this text. His refined sense of European history and its disturbing moral tensions have been of enormous value. During a particularly unsettled decade of my life Chip Briscoe and Ellen Bourdeaux made me feel at home at their farm in Richmond, Texas. They are generous and tolerant friends who gave me a place to live and work. I am very fortunate to have Amy Blakemore as a friend. She is one of the most complex humans I know whose deep humanity and pranksterism help keep me sane. Suzanne and Stephanie Cummings, each in their very distinctive ways, have been dear and faithful friends.

There are three other very close friends who helped at different points in the study. In many ways this project began with long conversations with Paolo Rondo Brovetto in Italy, when we wondered what a single European currency would mean to the political economy and politics of Europe. The way Paolo initially framed these issues based on his own work in public administration has continued to define the way I think about these questions. I met Nancy Rose Hunt in Brussels when she was finishing her research in the African colonial archives. She let me hear the voices and stories of her amazing informants and showed me how they could be woven into a compelling ethnographic text. I first heard about anthropology from Peter Wilson when I was an undergraduate. Through a wonderful coincidence we became reaquainted during my annual sojourns to Otago. In our regular Friday afternoon meetings Peter would remind me of the value of the anthropological archive and convey his enduring sense of excitement about the fundamental aims of anthropology.

My family was steadfast in its support of me during this project. My parents, my brother George Holmes, and my daughter Sarah Prouty have patiently seen this project through its various permutations, providing moral support throughout. My extended family in New Zealand has embraced me and my preoccupation with the manuscript with great warmth and understanding.

Day in and day out Barbara Butler brought a coherence to my work at the University of Houston. I am grateful for her constancy and care. This was all the more pivotal during the illness and subsequent death of our much loved colleague Mary Hodge. Christine Kovic and Mike McMullen have done much to generate a new intellectual project for our program and, in so doing, created not only a lively academic program but also a rich collegial environment. My students in Houston have been a responsive audience for my rehearsal of the ideas I pursue in the manuscript.

The final revisions for this manuscript were completed after my appointment to the Department of Anthropology at the University of Otago. I am grateful to Ian Frazer and the other members of the department for their welcome and their support in my completion of this project.

The National Science Foundation (BNS-9113545) funded the fieldwork in Europe. The College of Questors of the European Parliament granted me access to virtually all the Parliament's activities. Daniela DeTomas of the European Greens guided me through the bureaucratic complexities of this institution and began my introduction to the people who inhabit it. I am, of course, most indebted to the remarkable group of people who agreed to be interviewed for this study in Italy, the Parliament, and East London. They are all essentially public figures who have unusual perspectives on transformations of European society and for whom these transformations have unusual significance. I was very fortunate to be able to talk to these people as they were struggling to come to terms with the conflicting meanings and consequences of advanced European integration.

I benefited from participation in the Late Editions project organized by George Marcus. The LE annual meetings were always stimulating and they provided a forum in which I first presented and received critical commentary on issues that I developed in this text. Excerpts from "Exclusionary Welfarism," Late Edition 6 (1999), and "Society Lost, Society Found," Late Edition 8 (in press) appear in chapters 8 and 10. I am grateful for permission from the University of Chicago Press to reproduce these excerpts here.

The book is dedicated to my wife, Pamela Smart, and my son, Eli. Pam provided truly unflagging support in the preparation of this text. She applied her remarkable intellectual acuity to enrich the text and give it vibrancy. Her skillful reading of each draft provided the questions and queries that helped me, on one hand, to refine detailed arguments and, on the other, to frame the overarching structure of the text. Her love and generous spirit sustained me at every turn of this project, even when, as was often the case, we were separated by the Pacific. The text is also dedicated to Eli, who arrived only a few months ago, but who has enriched our lives from the first moment.

INTEGRAL EUROPE

# Chapter One

## INNER LANDSCAPES

DURING THE LATE 1980s, in what was a prelude to this inquiry, I studied a social milieu in the Friuli region of northeast Italy whose inhabitants had pursued a beguiling engagement with the symbolic and the material imperatives of modernity. Friuli is the terrain of Carlo Ginzburg's famous studies of sixteenth century agrarian cults and inquisitorial prosecutions as well as the battlefields of Ernest Hemingway's *A Farewell to Arms*. Over numerous generations these people, Friulani, had negotiated the intrigues of industrial wage work, traditional peasant farming, the bureaucratic apparatus of the nation-state, the material allures of consumerism, and the symbolic power of Roman Catholicism; many, particularly males, had engaged in long migrations traversing central Europe, Australia, and America in search of employment. To defy the alienation and anomie of industrial society, these Friulani pursued arduous strategies by which they perpetuated relatively autonomous domains of economic practice and cultural meaning. A commitment to a distinctive regional language, religious rites, folk beliefs, rustic tastes, and, above all, to the routines and intimacies of family life, allowed them to establish bastions of solidarity within which their ethnic identity was actively reaffirmed (Holmes 1989). Their commitment to traditional cultural forms was neither nostalgic nor residual; rather it formed the basis of a vigorous engagement with the modern world and it is this general response—this style of life—that I now refer to as "integralist" in form.

I observed ethnographically during twenty-two months of fieldwork how Friulani exercised a cultural awareness that allowed them to negotiate, if not overcome, the alienation of everyday existence while continuing to maintain manifold bases of solidarity. Though far from seamless, it was a consciousness and practice that offered them a dynamic framework within which domains of material existence, social life, and symbolic meaning were rendered coherent. Their integralist style of life was sustained by what was understood, at least by them, to be an inner cultural logic, and this logic was enacted as what John Borneman has elegantly termed a "praxis of belonging" (1992:339n). Integralism as I initially encountered it had four registers: as a framework of meaning, as a practice of everyday life, as an idiom of solidarity, and, above all, as a consciousness of belonging linked to a specific cultural milieu. I also recognized that within these integralist practices were intriguing, though usually quiescent, struggles that under certain conditions could assume a volatile political character. Those who conjured this type of political insurgency drew on *adherents'* fidelity to specific cultural traditions and sought to recast these traditions within a distinctive historical critique and an exclusionary political economy. What seemed to catalyze this transformation was a broadly experienced rupture in the sense of belonging on the part of members of various communities and collectivities. I also discerned that integralist sensibilities had affinities with those predispositions found at the center of what Isaiah Berlin calls the "Counter-Enlightenment," the European intellectual tradition that imbues romanticism, fascism, and national socialism. Berlin's conception of the Counter-Enlightenment came to provide both the basic intellectual structure for my rendering of integralism and a theoretical armature for the study as a whole.[1]

As I observed how integralist struggles were played out in people's daily lives in the rural districts of Friuli, I became increasingly interested in the potential of these dynamics to take wider political form. My encounters with the leaders of a small regionalist political movement, the Movimento Friuli, demonstrated that this was indeed happening and, notably, against the backdrop of European integration. These pivotal encounters began my gradual refocusing of the project to a full analysis of integral politics. My specific intention has been to link integralist aspirations—expressed in efforts to circumvent the alienating force of modernity by means of culturally based solidarities—to a broader political economy. More generally, I became convinced that the kind of struggles I had observed ethnographically in Friuli were emblematic of emerging political engagements taking shape across Europe. These new questions led me to relocate the study first to the bureaucratic and political precincts of the European Parliament, where I believed integralist aspirations were gaining halting expression in response to the project of European integration, and then to the urban wards of the East End of London, where I believed integralist politics were assuming a particularly fierce and incendiary articulation (Holmes 1999). At the core of this phase of the project are 140 interviews that I conducted with a broad spectrum of political leaders, technocrats, community organizers, and street fighters. My interlocutors ranged from a former prime minister of Belgium to neo-Nazis in inner London.[2] The first two parts of the text, "Europe" and "East End," reflect my research over twenty-four months in these remarkable locales. The third, "Atavism," concludes the text with an assessment of how integralism can emerge within dissonant theories of society and as revisionist narrations of history.

## FAST-CAPITALISM AND SOCIETY

This text is concerned with how integralist sensibilities have been translated into a broad-based politics by a cadre of committed partisans, most conspicuously by Jean-Marie Le Pen and his associates. These political leaders have shrewdly discerned ruptures in the experience of belonging that threaten various registers of European identity. They diagnosed a distinctive condition of alienation based preeminently on cultural rather than socioeconomic forms of estrangement. Two interwoven phenomena have played a crucial role in politicizing integralist fears and aspirations: first, the unfolding of advanced European political and economic integration that is manifest in the project to create a multiracial and multicultural European Union; and, second, the onslaught of what I term "fast-capitalism," a corrosive "productive" regime that transforms the conceptual and the relational power of "society" by subverting fundamental moral claims, social distinctions, and material dispensations.

I have drawn on the theoretical work of two distinguished anthropologists, Paul Rabinow and Marilyn Strathern, in pursuing these issues. In a sense their contributions are reciprocal: Rabinow (1989) provides a compelling framework for critically evaluating the science, political economy, and metaphysics of solidarity at the heart of the European Union, whereas Strathern (1992) has been the first to theorize the very specific ways that fast-capitalism (though she does not use the term) radically "flattens" those preexisting frameworks of social meaning upon which our understanding of industrial democracies rest. The work of these two anthropologists opened what are the most important theoretical issues of this study. They allowed me to see the innovation at the heart of the integralist insurgency. Specifically, those political actors who embraced an integralist agenda recognized the changed nature and shifting discursive status of "society" in late-twentieth-century Europe. They labored zealously to impose on European politics a radical delineation of society in which "cultural" idioms as opposed to abstract interests serve as instruments for expressing meaning and for deriving power (Strathern 1992:171). Whether or not their political project succeeds electorally, the impact of integralist ideas is already acute and consequential insofar as they have succeeded in recasting society as a realm of political engagement.

The specific design of the research grew out of conversations with a third distinguished anthropologist, George Marcus, and his conceptualization of what has come to be called "multisited ethnography" (1999). Most important for this text, what Marcus has captured by interleaving the "thick" and "thin" of ethnography is not so much a new "methodology" as an analytical approach that addresses the underlying conceptual problems posed by Rabinow and Strathern. What he has achieved and what is reflected at virtually every turn of this text is a means by which to engage ethnography with emerging resonances of society, with the contours of a nascent social.

What follows is a brief overview of the concepts that have guided the inquiry as well as a profile of the overall thematic structure of the text.

## INTEGRALISM: POPULISM, EXPRESSIONISM, AND PLURALISM

Isaiah Berlin (1976) in his classic essay on "Herder and the Enlightenment" sets out "three cardinal ideas," drawn from the work of Johann Gottfried Herder, which, I will argue, underpin integralist politics and give it form and content. Populism, expressionism, and pluralism both provide the basic conceptual structure of integralism and locate its roots in European intellectual history.

Berlin defines these three concepts with broad strokes: *populism* is simply "the belief in the value of belonging to a group or a culture" (1976:153). He draws from Herder's distinctive orientation to the vicissitudes of human association, an orientation that envisions patterns of association crosscut by the possibility of loss and estrangement. The stranger, the exile, the alien, and the dispossessed haunt the margins of this populism. "[Herder's] notion of what it is to belong to a family, a sect, a place, a period, a style is the foundation of his populism, and of all the later conscious programmes for self-integration or re-integration among men who felt scattered, exiled or alienated" (1976:196–97).[3] Although Berlin acknowledges that Herderian populism embraces views of collectivity that are not necessarily political and ideas of solidarity that need not be forged through social struggle, he is clear that populism, by taking dispersed human practices and beliefs and by endowing them with a collective significance, creates singular political possibilities.

He also defines *expressionism* in expansive terms implicating all aspects of human creativity. Yet, it is a definition that orients analysis of society toward inner truths and inner ideals:

[H]uman activity in general, and art in particular, express the entire personality of the individual or the group, and are intelligible only to the degree to which they do so. Still more specifically, expressionism claims that all the works of men are above all voices speaking, are not objects detached from their makers, are part of a living process of communication between persons and not independently existing entities. . . . This is connected with the further notions that every form of human self-expression is in some sense artistic, and that self-expression is part of the essence of human beings as such; which in turn entail such distinctions as those between integral and divided, or committed and uncommitted, lives. (1976:153)

Expressionism thus encompasses virtually the entire compendium of collective practices, the varied fabrications of culture, from rustic cuisine to high religion. Herder posits an inner logic and internally derived integrity to these creative enterprises and thus a unifying dynamic.

*Pluralism* is for Berlin "the belief not merely in the multiplicity, but in the incommensurability, of the values of different cultures and societies, and in addition, in the incompatibility of equally valid ideals, together with the implied revolutionary corollary that the classical notions of an ideal man and of an ideal society are intrinsically incoherent and meaningless" (1976:153). Significantly, Berlin's rendering of pluralism can yield tolerance of difference among discrete groups with their own enduring traditions and territorial attachments. However, when cast against a "cosmopolitan" agenda based on universal values and "rootless" styles of life, it is a "pluralism" that can provoke fierce intolerance. In its embrace of "incommensurability," it creates a potentially invidious doctrine of difference, which holds that cultural distinctions must be preserved among an enduring plurality of groups and provides, thereby, a discriminatory rationale for practices of inclusion and exclusion.

Berlin also derives from Herder one more concept, already alluded to, that has relevance for this study, the concept of alienation. Herder's portrayal of alienation as the outcome of uprooting, of a deracination, had enormous influence on subsequent scholarship, most notably in the theoretical writings of Marx and Engels. Berlin notes that it "is not simply a lament for the material and moral miseries of exile, but is based on the view that to cut men off from the 'living center'—from the texture to which they naturally belong—or to force them to sit by the rivers of some remote Babylon . . . [is] to degrade, dehumanize, [and] destroy them" (1976:197). This view of alienation emphasizes cultural estrangement over and above socioeconomic oppression. Crucially for this text, estrangement can also be figurative: it can be instilled by the "emptiness of cosmopolitanism" without entailing any physical dislocation (198–99).

These ideas delineated by Berlin are not in themselves political assumptions; as I demonstrate in this text, they are postulates about the essence of human nature and the character of cultural affinity and difference that can potentially imbue fervent political yearnings and foreshadow a distinctive political economy. Berlin further notes: "Each of these three [populism, expressionism, pluralism] . . . is relatively novel; all are incompatible with the central moral, historical, and aesthetic doctrines of the Enlightenment" (1976:153). In other words, they form the basis of a distinctive intellectual and cultural movement in European history, again, what Berlin refers to as the "Counter-Enlightenment," which assumed its most sophisticated manifestation within the artistic triumphs of romanticism and most malevolent expression in the politics of fascism.[4] Fundamentally, the three postulates formulated by Berlin and the fourth that I added represent an alternative theory of society, an alternative project of human collectivity.

Thus, integralism, as I develop it in this text, is a protean phenomenon that draws directly on the sensibilities of the Counter-Enlightenment for its intellectual and moral substance. Its general trajectory is toward "an organic approach to life and politics," and, to the extent that integralism relies on enigmatic "inner truths" for its legitimacy, it can defy rational appraisal and frustrate external scrutiny (Mosse 1978:150). Indeed, as one of the most formidable contemporary practitioners of integralist politics avows darkly, "there are other reasons for our fate than Reason" (Le Pen 1997).[5]

The term "integral" itself has an historical pedigree that links it with various movements associated directly with the lineages of the Counter-Enlightenment. Specifically, it has a broad association with various French right-wing intellectual movements. There is the "integral nationalism" of Charles Maurras, "integral experience" of Henri Bergson, the "integral humanism" of Jacques Maritain, and, more recently, the "integral Catholicism" of Monseigneur Marcel Lefebvre. In general, "integralists" are seen as staunchly traditionalist or fundamentalist in their outlook. They themselves tend to view their integralism as a defense of some form of "sacred" patrimony. There are also more generic political designations of integralism, as in "integral nationalism," to refer to formations of ultranationalism that intersected, most notably in Germany, with Nazism (Alter 1994:26–38), and in "integral socialism," an effort to fuse "a primitive idealistic socialism and Marxist realism" (Sternhell 1996:72). Thus, the term is generally used to designate a range of idiosyncratic "fundamentalisms," most often, though by no means exclusively, of a right-wing provenance. Alberto Melucci emphasizes this "fundamentalist" and "totalizing" character of integralist agendas, as he encountered them on the left and the right, within the Italian Communist Party and the Roman Catholic Church respectively, and links this experience of prejudice as expressed in integralist agendas to his own scholarly interest in social movements:

> Under the influence of integralism, people become intolerant. They search for the master key which unlocks every door of reality, and consequently they become incapable of distinguishing among the different levels of reality. They

long for unity. They turn their back on complexity. They become incapable of recognizing differences, and in personal and political terms they become bigoted and judgmental. My original encounter with totalizing attitudes of this kind has stimulated a long-lasting interest in the conditions under which integralism flourishes. And to this day I remain sensitive to its intellectual and political dangers, which my work on collective action attempts to highlight and to counteract. (1989:181)

What I seek to accomplish by recontextualizing integralism explicitly within the tradition of the Counter-Enlightenment is to demonstrate how the concept can encompass far more than mere fundamentalism. This juxtaposition reveals that intregralism has a complex conceptual and moral structure with deep roots and a distinctive genealogy in European intellectual history, a history that Eric Wolf has noted intersects with that of anthropology:

> At the root of this [Counter-Enlightenment] reaction lay the protests of people—self-referentially enclosed in the understanding of localized communities—against the leveling and destruction of their accustomed arrangements. Together these varied conservative responses to change ignited the first flickering of the relativistic paradigm that later unfolded into the key anthropological concept of "culture." (1999:26–27)[6]

I have suggested thus far that integralism can serve as a framework to examine how mundane forms of collective practice can be linked to sublime political yearning, how varied and contradictory political ambitions can be synthesized within an overarching integralist agenda, and how integralism can draw on a specific European intellectual tradition for its form and substance. A fourth element to this preliminary portrayal draws together the first three within an oppositional configuration—opposition to the subversive capacity of what I term "fast-capitalism."

I have taken the idea of fast-capitalism from Ben Agger's nettlesome text *Fast Capitalism: A Critical Theory of Significance* (1989). Though he steadfastly refuses to define fast-capitalism in any extended fashion, Agger frames it as a phenomenon that promotes a wide-ranging "degradation of significance." In the following section I have set out a preliminary depiction of this regime assessing its dissonant impact on society and its potential to inflame an integralist political imaginary.

## INVIDIOUS HANDS

I use the term fast-capitalism to refer not just to the pacing of a technologically advanced and fully globalized economic regime, but rather to designate a phenomenon that can unleash profound change that circumvents classic domains of political decision making and social control. Speed is a crucial aspect of this regime.[7] However, its velocity is sustained not by sheer technological dynamism, but by a chain of profoundly corrosive ethical, moral, and social maneuvers; this is the monumental process that Max Weber refers to as the "disenchantment of the world."

Its most overt and cataclysmic impact has been the sequelae of financial crises that have insinuated themselves with breathtaking rapidity during the 1990s within a range of economies, including those of Mexico, Brazil, Britain, Indonesia, South Korea, and Russia. Literally overnight, principally through the operation of exchange rates, the economic structures and policies of these nation-states have been overruled with, in some cases, calamitous consequence for their citizenry. Astonishingly, within the course of a few hours, not just the legitimacy of a particular regime but the fundamental sovereignty of a nation-state can be usurped by international financial markets, the agents of fast-capitalism. This deeply subversive potential is the focus of this study. By that I mean this analysis is not concerned with fast-capitalism as a system of production or exchange, but rather as an austere cultural phenomenon that degrades moral claims, subverts social consenses, and challenges various forms of political authority. In other words, the analysis focuses on the operation of fast-capitalism upon and within society and the integralist politics that can take shape in opposition to what Joseph Schumpeter described famously as this "gale of creative destruction."[8]

The ethos of fast-capitalism—by which the abstract principles of market exchange are rendered as overriding ethical imperatives—supersedes other socially derived moral frameworks and political programs. Ulrich Beck and Anthony Giddens characterize this general process as "reflexive modernization." The consequence of this type of modernization means "that high-speed industrial dynamism is sliding into a new society without the primeval explosion of a revolution, bypassing political debates and decisions in parliaments and governments" (Beck, Giddens, and Lash 1994:2). Centrally, fast-capitalism obscures its own transformative dynamic by disrupting the social "distinctions," particularly those based on "class," that engendered the rich critical "perspectivism" vital to the modern European project of society (Rabinow 1989):

> The nineteenth-century concept of social class, we might say, also came to embody the permanent representation of different viewpoints. . . . In the late twentieth century, however, there has been a further and curious flattening effect. Class no longer divides different privileges. For anything that looks like privilege is nowadays worthy of attack, including the "privileges" of those on state benefit. . . . To put it in extreme terms, there is no permanent representa-

tion of different viewpoints any longer, because such viewpoints are no longer locked in class dialogue. Class dialogue has collapsed. (Strathern 1992:140–42)

Although fast-capitalism at the close of the twentieth century is generating and destroying wealth on a truly staggering scale, its character, for the purposes of this study, is defined by the way it impoverishes preexisting frameworks of social meaning.

How this has happened is hardly a mystery; it is the direct result of overt political decision making. The aggressive programs of liberalization and structural reform—initiated by the weakening and collapse of the Bretton Woods agreements and then advanced in the 1980s under the guise of Reaganism and Thatcherism—have accelerated the flows of goods, services, labor, and capital on a worldwide scale. As Karl Polanyi (1957) pointed out many years ago, far from being natural or inevitable, "the market is an instituted process." Within the European Union the three hundred or so legislative provisions that resulted from the Single European Act (1986), in concert with the "convergence criteria" for monetary union established under the provisions of the Maastricht Treaty (1992), are the means by which a "borderless" European capitalism is given ever increasing speed and freedom of operation among its member states.[9] Though it is the outcome of very clear programs of technocratic reform, once given life this regime has elusive and far-reaching consequences, which are difficult to predict, let alone control politically.

Zygmunt Bauman (1997a) has focused on perhaps the single most important instance of this type of flattening and devaluation of social meaning, a type that can engender an epochal transformation of political economy. He shows that it is precisely in the definition of the "new poor" that the austerities and destructive force of fast-capitalism gain clarity:

> The prospect of solidarity with the poor and desolate may be further, and decisively, undermined by the fact that, for the first time in human history, the poor, so to speak, have lost their social use. They are not the vehicle of personal repentance and salvation; they are not the hewers of wood and drawers of water, who feed and defend; they are not the "reserve army of labour," nor the flesh and bones of military power either; and most certainly they are not the consumers who will provide the effective "market clearing" demand and start-up recovery. The new poor are fully and truly useless and redundant, and thus become burdensome "others" who have outstayed their welcome. (Bauman 1997a:5)

As fast-capitalism nullifies the instrumental relationships binding the poor and disadvantaged to a wider social nexus, an all encompassing conception of society is increasingly difficult, if not impossible, to sustain.

Rendering the new poor socially and morally "useless" demolishes the fulcrum on which classic formulations of social justice have historically been conceived. The apotheosis of a stark individualistic ethic, which promotes a disregard bordering on contempt for the disadvantaged, coincides with the creation of new ill-defined realms of alienation. Its consequence is the virtual expulsion of the "new poor" from the public sphere; the lives of these people only attain social recognition as the problem of the "underclass" who live an increasingly marginal and semilegal existence. Of course, it is not just the poor who are subject to this transmutation, who find their social claims undercut and social security compromised. Social mediation offered by class and status is broadly under threat, while conventional forms of protest and resistance are muted. As Baroness Thatcher has astringently averred, "society" itself appears increasingly implausible under the onslaught of this dissonant regime.

Strathern remarks on the radical implication of this disavowal of society, "What is breathtaking is that the leader of an elected political party [Margaret Thatcher] should have chosen the collectivist idiom to discard. What vanishes is the idea of society as *either* a natural *or* an artificial consociation. What also vanishes, then, are the grounds of class dialogue (the naturalness or artificiality of social divisions) that has dominated political debate and reform for the last two centuries" (Strathern 1992:144). She goes on to assess the consequences of this progression for political legitimacy and the resulting impoverished status of personhood within a degraded public sphere:

> A government that does not identify with "society" not only out-radicalises the radicals, but consumes its mandate to govern. To bypass the idea of social legitimation, to interpret the electoral mandate as no more than the outcome of individual acts of choice, like so many multidimensional pathways, contributes to a kind of greenhouse effect. All that requires is maintaining our present levels of consumption. And all that requires is continuing to assimilate our own precepts—in this case for public figures to make explicit already held values concerning the propriety of individual choice. The self-gratification of the individual as consumer is then bounced back to the consumer in the form of publicly sanctioned individualism ("privatisation"). The exercise of individual choice becomes the only visible form of public behaviour. . . . [T]he result is to extract the person from its embedding in social relationships. (Strathern 1992:168–69)

Thus, the basic issue that links the first and second parts of the text is how we understand the broad-based transformations of society instilled by the operation of fast-capitalism. This issue is examined through the lens of an integralist politics, whose agile proponents decry these invidious transformations while exploiting the resulting disorder for their own unsettling political ends. Indeed, these integralists assert a highly contentious theory of society—an illiberal, antimaterialist, authoritarian socialism—by which they propose to thwart the advance of fast-capitalism and its wide-ranging social repercussions.

## FASCISM AND RACISM

Why not call integralist politics by a more conventional term like right-wing nationalism or fascism? There are, I believe, clear empirical, ethical, and theoretical reasons for this alternative usage. From observations and conversations with those partisans who articulate this kind of agenda—I interviewed the founders and/or leaders of nine of these political movements—to view them as either "right" or "left" wing is not simply misleading, but wrong. Drawing on populism, expressionism, and pluralism they create political orientations that defy easy placement along a single axis. In an emendation of George Valois's famous pronouncement on fascism, as "neither right or left," I argue in the following chapters that "integralism" creates a space in which an entangled politics arises that is *both* right and left. Indeed, it is precisely the unsettling potential of this kind of politics to join, fuse, merge, and synthesize what might appear to be incompatible elements that is at the heart of its distinctive power.

Integralism is often cloaked in the rhetoric of "nation," but it diverges from what are understood to be more conventional formulations of "nationalism." First, integralist nationalism is not oriented toward the progressive state-building, the *risorgimento,* of the nineteenth century or, for that matter, the postcolonial nationalism of the second half of the twentieth century (Anderson 1991; Gellner 1997; Greenfeld 1992). Indeed, as suggested earlier, it often materializes as a disparaging assessment of the secular nation-state. Second, when integralist agendas are scrutinized, it becomes clear that they encompass far more than fidelity to the idea of nation; rather, they draw authority from a wide range of collective practices that implicate family, town and country, language groups, religious communities, occupational statuses, social classes, and so on. The nationalism that imbues integralism consequently has a very specific intellectual character drawn from the proclivities of the Counter-Enlightenment and defined historically through an explicit repudiation of the principles of the French Revolution (Alter 1994:1–38; Berlin 1979:6–24; Herf 1986; Meinecke 1970).

Fascism poses a related set of challenges. Integralist groups often draw aggressively on the most forceful and unsavory elements of the fascist legacy, without themselves being or becoming "fascist," much as socialist groups have historically drawn on Marx's ideas without becoming Marxist. What this demands analytically is the scrutiny of various integralist agendas in terms of their specific affinities with "fascism" without necessarily or definitively classifying them as such. To designate a cultural practice or political movement as "integralist" has, therefore, pragmatic value, insofar as it can circumvent disabling disputes over whether or not a phenomenon is, in fact, "fascist."[10] That said, there is no doubt that fascism is a form of integralism, as we will see in the second part of the text.[11] To negotiate this interface between integralism and fascism, I draw on the scholarship of Roger Eatwell, Roger Griffin, George Mosse, Stanley Payne, and, most important, Zeev Sternhell.

Thus, integralism, as I portray it in the following chapters, can veer toward a radical intellectual tradition that took form initially in France at the close of the nineteenth century, ostensibly as a broad-based, anti-materialist revision of Marxism.[12] Sternhell describes the characteristics of this Counter-Enlightenment movement that ultimately gave birth to fascism in the 1920s:

> This political culture, communal, anti-individualistic, and antirationalistic, represented at first a rejection of the heritage of the Enlightenment and the French Revolution, and later the creation of a comprehensive alternative, an intellectual, moral, and political framework that alone could ensure the perpetuity of a human collectivity in which all strata and all classes of society would be perfectly integrated. Fascism wished to rectify the most disastrous consequences of modernization of the European continent and to provide a solution to the atomization of society, its fragmentation into antagonistic groups, and the alienation of the individual in a free market economy. Fascism rebelled against the dehumanization that modernization had introduced into human relationships, but it was also very eager to retain the benefits of progress and never advocated a return to a hypothetical golden age. Fascism rebelled against modernity inasmuch as modernity was identified with the rationalism, optimism, and humanism of the eighteenth century, but it was not a reactionary or an antirevolutionary movement. . . . Fascism presented itself as a revolution of another kind, a revolution that sought to destroy the existing [bourgeois] political order and to uproot its theoretical and moral foundations but that at the same time wished to preserve all the achievements of modern technology. It was to take place within the framework of the industrial society, fully exploiting that power that was in it. (1994:6–7)

Sternhell further notes, "fascism was only an extreme manifestation of a much broader and more comprehensive phenomenon" and "fascism was an integral part of the history of European culture" (1994:3). It is this broader phenomenon, deeply rooted in European cultural fears and aspirations that I seek to capture with the notion of integralism.[13] By depicting the broad field of European integralism I have tried to show how this kind of politics can, but need not, follow a trajectory toward fascism. Indeed, as I argue in subsequent chapters, the degree to which integralist agendas can influence and shape mainstream political discourse can render them a far more significant peril than any overt "fascist" or "neofascist" movement.

To deal with the specific issues of racism and anti-Semitism I have drawn on the vigorous contemporary scholarship of Gérard Noiriel, Verena Stolcke, Ann Laura Stoler, Pierre-André Taguieff, and Michel Wieviorka. By foregrounding the notion of integralism, however, my approach takes two unusual turns.

First, and most important, I have tried to treat the racism and anti-Semitism expressed by my informants, at least in part, on *their* terms. That is to say, I have sought to let them define the nature of human racial and cultural difference from the perspective of their own political positions. In some instances this yielded overt bigotry, in other cases, far more ambiguous, though no less troubling, testimony. In "giving voice" to what are obviously offensive and, at times, despicable political positions, I have by no means relinquished my responsibility to scrutinize them critically. My main concern, however, is to explore how critical perspectives can be formulated to understand the overarching integralist politics that frame these potentially malevolent representations of human difference.

Second, I have approached the question of racism and anti-Semitism from the standpoint of fundamental shifts and realignments of the concept of society itself. Gérard Noiriel's work is relevant here because he sees Emile Durkheim's endeavor to define "society" as an overt effort to thwart specifically a French integralist construal of the social order espoused most notably by Maurice Barrès. This confrontation provoked Durkheim's classic distinction between "organic" and "mechanical" solidarity:

> The Division of Labor in Society should be seen as the most radical critique ever written of rootedness in the land (*enracinement*). For Durkheim, the topics most often emphasized by his adversaries—the family, "ethnic group," local environment, worship of ancestors, and heredity—belonged to the past, to the era of "mechanical solidarity," when individuals were subordinated to groups and therefore deprived of true freedom. The modern world, he argued, had witnessed the triumph of organic solidarity. Progress in transportation and greater human mobility had gradually eroded the social function of attachment to the land. Values and knowledge were no longer transmitted directly by the family or through genealogy, from one generation to another, but *indirectly*, the past having become crystallized in the present through the materiality of monuments, of rules of law, and so on; hence the role of institutions (above all schools) in transmitting to "untamed" children (that is, children deprived of heredity) the culture of the society in which they were born. (Noiriel 1996:15)

Thus, one of the most influential modernist theories of society took form through a radical engagement with one of the most formidable integralist traditions rooted in the dark inner landscapes surveyed by Barrès and later Charles Maurras. The legacy of Durkheim's theory—predicated on the triumph of "organic" solidarity—gained moral force as a central element in the project of social justice; it achieved organizational expression in the European labor movement; as a social democratic agenda it implanted welfarism at the heart of the project of the nation-state; and as a technocratic practice it shaped the political economy of the European Union (Rabinow 1989). The unforeseen retreat of this wide ranging societal agenda has opened the way for a tortuous resurgence of integralist politics and its tainted discrimination of human difference. Thus the formulation and the propagation of malevolent distinctions are examined in this text as linked intimately to a broader political struggle over fundamental definitions of society.

In sum, integralism can provide an analytical perspective from which various atavistic political formations are rendered as disconcertingly familiar rather than as alien phenomena. As I sought during the early phases of the research to distance myself from my informants' darkest demiurges, I found my analysis increasingly truncated and disabled. I also noted that it was precisely the impulse to denounce them as "racists" and "fascists" that has been shrewdly exploited by the leaders of these movements with what are potentially grave consequences. Integralism furnished an alternative stance; it allowed me to explore the precarious proximity of the ideas that infuse these cultural agendas to conventional political values, and hence to reveal their true danger and our abiding vulnerability to them.

# PART ONE

EUROPE

# Chapter Two

## FLOWERING OF CULTURES

IN LATE AUGUST 1987, I traveled to a small town in northeastern Italy to interview Marco de Agostini, general secretary of a tiny autonomist party, Movimento Friuli. I drove along the back roads through densely foliaged country from Cividale to Tricesimo skirting the pre-Alps. Interspersed among the vineyards, farmlands, and rolling landscape were the small workshops and factories that powered the economic boom of the late 1980s in northeast Italy. It was on this journey that I first encountered elements of a marginal politics, which, in subsequent years, would assert itself forcefully on European political consciousness.

After a decade of research in the area around Cividale del Friuli, the inquiry came together in an unanticipated way. That study examined a rural population that had an enduring commitment to wage earning—whether it be in agriculture, in nearby factories, in distant urban centers, or in frontier settlements—without becoming a "true" working class. I found that intricate bonds tied these people to both a traditional peasant routine and wage work. The fabric of their relations constituted a peculiar type of society, a worker peasantry, which was difficult to bound in time and space: it could be observed from a locale but was not confined to a place. For three centuries this society had mediated fundamental social transformation, from proto-industry to the welfare state, yet the society itself was not transitional.

The people who inhabited this landscape were preeminently sojourners, traversing regional and national frontiers as easily as they trespassed the conceptual boundaries fabricated by social scientists. Their odysseys entailed long itineraries spanning central Europe and the New World. Yet, these same sojourners still managed to maintain identities rooted in the ethnic practice of their Friulian homeland. With great shrewdness and courage, these Friulian country folk had discovered ways to circumvent the material insecurities of industrial capitalism only to find themselves confronted with a central cultural bind of modernity.

In portraying the character of livelihood in this Italian social milieu, an arresting cultural orientation emerged. I found that the habit of exile, which punctuates the lives of worker peasantries, mediated a distinctive consciousness. In their accounts, cultural motives defined experience in ways that cannot be reduced to the interplay of socioeconomic interests.

Again, the commitment to Friulian ideals as expressed in the language, religious rites, folk beliefs, rustic tastes and, above all, the routines and intimacies of a modest farmstead sustained bastions in which ethnic identity was actively reaffirmed. To preserve such enclaves, however, these sojourners were ironically compelled to set out on daunting circuits into the wage economy and risked entanglement with its dangers and allures.

On the eastern periphery of the northern Italian plain was a domain where the political dramas that have dominated Europe since the late nineteenth century were reconfigured; the great allegories of material inequality that have infused working-class consciousness were abridged. Rather than embracing the transcendent ideals of a true proletariat, worker peasantries here formulated an awareness embedded in highly personal struggles and expressed in arcane cultural idioms. These struggles were more likely to be enacted, in the strategies of livelihood and routines of ethnic practice, than to be articulated, let alone politicized. They yielded a sovereignty enmeshed in largely unvoiced sentiments, rather than rational programs. Raymond Williams captures this kind of immanent awareness in a yet to be defined "social present":

> We are talking about the characteristic elements of impulse, restraint, and tone; specifically affective elements of consciousness and relationships. . . . We are then defining these elements as a "structure": as a set, with specific internal relations, at once interlocking and in tension. Yet we are also defining social experience which is still in process, often indeed not yet recognized as social but taken to be private, idiosyncratic, and even isolating, but which in analysis (though rarely otherwise) has its emergent, connecting, and dominant characteristics, indeed its specific hierarchies. These are often more recognizable at a later stage, when they have been (as often happens) formalized, classified, and in many cases built into institutions and formations. By that time the case is different: a new structure of feeling will usually already have begun to form, in the true social present. (Williams 1977:132)

In my attempt to explicate the idiosyncratic dynamics of Friulian livelihood, an approach to cognition and affect emerged to reveal a distinctive consciousness, a distinctive "structure of feeling."[1] Woven through the social experience of these countryfolk I began to discern quiescent struggles over identity and belonging that encompassed an inchoate integralist politics.

Integralism was manifest in these people's endeavors to align their experience along a particular axis of meaning and significance. Their world view, though highly sensitive to injustice, was largely aloof from the epistemologies of class struggle. What was arresting in their accounts was that cultural aspirations defined their experience in ways that challenged explanations based on conventional conceptions of social distinction. At the core of this social formation I found struggles that I now pose as paradigmatic, struggles by which the material insecurities of industrial capitalism and the secularizing accountabilities of the nation-state were pitted against deeply held sentiments inlaid in what social scientists generally abstract as "ethnic" or "national" identity. Ultimately, they sought a cultural framework of solidarity in response to various registers of alienation. Only after the journey to Tricesimo did I fully recognize how these integralist sensibilities could unleash an incipient politics.

## INTEGRALIST POLITICS

Interviews with the leadership of the Movimento Friuli (MF) were the last task, almost a postscript, of the earlier study. The day before the trip to Tricesimo, I met with the president of the MF, Roberto Jacovissi, in Udine, the provincial center. The interview caught me off guard. Unlike the conversations I had with other political figures, I spoke to Jacovissi in his home. I found his personal warmth engaging. His library was lined with books in the regional language, Friulian. Displayed were awards and citations from various organizations, acknowledging Jacovissi's contribution to the promotion of Friulian cultural life. The walls of the house were replete with examples of local arts and crafts. The sounds and smells were familiar. Here, in the urban precincts of Udine, a middle-class household held the qualities I associated with the modest farmsteads of the countryside: boisterous children, social interchange that gravitated toward the kitchen, dark middle rooms with heavy furniture, smells of spice and oil, a familiar dampness. Through the windows came the late August light that follows the heavy rains that mark the end of a Friulian summer. The only thing absent was the pervasive scent of wine and sweat that permeate the country dwellings. It was here that I first heard talk of "Friulian nationhood."[2]

The next day, I met Marco De Agostini, general secretary of the MF, and his wife in a café in Tricesimo. The interview began with a brief history and prehistory of the Movimento Friuli and its founding in the late 1960s out of student demands for the creation of a university in Udine. The efforts of clerics and intellectuals, committed to linguistic and cultural preservation, were prominent in the founding of the party. De Agostini described the spirit of the movement as a party of neither the "right" nor the "left," but as an "avant-garde," a party of ideas. He talked about the Catholic roots of the MF and the "mythical socialism" that informed this political imaginary. He also portrayed a dark side to the MF's vision, one oriented toward establishing special rights and privileges for those who are judged ethnically "Friulian": specifically, the insistence on discriminatory preference in employment of civil servants that favored Friulani by requiring a minimum five-year residence before appointment to government positions. The purpose, which was openly expressed, was to exclude southern Italians from government bureaus. There was also preoccupation with redrawing the borders of eastern Friuli through urban neighborhoods of Gorizia, dividing what are believed to be "Slavic" and "Friulian"-speaking districts.

The quixotic political narrative was broken when De Agostini asserted the aspiration of the MF for Friulian autonomy. "We are Europeanistic. . . . Borders are political, not cultural." He described the goal of a Friulian "nation": as "European," but at the same time, independent of any state. The European Community was seen as the supranational context in which the movement could achieve its autonomous aspirations. Embedding ethnic autonomy within a European context—rendering the Italian nation-state largely irrelevant—represented a distinctive conceptualization of community and polity. The aspirations that informed this vision were at odds with the trajectory of western European political development in the late-1980s. The unvoiced sentiments that pervaded rural consciousness seemed to gain rough political expression in De Agostini's words. His vision extended further, hinting at a new political discourse on Europe, one unhinged from the civic imperatives of the nation-state. He formulated a distinctive rendering of ethnic autonomy, framed institutionally by the European Community and free of the encumbrances of any nation-state.[3] I was struck by this formulation because it hinted at a radical political vision based on an arresting, pluralist conception of Europe.[4]

The program articulated by the leadership of the MF cogently recapitulates Berlin's Counter-Enlightenment doctrines. The MF's populism was founded on a commitment to a collectivity manifest in an intricate tableau of shared Friulian values, to a cultural "grass roots." Its expressionism was evidenced in the array of ethnic idioms and practices by which Friulian humanity and solidarity were rendered intelligible. Its multilayered pluralism was predicated on the marking of differences among peoples—Slovenes and southern Italians—along tangents of incommensurable cultural values, while at the same time permitting the MF to participate in a European Community composed of a multiplicity of cultural groupings. The leadership of the movement was keenly aware of the unconventional nature of their political agenda and its incompatibility with conventional political strategies and practices. Their cultural aspirations emerged initially not as a "power politics" but as a diffuse populism. "It is this that acquired such momentum among the oppressed people of Eastern Europe, and later spread to Asia and Africa. It inspired not *étatistes*, but believers in 'grass roots'—Russian Slavophiles and Narodniks, Christian Socialists and all those admirers of folk art and popular traditions whose enthusiasm assumed both serious and ridiculous shapes" (Berlin 1976:183). By moving the project to Strasbourg and later to Brussels I sought to investigate how what appeared to be an inherently self-limiting populism might be recast as a powerful politics in response to the project of European economic and political integration.

STRASBOURG

In the spring and summer of 1989 the last moves of the Cold War were unfolding, the two hundredth anniversary of the storming of the Bastille was commemorated, democracy protests in Tiananmen Square were brutally quashed, and tourists surged through Strasbourg. I was staying in a hotel on the south bank of the L'ill just below the great locks that regulate the level of water as it flows around the city and into the Rhine. My room had a clear view on the pink sandstone west facade and the single towering spire of the Strasbourg Cathedral, the site and subject of a famous encounter between Herder and Goethe.[5] On most days I took a bus away from the center city past the university to the European Quarter, setting of the modernist Palais d'Europe housing the Council of Europe and the European Parliament. It was the latter institution that I was in Strasbourg to study.

At that time the European Parliament was considered a rather mysterious body moving between Brussels and Strasbourg, operating ostensibly as the consultative body of the European Community (EC), yet lacking any real political power. In June 1989 an election of the Parliament was scheduled. I was in Strasbourg to observe the campaign because I thought it would give insights into the emerging *politics* of European integration. Integration was poised to accelerate in the wake of the passage of the Single European Act (SEA), which legislated the establishment of a single market among the member states of the Community. It was clear, however, that market integration presaged a far more sweeping political project aimed at the creation of a new type of polity, a European Union (EU).

I spent much of my time across the street from offices of the Parliament in the splendid Parc de l'Orangerie. Each day I took with me to a bench under a stand of pine trees copies of the treaties that serve as the constitutional instruments of the European Community as well as the official reports and documents of the Parliament pertaining to the technical requirements of creating the single market. In a garden designed by Louis XIV's landscape architect, André Le Nôtre, I became familiar with the arcane project of European integration. Occasionally, I caught glimpses of the complex historical vision that had impelled integration since the 1950s, but my general impression was different. With each day's readings I found it more and more difficult to see the European Community as anything other than a vast, uninspired technocratic undertaking, its historical imperatives rendered increasingly obscure. This view was furthered as each day I also scrutinized European press coverage of the dismal course of the campaign for the new Parliament. The reports failed in general to capture the remarkable issues at stake in the election. Indeed, during late June another important event in the development of the European project was taking place that similarly escaped public attention.

In Madrid the European Council, composed of all the heads of state or government of member states supported by their ministers for foreign affairs along with the president of the European Commission, had a two-day meeting. In the unusual structure of the EU, the European Council has since the early 1970s set the course for integration by convening intergovernmental conferences to draft revisions of EC treaties. During this brief gathering on June 26 and 27, a proposal tabled by the governors of the central banks of the twelve member states under the direction of Jacques Delors, then president of the European Commission, was considered. The proposal, known as the "Delors Plan," called for the convening of an intergovernmental conference, an IGC, that would plan the specific revisions to the Treaty of Rome and subsequent treaties to make possible European Monetary Union (EMU). The plan was approved at the December 1989 meeting of the European Council in Strasbourg. In the closing months of 1989, however, the fall of the Berlin Wall dramatically recast this priority. The German government forcefully argued that monetary union must be pursued in concert with further political integration. More specifically, it demanded at the insistence of the German regional assembly, the Bundesrat, an expanded federalist agenda with the allocation of powers based on the application of an obscure concept drawn from Catholic social doctrine, subsidiarity.[6] At a subsequent meeting in Dublin in April 1990 the European Council acceded to the German demands and called a second IGC to consider simultaneously this expanded agenda of political integration. The work of these two IGCs yielded documents that became the basis of the Maastricht Treaty on European Union. Advanced European integration has been legislated via this incremental process by which complex treaties are drafted that bind member states in increasingly comprehensive relationships to further "an ever closer union." These intricate and unwieldy agreements, which result from this "intergovernmental" bargaining process, thus serve as the constitutional instruments upon which the European project is legally based (Moravcsik 1998:391, 398–400, 435–38; Weiler 1999).

It was in retrospect an eerie episode of research given the awesome changes in the contours of Europe that were impending, though barely imaginable, in the spring and summer of 1989. There was, nonetheless, a series of notable challenges that emerged during this period of research.

Most important, it became clear that, despite its ardently technocratic appearance, there were powerful urgencies at the core of the European project that needed elucidation. Thus, the first challenge of this new phase of the project was to begin to depict the relationship between the economic imperatives and technocratic practices of the European project and how this relationship was defining axes of struggle over the emerging European social order.

I found in Strasbourg that for various intended and unintended reasons the institutions of the EC, and now the EU, obscure their own operation and define themselves outside of clear-cut civic accountabilities. Vast economic and political power was being transferred from the member states to the European Community, as a result of the Single European Act, with a striking lack of public awareness, much less debate. Under the leadership of Jacques Delors at the European Commission, the diplomatic and institutional dynamics were being set in motion to pursue what seemed then to be the extravagant ambitions of full monetary and political union. This raised questions of how this complex entity, this embryonic polity, was spliced to a wider European society. Or, put reciprocally, what kind of social order would the project of European integration engender? This led me to examine what I call "surrogate discourses of power," which, though neither official doctrines nor policies of the EU, have nonetheless defined its organizational makeup and its technocratic practice and, most centrally, its wider societal premises. These two discourses—French social modernism and Catholic social doctrine—defined a science, political economy, and metaphysics of solidarity that established a very specific architecture for the European project that operates, as Perry Anderson (1996) puts it, "under the sign of the interim." It is the character of this social order that became the focus of my subsequent research in Brussels.

There was one final element to the work in Strasbourg that was significant. During the campaign for the Parliament in the summer of 1989 I also became interested in a small political movement in France that espoused an agenda at odds with the project of European integration, the Front national, led by the mercurial figure of Jean-Marie Le Pen. At that time, however, I did not yet fully grasp the radical nature of Le Pen's integralist insurgency nor did I recognize its capacity to define the debate on a pluralist Europe.

## BRUSSELS

Exiting the Brussels metro at Place Schuman in the early 1990s, one might have noticed an inconspicuous black-and-white transparency at the end of the platform set amid a display of advertisements. Portrayed in the picture dating from the 1950s is a distinguished looking French politician Robert Schuman (1880-1963), after whom the stop is named, in the company of his assistant Jean Monnet (1888-1979). Schuman, former French foreign minister and leader of the Christian Democratic Mouvement Républicain Populaire (MRP), is credited with formulating the plan upon which the European Community was founded.[7] Konrad Adenauer, first postwar chancellor of the Federal Republic of Germany, provoked the plan; Jean Monnet, Pierre Uri, Etienne Hirsch, and Paul Reuter authored it; and Schuman appended his name and gave the plan political viability (see Duchêne 1995; Milward 1992; Monnet 1978).[8]

In a few pages of text, what has come to be known as the Schuman Plan, an agreement to bind French and German production of coal and steel under a common administrative authority, was established. Woven through the document, however, was a far more militant aim. The plan specified an open-ended institutional schema that sought to eliminate national rivalries and establish an architecture for a new social construction of European power. In its subdued wording: "The solidarity in production thus established will make it plain that any war between France and Germany becomes not merely unthinkable, but materially impossible. . . . [T]his proposal will build the first concrete foundation of a European federation which is indispensable to the preservation of peace" (Schuman, May 9, 1950, quoted in Pinder 1991:1). Schuman and Adenauer sought to begin to construct a lasting peace in Europe with coal and steel. The insurgent motive was fundamental, manifest in a comprehensive assault on the sovereignty of the nation-state (Adenauer 1966; Duchêne 1995):

> The indispensable first principle of these proposals is the abnegation of sovereignty in a limited but decisive field. . . . Any plan which does not involve this indispensable first principle can make no useful contribution to the solution of the grave problems that face us. . . . What must be sought is a fusion of interests of European peoples and not merely another effort to maintain equilibrium of those interests. (Monnet 1978:316)

The signing of the Schuman declaration (April 18, 1951) established the institutional imperatives for what is now the European Union.[9] It substituted "pooled sovereignty" for indivisible national interests, permitting the coordination of policy and action around fundamental economic issues. Implicit in this arrangement was a rejection of the narrow and potentially rapacious interests of the nation-state. Yet there is also a recognition that displacing the authority of the state must proceed at a gradual pace with circumspection and tact. "The solution . . . was to seek to bridge the gap between national autonomy and European federation in a gradual process. Rather than relinquish all sovereignty overnight, the member states were asked merely to abandon the dogma of indivisibility" (Borchardt 1989:25). Subsequent treaties further endowed the project "with sovereign powers of its own, independent of the member states, which it can exercise to adopt acts which have the force of national law. This novel approach of pooling national sovereignty and policies is commonly referred to as 'integration'" (Borchardt 1989:9). More important, this approach established, in embryonic form, an institutional method to "broaden" its membership and "deepen" political and economic convergence (Fontaine 1990:18).

The nature of European institutions that evolved from the Schuman Plan veils this radicalism. Moral urgencies do not adhere to the daily work of the EU. On the contrary, the vision that it projects is that of a sweeping technocratic undertaking couched in the reassuring terms of social progress and economic betterment. Remarkably, Jean Monnet acknowledges the prominence of this ambiguity from the earliest moments of the project's history. Commenting on the journalists covering the announcement of the Schuman Plan, Monnet notes their bafflement: "They were still uncertain about the significance of the proposal, whose technical aspects at first sight masked its political meaning" (1978:304). It is precisely the incongruent nature of the European project's insurgency that creates unusual possibilities for interpretation.

I returned to Europe during the period of the drafting of what came to be known as the Maastricht Treaty on European Union and immediately thereafter specifically to investigate the struggles over the definition and character of this emerging polity.[10] My aim was to examine what I understood to be a looming confrontation between the politics of integration and an opposed, yet still nascent, European integralism. I interviewed scores of elected members of the European Parliament (MEPs) including the leaders of all the political groups represented in the Parliament. I sought to capture the ways in which they, that is, *participants* themselves, endowed evolving struggles with political meaning.[11]

I found that for most of the senior cohort of politicians, who fill leadership roles in the Parliament, the moral imperative and historical critique upon which the European Union is founded remained implicit. A few of these politicians were directly involved in the early construction of the Union, working with Schuman and Monnet in the wake of the Second World War; they built a political agenda that held enormous immediacy and embraced a distinctive logic of power. They understood intimately the texts, subtexts, and intertexts of the treaties that form the constitutional foundations of the EU. Moreover, they institutionalized the EU's agenda in layer upon layer of informal agreements that rarely came under journalistic or academic scrutiny or made their way into public debate. What is most prominent in the EU's development is its commitment to a series of far-reaching economic agendas that conceal its underlying social and moral urgencies.

This gives rise to a central disparity; the European project is predicated on a broad-based societal theory blending a complex moral vision and technocratic practice, yet it lacks virtually any formal constitutional theory of its own. François Duchêne is emphatic about this haphazard historical character, whereby the power of the EU appears to operate through fragmented and partial arrangements:

> [T]he European Communities were steps to a federation that might have to operate indefinitely in intermediate zones. It was federal minimalism confined to certain economic areas. New instruments and ideas had to be devised for dealing with such a partial condition of life. The creators of the Community were surprisingly ignorant of, and indifferent to, historical precedent. The system corresponds closely to no previous constitutional norm. (Duchêne 1995:407)

As I read the treaties that serve as constitutional instruments for the construction of the EU, I was struck by a highly pragmatic organizational emphasis and an arresting lack of any overarching theoretical vision. Tony Judt is more forceful, positing a vacuous fanaticism at the heart of the project:

> [T]he history of the formation of an "ever-closer union" has followed a consistent pattern: the real or apparent logic of mutual economic advantage not sufficing to account for the complexity of its formal arrangements, there has been invoked a sort of ontological ethic of political community; projected backward, the latter is then adduced to account for the gains made thus far and to justify further unificatory efforts. It is hard to resist recalling George Santayana's definition of fanaticism: redoubling your efforts when you have forgotten your aim. (1996:23-24)

Through my interviews with senior political leaders I began to see how this apparent discrepancy between theory and practice is resolved. As suggested earlier, there are in fact two surrogate discourses of power that are entirely independent of the EU, yet have imparted a moral perspective, organizational theory, and technocratic practice to the construction of this federal polity. Catholic social doctrine and French social modernism serve as the symbolic frameworks that have sustained this wide-ranging political development. Both permit the conceptualization of a highly contingent political program based on the pursuit of a comprehensive agenda of solidarity. Again, they are both conceptual approaches, which are intimately involved in the development of European federalism and yet are independent of it.

Paul Rabinow has examined the remarkable lineage of administrative engineering at the heart of French social modernism as it developed between 1832 and 1939. Since the 1950s, what Rabinow terms "middling modernism" has been superimposed on Europe. "[T]he . . . focus is not on 'high culture' nor the practices of everyday life, but on a middle ground where social technicians were articulating a normative, or middling modernism. In their discourses, society became its own referent, to be worked on by means of technical procedures which were becoming the authoritative arbiters of what counted as socially real" (Rabinow 1989:13). Jean Monnet and, more recently, Jacque Delors were the preeminent carriers of the tradition of French modernist planning and practice from Paris to Brussels (Delors 1992; Duchêne 1995; Haas 1964; Ross 1995).

The project of French social modernism, as it took form in the last two decades of the nineteenth century, was centrally about conceptualizing society as a field of human interdependence susceptible to planning and administration through the application of "scientific" norms and principles. With roots in de Tocqueville, Le Play, Proudhon, and Durkheim a highly pragmatic socialism coalesced in France as a "school of solidarity" (Rabinow 1989:182). This peculiar configuration of "socialism" was impelled not by a revolutionary elite, but by a cadre of social technicians— middling modernists—who through their administrative interventions sought to arbitrate a distinctive social order. The subject of their interventions encompassed infrastructures of industry, public services, and social welfare. What these theorists and planners devised was a comprehensive technocratic politics of a modern industrial society that circumvented what they saw as disabling clashes between the ideologies of left and right. They sought a degree of independence from the give-and-take of parliamentary politics, and thereby from democratic accountabilities. The elite technocratic practice of the EU, examined in the next chapter, draws directly on the legacy of middling modernism for its method of "convergent action," which has come to serve as the paradigm for institutional decision making.[12]

Social Catholicism, with its roots also in the emergence of industrial societies of the late nineteenth century, has imparted to the EU not just a metaphysics of solidarity but a model of federalism. The ecology of power is difficult to schematize in an evolving polity like the EU. It spreads over institutional competencies, the boundaries of which are ill defined; it resides in executive bureaus that translate abstract legislative formulas into administrative practice; and it adheres to the informal agreements and understandings that coordinate political contests. "Subsidiarity," a pivotal concept in Catholic social doctrine, serves as a central axis in the struggle over the definition and the disposition of power. The effort to define subsidiarity discloses not merely a single concept but a range of concepts and formulations that constitute a comprehensive societal theory.[13] Subsidiarity denotes a means for circumscribing domains of action for public authorities, establishing formulas for allocating governmental powers, and defining norms of societal stewardship and the conditions of individual freedom.

French social modernism and social Catholicism confer a distinctive conceptualization of society and political economy on the European project. They have also imparted striking cultural contradictions, which pose fundamental questions about the legal status and political character of a multiracial and multicultural Europe.

## ORIGINAL SIN

Principles governing the creation of a pluralist European Union are virtually absent from the treaties upon which the political project is based. "Until the Treaty on European Union came into effect there was no explicit treaty basis for cultural affairs and cultural policy within the framework of the European Community" (Weidenfield and Wessels 1998:58). What the treaty provides is a limited acknowledgment of issues of cultural diversity setting out a modest consultative procedure for their institutional scrutiny by the EU. "[T]he advent of the Treaty on European Union, Article 128 . . . provides a treaty basis for the inclusion of culture as a sphere of activity requiring, on the one hand, that the [European] Council reaches its decisions unanimously and, on the other, that the . . . Committee of the Regions be consulted" (Weidenfield and Wessels 1998:58). The only area of vigorous engagement with "culture" is within the context of a "European culture industry," where culture, here reduced to mass culture, can be understood in commercial terms and where the influence of the United States looms large.

There is an abiding respect for the United States as a model of an integrated economy and a federal system among the leadership of the EU. There is also a strident rejection of what is viewed as a virulent philistinism and consumerism unleashed by the United States, which is seen as threatening the integrity of European cultural distinctions and social practices. Although it is rarely articulated openly, the United States operates in the minds of many leaders as a foil against which they struggle to find meaningful alternatives for the preservation of European languages and cultural traditions. The United States, however, is not merely a foil; its dominance of popular culture and the mass media makes it an adversary. Protectionist directives limiting access to European media markets have, in effect, become the core of the EU's cultural policy.[14]

Culture, as ethnic or national identity, is, nonetheless, alluded to in the elliptical language of the Treaty of Rome. In the preamble, "an ever closer union among the peoples" [of Europe] is established as the supreme aim of the European project. The preamble also rejects both the idea of a cultural "melting pot" and the idea of nation building (Weiler 1999).[15] Yet, as Cris Shore points out, the Rome treaty does not provide a definition of Europe, nor does it designate its boundaries. This raises the fundamental question for those who hold ardently to notions of European cultural preeminence: where does Europe end and Asia begin?

Forced to address the issue of identity, the European Commission is evasive:

> The term "European" has not been officially defined. It combines geographical, historical and cultural elements which all contribute to the European identity. The shared experience of proximity, ideas, values and historical interaction cannot be condensed into a simple formula and is subject to review by each succeeding generation. The Commission believes that it is neither possible nor opportune to establish now the frontiers of the European Union, whose contours will be shaped over many years to come. (Shore 1993a:786)

What makes these otherwise naive pronouncements pernicious, if not racist, is the way they obscure the EU's own administrative practices—its praxis of exclusion (Stolcke 1995). Again, Shore puts it elegantly:

> [W]hile the Commission dismisses the notion of an "official" category of "European," evidence of a more coherent "applied" definition can be seen emerging at the borders and boundaries of the new Europe, particularly in the spheres of immigration control and external customs barriers. The . . . terms "non-EC nationals," "third countries" and "non-Europeans" are being defined with increasing precision and thus, as if by default, an "official" definition of European is being constructed. (1993a:786)

To the extent that the new Europe lacks a principled and political coherent definition, it achieves a de facto reality through the administrative processes of establishing directives governing the statuses of immigrants and refugees and the related issues of working out a bureaucratic framework for European citizenship (Balibar 1996).

Thus, one of the most crucial dimensions of the emerging social order underpinning integration is the consolidation of a vast multiracial and multicultural Europe. Yet the creation of a radically pluralist Europe is not being devised through fundamental constitutional postulates or direct political decision making; rather, it is achieved through a derivative process, nested most notably in the challenge of instituting an integrated labor market. The Treaty on Union does little to correct these deficiencies. Article 128 states the constitutional means for promoting European cultural unity and diversity:

> The Community shall contribute to the flowering of the cultures of the member states, while respecting their national and regional diversity and at the same time bringing the common cultural heritage to the fore. Action by the Community shall be aimed at encouraging cooperation between members states and, if necessary, supporting and supplementing their action in the following areas: improvement of the knowledge and dissemination of the culture and history of European peoples; conservation and safeguarding of cultural heritage of European significance; non-commercial cultural exchanges; artistic and literary creation, including in the audiovisual sector.

Its insipid declarations to the contrary, full legal recognition of the right to cultural difference is, in fact, treated with intense suspicion by the leadership of the EU. Michael Herzfeld (1987) notes that assertions of European cultural diversity are often nothing more than justifications for the retention of powers of the nation-state.

The creation of a vast multiracial and multicultural society has to an important degree taken place independent of any formal political agenda in its own right. This is a pivotal example of reflexive modernization, in which the intricately legislated course to economic and political integration precipitates a pluralist Europe as a derivative process largely outside the institutional scrutiny and control of the EU. "The idea that the transition from one social epoch to another could take place unintended and unpolitically, bypassing all the forums for political decisions, the lines of conflict and the partisan controversies, contradicts the democratic self-understanding of this society just as much as it does the fundamental convictions of its sociology" (Beck 1994:3). This "radicalization of modernity" is antagonistic to the constructivist tradition of the European project. Aggressive commercial dynamism is thereby creating a pluralist Europe "surreptitiously and unplanned." Indeed, to conceptualize politically this multiracial and multicultural Europe is by no means easy.

## Four Strands of Pluralism

What I found early in my work at the Parliament were elements of a political debate on a multiracial and multicultural Europe emerging in fragmentary form and with varying degrees of emotional intensity and conceptual rigor. There appeared to be four strands—at times rather loose strands—to the debate. The first strand aligned pluralism with an idealized view of European civilization on the one hand and with pragmatic elements of Catholic social teaching on the other. The second strand pursued a pluralism manifest institutionally in a decentralized and socially progressive "Europe of regions." The third strand encompassed opposition to forces seen as hostile to the emergence of a humane and tolerant European pluralism: that is, racism, xenophobia, anti-Semitism, and neofascism. The fourth gained expression in agendas that emphasized cultural incommensurability as the defining principle of European pluralism, a position antagonistic to a cosmopolitan embrace of human difference. I briefly portray the first three strands of this debate here, mainly to clarify why the fourth, the integralist approach, became decisive for this study.

I sought out a peculiar figure in the Parliament, a member of the European Peoples Party (the Christian Democrats), Otto von Habsburg. I wanted to know about the institutional design of the multinational empire over which his family historically ruled. Rather than a critical account of the dual empire that I sought, he recounted for me his return to postcommunist Budapest as head of a parliamentary delegation to Hungary. His story epitomized an idealized vision of European civilization and its embrace of cultural diversity. He and his colleagues traversed territories once part of the old, multinational empire. As the old man peered out the train window, what passed through his mind was the layout of cities. It occurred to him that these urban centers were not dominated by towering commercial structures, stock exchanges, or vast stadia. What he saw at their heart were cathedrals. It led to the simple—though, for him, indisputable—conclusion that Europe was culturally unified by Christianity, its cultural diversity transcended by religion. For Habsburg this spiritual unity was fundamental and indivisible. This very simple, almost quaint construal of "a closer union among peoples" of Europe unified by Christendom is widely held and rarely debated and by no means limited to members of confessional political groupings.[16]

Despite the impressionistic character of this Christian vision, when fused with key concepts of Catholic social teaching it can supply the essential elements of a modern theory of pluralism. Although its theoretical assumptions are abstruse, the Catholic framework can generate political agendas with broad popular appeal across Europe. Indeed, the European Peoples Party, dominated by Christian Democrats, is the largest group in the Parliament elected in June 1999, with 224 of the 626 seats.

Full constitutional acknowledgment of a pluralist Europe opens other possibilities and limitations, as suggested in the following account of Jaak Vandemeulebroucke. Vandemeulebroucke was the leader of a small political group in the Parliament committed to a socially progressive Europe of regions in which ethnic, religious, and cultural distinctions could be preserved, if not enhanced. He articulated in an interview with me in 1991 in Brussels essentially the same dream of cultural autonomy within a European framework that I had heard originally among the leaders of the Movimento Friuli:

> If you are seeking cultural rights, to preserve your own tradition, you must be committed to a positive nationalism open to all forms of diversity and the rights of all minorities. . . . We should write into a constitution of Europe that minorities [including non-European minorities] have the right to preserve their culture, their beliefs, the convictions of their religion. It must be on the same terms as for dominant European cultural groups. If you do not do that you will only have negative forms of nationalism, in which you create ghettos. . . . I think we can place nationalism within a European framework and make it a force for good. Nationalism can become a basis for a new form of democracy, decentralization, restoring governmental powers to the people. . . . The Jacobinistic system does not work anymore. For an alternative to develop, however, there must be solidarity between regions [and small states like Denmark]. . . . You need regional dialogue. Nationalism must be linked to internationalism.

Central to this vision is a federal Europe committed to devolution with, as in the Catholic model, the concept of subsidiarity as a constitutional guarantee protecting fundamental cultural rights.

What obstructs this kind of constitutional solution within the EU is the deep rejection of nationalism that underpins the modernist logic of institution building from the Schuman Plan forward. More fundamentally, there is an inherent disharmony posed by advanced European integration and the specification of "cultural rights." The problem, as suggested already, is inlaid in the disparity between the economic forces of expanding integrated markets, particularly a European-wide labor market, and the maintenance of cultural traditions held by more or less discrete peoples of Europe. The free movement of people, goods, and services—at the heart of the Single Market and the project of European Monetary Union—is difficult to reconcile with constitutional provisions guaranteeing the rights of variously defined cultural groupings to a differential national, ethnic, or religious autonomy. This cultural anomaly posed by advanced European integration is pivotal.

The third strand of the pluralist debate starts from a very different perception of political opportunities and perils. The Parliament convened a series of committees of inquiry into the reemergence of racism and xenophobia in the late 1980s and early 1990s, and their reports galvanized this critical strand to the pluralist debate. Glyn Ford, at the time the leader of the Socialist Group in the European Parliament, was *rapporteur* of the Committee of Inquiry and became closely identified with one of these parliamentary documents. The text of the "Ford Report,"[17] particularly for the left, became the starting point for the fight against the "new racism" in Europe in the 1990s. The committee drew heavily on the expertise of outside activist groups, notably SOS-Racisme. The document chronicled the rise of racism, neofascism, and extreme right-wing movements across Europe, with substantial attention to the practices of the Front national and the motives of its leader Jean-Marie Le Pen, MEP. It conveyed a thoroughly disparaging appraisal of Le Pen's "cultural agenda" by representatives of the main political groups within the Parliament. The critical labor performed by the Ford Report was conspicuous: to position nationalist agendas, like that articulated by Le Pen, within the discredited history of *European* fascism. As a practical matter, it conceptualized the struggle to achieve a multiracial and multicultural Europe in terms of silencing those individuals and movements seen to espouse intolerance and to promote bigotry.

In many respects this was a courageous stance that was pursued with great conviction and energy by its adherents. It also defined an agenda that generated broad support across the major political groups in the Parliament. By invoking the horrors of the Second World War and the Holocaust as the moral basis of this intervention, however, it had the inadvertent effect of obscuring the contemporary ideal of European pluralism and thereby restricting its status as a political agenda in its own right. In other words, by tethering the debate on a multiracial and multicultural Europe to the disquieting history of European racism and fascism, it perversely conceded to that history the power to define many of the terms of the contemporary debate. It was this weakness that integralists, who created the fourth strand of the debate, aggressively exploited. Their approach to pluralism entails a comprehensive rejection of the supranational aims of the European project.

The partisans of this fourth approach were skeptical of the enigmatic comment attributed to Jean Monnet: "if we were to do it all again we would start with culture" (quoted in Shore 1993a:785). For them the European project *did* begin with "culture." They believe that from the outset, a universalistic metaphysics and practice have been embraced as the foundational architecture of the European project and at virtually every turn populism, expressionism, and a pluralism rooted in cultural incommensurability have been overruled. Those who were designing an *integralist* politics for Europe at the end of the millennium understood acutely the genesis of this original sin and against it they cast their atavistic politics. They have devised what they believe to be a fully developed theory of pluralism with deep historical resonance: a theory that they are willing to articulate openly and emphatically. What is at stake for them in this debate is the fundamental nature of society.

In the next chapter I briefly summarize the traditions of French social modernism and social Catholicism—the modern and the sacred—in terms of the distinctive dynamics they have conferred on the European Union.[18] As suggested earlier, these two traditions are both consummate discourses on society, yet, as they came to be fused with the economic agenda of the EU, their integrity was challenged. This fusion, underwritten in the provisions of the Single European Act and the Maastricht Treaty, implanted a fast-capitalism and unleashed reflexive modernization at the heart of the European project. It was precisely the success of market and monetary integration that eroded the authority of a modernist politics of society, making the sharply divergent potentialities of integralism manifest. These circumstances are pivotal for this study insofar as they opened the field of "society" as a domain that integralists can colonize politically.

# Chapter Three

## SCIENCE AND METAPHYSICS OF SOLIDARITY

THE BUILDINGS of the European Union undulate over the hills of Brussels. The gleaming headquarters of the European Parliament looms over the city's quartier Leopold. If one walks through this complex of buildings, one can observe the members of Parliament, their staff, and parliamentary personnel doing what appears to be rather conventional legislative work. The 626 elected MEPs are drawn from fifteen member states and represent almost one hundred political parties. They are divided into four major European political groupings: the European People's Party, the Socialists, the Liberals, and the Greens. They serve on parliamentary committees, draft reports, debate issues, and vote on European legislation. Two things might initially strike the observer as somewhat unusual: first, the Parliament conducts its business at two venues in Brussels and Strasbourg with the day-to-day work of the Parliament conducted in Brussels and most of the voting in plenary sessions held monthly in Strasbourg.[1] Second, the work of this supranational institution is conducted in eleven official languages creating a staggering translation burden for all parliamentary work. What might be overlooked by the casual observer is the fact, the glaring fact, that the legislative power within the peculiar structure of the EU is not exclusively or primarily held by Parliament.

The European Commission and the Council of Ministers are vested with the power to propose legislation while the authority to pass legislation is held primarily by the Council of Ministers and secondarily by the European Parliament. The Parliament has the power to approve the EU's budget in a simple up or down vote. Under the expanded "codecision" procedure conferred on the Parliament by the Amsterdam Treaty (1997), it can now compel amendments of proposed bills with an absolute majority vote of its members. About three-quarters of the EU's law making is subject to the Parliament's codecision powers and thereby to a de facto veto. The Parliament also gained the power to vote on the accession of new member states and to block the investiture of the European Commission. It can also remove the commission with a two-thirds vote of censure. Although this latter power was not officially invoked, parliamentary scrutiny of mismanagement, nepotism, and alleged corruption within the commission resulted in the resignation of all its members, including its president Jacques Santer, in early 1999. Romano Prodi, former Italian prime minister, was appointed as the new president and he in turn nominated the new College of Commissioners, which was reviewed by the Parliament and approved in the fall of 1999.

Historically, the main challenge facing the Parliament has been to wrest for itself a wide-ranging democratic role. Many MEPs insist this can only be achieved through a written federal constitution, which would establish democracy as a first principle of the European Project. The parliament has always been the institution within the EU most committed to federalism—the issue that, in many respects, drew me to this unusual institution. I viewed the discourse on federalism from a peculiar perspective, not merely as a question of supranational institutions and powers, but as a much broader and far older set of questions. The discourses at the Parliament that coalesce around the issue of federalism permitted inquiry into the character of a European social order that long predates the EU. The natural history of this discourse is crucial for an anthropology of Europe in general and for the issues explored in this study in particular.[2]

The purpose of the analysis that follows is to provide a depiction of the European project against which integralists formulate their political insurgency. Again, the premise of this analysis is that integralist politics is taking shape in response to transformations set in motion by advanced European economic and political integration, most centrally the retreat of a specific modernist delineation of society. To grasp the broader significance of the recrudescence of integralism at the close of the century requires a prior understanding of the social imperatives that have defined the European Union.

## SOCIAL ORDER

For a cohort of politicians and civil servants who had experienced the devastation of the First and Second World Wars, the European institutions that took form in the early 1950s gave expression to their deep distrust of politics rooted in national agendas. Indeed, the first principle of the EU is the rejection of the nation-state as the preeminent institutional vehicle for defining economic interests and achieving political ends. The federalism that took root in Brussels was designed to thwart deformations of power—specifically, those based on unbridled nationalism, fascism, and Nazism. The great advantage of the new European Community was that it lacked history: it could configure policies sensitive to the traditional interests, affinities, and antagonisms of its member states, while not becoming hostage to those histories. Indeed, the project seemed to permit an escape from history.[3]

I found a core of senior politicians who were distinguished by their restlessness and intensity. They are the "federalists." Impatient and driven, they were the ardent believers in "Europe"; they identified with the project's historic mission. These apparently conventional politicians harbored surprisingly subversive convictions. They believed, often from direct personal experience, that the European nation-state was an inadequate—if not a failed—framework for addressing contemporary political challenges. They had formulated an alternative vision, of a federal Europe. To mediate their vision, they embraced two surrogate frameworks of power. French socialist modernism and Catholic social doctrine operated as surrogates, insofar as they profoundly influenced the architecture of the emerging polity, yet they were not doctrines or official policies of the EU.

There was one person whom my interlocutors deferred to when I asked them about the philosophical and practical tasks of interweaving these two traditions, Jacques Delors, then president of the European Commission (1985–94).[4] Delors is generally portrayed as the transcendent "Eurocrat"; like Jean Monnet, he is a carrier of the technocratic tradition of French socialist modernism from Paris to Brussels (Delors 1992; Ross 1995).[5] But he is more. There were few people within the European Community who had a more subtle and far-reaching understanding of Catholic social teaching than Delors.[6] I asked Leo Tindemans, a highly respected Christian Democrat, why Delors, a French Socialist, was such a passionate champion of "subsidiarity," the key principle of the Catholic discourse on political power and social justice. Tindemans pointed out the crucial importance of Delors's formative experience in the 1950s and 1960s, when he had been deeply involved in the modernization of the Catholic labor movement in France.[7] While engaged in that endeavor, Delors developed a thorough understanding of social Catholicism, particularly the theory of "personalism" as interpreted by Emmanuel Mounier.[8] From Mounier, Delors derived a distinctive sociological perspective:

> Society according to Mounier could not be reduced to a market writ large or a utilitarian agglutination of isolated individuals. . . . Society grew from delicate interdependence in which different social groups owed one another active solidarity. . . . The state and politics had a role, but in facilitating, rather than substituting for, the active agency of groups and moralized individuals working together. Delors was thus not immersed in, and did not emerge from France's secular Left tradition, whether socialist or communist." (Ross 1995:17)

Delors, in fact, only became a member of the Parti Socialiste in 1974 during the party's reconstruction under François Mitterrand and served as Mitterrand's minister of finance in the early 1980s before his appointment to the European Commission (Ross 1995:253n9). In the person of Jacques Delors, the two traditions—social Catholicism and French social modernism—intersected, and through his leadership both were brought to bear on the construction of the European Union.

## MIDDLING MODERNISTS

The project of French social modernism was centrally concerned with the conceptualization of society as a field of human interdependence susceptible to planning and administration through the application of "scientific" principles. Paul Rabinow has examined the remarkable history of this type of administrative engineering as it took shape in France between 1832 and 1939. For the very foreshortened summary that follows, however, I have selected three figures as distinctively illustrative of this technocratic tradition: Henri Sellier (1883–1943), Etienne Clémentel (1864–1932), and Jean Monnet (1888–1979).

Rabinow locates the basic conceptual innovation that opened the way for this modern political engagement with society around the rise of the "social question" in nineteenth-century France: that is, the fundamental problem of societal cohesion in the face of widening material inequalities between classes. "During the last two decades of the century, a range of reform groups extending from Social Catholics to non-revolutionary socialist factions attempted to map antagonistic classes onto a common space regulated by social and scientifically derived norms. Moving toward such a world required recasting century-long practices and assumptions about the nature of the individual, the state, space, and society" (1989:169). The idiom which would mediate the transition from "moralism" to the political economy of "welfarism" was "solidarity." Various reformers sought to orient the project of the French state around issues of social interdependence and integration. They sought to make the notion of collectivity—the idea of "society"—the dominant preoccupation of the state:

> The period between the International Exposition of 1889 . . . and the International Exposition of 1900 (held under the banner of Solidarity, a discourse of social interdependency that spanned the center of the political spectrum) marks the beginning of a major shift in the discourse of the social sphere. Just as these groups [of reformers] were arguing that society, and not the individual, constituted the *real*, so too the state (along with new social sciences) was beginning to replace both the church and industry as regulator of social relations. (1989:169–70)

This ambitious political movement was led by social theorists and planners who devised a comprehensive technocratic politics of a modern industrial society. The subject of their interventions encompassed a broad field covering infrastructures of industry, transportation, public works, and social welfare. This development was personified by Henri Sellier, socialist politician, minister of public health, and a major figure in French urban planning:

> The norms guiding Sellier's emerging socialist modernism were the welfare of the population, the maximizing of individual potential, and the linkage of these two engineered by an efficient administration manned by committed specialists dedicated to the public good. . . . [He] conceived of the problem in terms of mobilizing political support for this flexible, new administrative structure—based on statistical projections and abstract social unities—while retaining traditional political accountabilities and social bonds. While explicitly concerned with social justice, Sellier sought to move beyond right/left political distinctions as well as traditional class divisions. (Rabinow 1989:320)

Out of the work of a group of highly pragmatic socialists like Sellier, a movement emerged with cadres of social technicians—middling modernists—at its center, who, through their analyses and administrative interventions, sought to arbitrate a distinctive social order, through a "science of solidarity."[9] What gave the movement vibrancy was a spirit of "experimentation"; its legitimacy derived from a thorough engagement with the nuance of the contemporary political and cultural "milieu." Social intervention was understood as historically contingent: "History was never finished; each battle was only temporary, even if particular moments lasted centuries. This was *la longue durée* with a vengeance: a picture of constant change, open to modest modification through wisdom and patient intervention" (1989:196). These early French modernists, attentive to human geography and urbanistics, pursued a "humanistic, historically mediated conception of spatial and social forms. They sought to identify forms guided, at least in part, by norms—norms articulated by modern science and applied by disinterested public servants." They also embraced the concept of *genres de vie* "emphasizing the milieu as active variable linking society, nature and history" (1989:195).

A crucial change began to ensue at the turn of the nineteenth century as the field of administrative planning shifted from the highly differentiated "historico-natural milieu" to an "anonymous space of regulation and rationalization." In other words, the laboratory of social intervention for middling modernists was no longer *la cité*—a public space of politics—but increasingly an administrative abstraction, a "socio-technical" *agglomération*. "While Sellier clung to history and locale as sources of legitimacy and solidarity, his younger assistants and successors were more relentless, gradually stripping away such architectural, historical, and social references in the name of efficiency, science, progress, and welfare: middling modernism" (Rabinow 1989:322). The shift in Sellier's technical approach had fundamental political consequences: "local-level political participation" was superseded by "social-scientific administration and the exigencies of cost analysis" (1989: 321). This move disenthralled socialist modernism from an engagement with the social and cultural specificity of the small towns, the urban districts, and the regions of France and required that its principles and practices be universalized.

This brings us to Etienne Clémentel (1864–1932), who as minister of commerce (1915–20) established a program of state-directed management of the French economy by a small group of what Rabinow calls "unbureaucratic bureaucrats" (1989:326). The First World War was a profound catalyst for this transmutation. During the war Clémentel assumed vast powers, spanning control of industry, trade, transportation, supply, and postal services. He was the real organizer of the French war effort and Jean Monnet, still in his twenties, became his *directeur de cabinet*:

> Clémentel was an ardent advocate of increasing the role of bureaucratic technicians in order to rationalize the economy. He planned a considerable expansion of the research and information components of the Ministry and enforced compliance on the part of reluctant industrialists through his control over the allocation of resources. Clémentel proposed the annual publication of production statistics, the creation of a prices board to determine normal prices through the expert assessment by bureaucrats of production costs, and the establishment of an industrial council, which was to be a state-supervised alliance of industry and science to ensure that French industry would remain in the vanguard of modern technological advance. (Rabinow 1989:325–26)

In fact, Clémental's work went much further in the direction of an international regime of planning and coordination broaching a new dimension of the "science of solidarity." He and Monnet were confronted at the outbreak of the war with the intrinsic limitations of economic management under the domination of competing nation-states. In response they organized an integrated supranational system of cooperation among the Allies that managed with great efficiency wartime allocations of food and transport (Monnet 1978:53–77). They constructed a remarkable arrangement to handle the distribution of vast resources among France, Italy, and Britain under the cooperative control of a tiny coterie of managers.

It is no surprise that with peace Clémentel and Monnet advocated an extension of their planning regime for the reconstruction of Europe. The United States refused to support the Clémental Plan, insisting on free-market arrangements, and leaving Clémental to lament: "That's the end of the solidarity we worked so hard for. Without it, and without the altruistic, disinterested co-operation that we tried to achieve among the Allies and should have extended to our former enemies, one day we'll have to begin all over again" (quoted in Monnet 1978:75). Monnet, however, continued to struggle for a few more years with the technical operation of another ill-fated supranationalism. As deputy to the secretary-general of the League of Nations, he helped to prevent the partitioning of Austria, while witnessing the dismal struggles over Upper Silesia, the Saar, and German reparations. Monnet's experience at the League confirmed the conviction expressed earlier by Clémental, that peace in Europe based on national sovereignty was impossible (Monnet 1978:84). He left the Secretariat in 1921 and returned to his family's ailing cognac business.[10]

By 1938 Monnet was already intimately involved in the preparation for war, and for the duration of the Second World War he filled a series of important posts in London and Washington. Much of his work in exile focused, as it had during World War I, on the management of high-level military supply and coordination among the Allies.[11] This was punctuated in 1943 with eight months in Algeria during which he participated in the founding of a de facto French government under the Comité français de libération nationale (CFLN), which quickly came under the control of Charles de Gaulle (Monnet 1978:150–211).

## A METHOD

Monnet returned in 1946 to formulate what was to become the penultimate expression of the French social modernist project: the French Plan—also known as the Monnet Plan—for the reconstruction of postwar France.[12] Monnet and his close advisors laid out a "philosophy" and "method" for the plan with technical management of the economy at its center, though its modernist aims went much further: "To transform France, we must first transform the French Establishment" (Monnet 1978:245).[13] The plan reiterated a familiar litany of the science of solidarity, however it also advanced a logic of power increasingly under the sway of a technocratic universalism, that prepared the way for French social modernism to assume a European scope. Rabinow describes precisely this dynamic:

> [B]oth the norms and form of [French modernism] were becoming increasingly autonomous—freed from previous historical and natural constraints, defined by their own operations, and claiming universal status. This universalism, in turn, formed the ground of legitimacy for bypassing a political

participation seen as shortsighted, self-interested, and destructive of the public good. (1989:13)

Monnet self-consciously devised what he conceived of as a "democratic method," one that was intended to undermine ideological differences and promote what he referred to as "participationism."[14] The plan "is essentially a method of convergent action and a means whereby everyone can relate his own efforts to those of everyone else. It is concerned as much with orientation as with control" (1978:258). The first French Plan (1947–52) was well suited to bringing to bear the practices of middling modernism on the political economy of postwar France:

> Time was propitious for experiments in collective effort: the patriotic impulses released by the Liberation were still powerful, and they had not yet found an adequate outlet. The nationalization of various industries, long awaited and recently achieved, was no longer a goal, but a vehicle for making collective progress in ways that now only had to be defined. Everyone felt that progress was possible, but no one knew precisely what to do. In this situation, the Plan could be a genuinely "national enterprise"—an expression that could at last take on practical meaning. (Monnet 1978:239)

This stage of the social modernist project was accompanied by a shift in rhetoric substituting contingent notions of "interdependence," "participation," and "convergence" for the monolithic ideal of "solidarity." An open-ended "method" was formalized, as modernist planning was superseded by more routinized technocratic practice. The persuasive power of the method would render political pressure or coercion unnecessary. Monnet quotes himself describing to his associates how convergence would take hold: "When you take people from different backgrounds, put them in front of the same problem, and ask them to solve it, they're no longer the same people. They're no longer there to defend their separate interests, and so they automatically take a common view. You'll see: the Plan will work without imposing anything on anyone" (1978:248). This "empirical attitude" and faith in progressivism was unassailable. "The Plan, like life, is a continuous creation" (1978:259). "Once it [the Plan] was set in motion, its own impetus would create the internal and external conditions that were essential to its success" (Monnet 1978:254).[15]

Two institutions were at the center of the French Plan, the council and the commission. Both institutions, with modest changes, were ensconced as the core structures of the EC in 1967. The Planning Council, which was the supreme political body, was headed by the prime minister, and composed of twelve government ministers and twelve public figures chosen for their special expertise (Monnet 1978:240). The role of the council was to direct and oversee the wide-ranging activities of the Planning Commission. Monnet described the planning commissioner's remarkable role—which he both created and filled—and its sweeping administrative powers: "He was to be the Head of Government's permanent delegate to all Ministerial departments; he was given extensive powers of inquiry, and the Commissariat which he headed was empowered to enlist help from the staff of all Ministries and in particular from the statistical institutes."(1978:240). By virtue of this audacious maneuver, Monnet established his newly created position in the prime minister's office but independent of the bureaucratic structure of the ministries. His shrewd insistence on ambiguous accountability for the planning commissioner created a radical basis of power, which he subsequently superimposed on the organizational structure of the European project:

> Traditionalists would have placed the Commissariat under one of the economic Ministries, and the whole weight of civil service tradition tried to drag it back into this state subordination every time there was a Cabinet change. . . . No Ministerial post would have offered as much scope as the indefinable position of Planning Commissioner, attached to the Prime Minister's office. I was taking no one's place and becoming no one's superior. I was moving into territory that had hitherto had neither occupant nor name. (1978:240–41)

As commissioner, he defined the role of the paramount *technocrat* with enormous latitude for intervention, wide-ranging spheres of authority, and an overriding set of political aims and goals. He "invented" a tightly designed institutional structure, independent of direct ministerial jurisdiction and bureaucratic scrutiny, yet capable of influencing, if not compelling, change focused directly on the power elite of France. Above all, his institutional innovations recast the full domain of political economy as a field of "convergent action" under sway of technocratic surveillance. It was a deceptively simple and profoundly innovative formula.

Monnet as first planning commissioner set the imperatives governing the technocratic method:

> Production must be adjusted to requirements, or else there would be economic and social chaos. Such precise adjustment, allied to such massive efforts, at a time when there were no computers, could neither be decreed and supervised by a few civil servants nor left to the judgement of thousands of entrepreneurs. Our action had to be at once less dictatorial and more specific: we had to persuade, not compel, private enterprise to act in accordance with public needs. The best way, surely, was to bring together all the parties concerned, so that they could jointly seek the common interest, which no one of them could

determine alone, but in which all of them had a share. We agreed that what mattered above all was to work out a democratic method of action along these lines. (Monnet 1978:236)

Key to this method was a broad definition of societal problems that brought together what might otherwise be considered opposed parties and incompatible interests. It was implacably antibureaucratic, an approach supremely adroit at circumventing conventional divisions of power and patterns of authority. Monnet had created in the spirit of French social modernism an entirely new framework for the conceptualization of issues, the formation of broad and unlikely alliances, and the delineation of unusual possibilities for intervention. He portrayed his formulation of the "science of solidarity" as follows:

[T]he underlying philosophy of the French Plan was clear in my mind. What remained was to give it practical form: a method of concerted action whereby everyone could see where his own efforts fitted in with everyone else's. We had to ensure that everything—the most pressing needs and the most distant ambitions—obeyed the rule we had set ourselves: always start with an overall view. The experts who brought us their statistics, the industrialists with their dossiers, the trade unionists with their programs—all went away with extracts from our "Treatise on Method." We wanted them to digest it first and come back later, when we had established the framework within which we could all confer. Nor did it merely have to be established: it had to be invented. As I have said, civil servants, producers, and workpeople had never sat down together around the same table. If they had sometimes negotiated, they had done so bilaterally, on opposite sides of the table and in an atmosphere of confrontation. There had been a winning side and a losing side, so that the underlying problem had merely been postponed. (Monnet 1978:236–37)

He proudly notes: "there were never more than thirty senior officials on the Planning Commissariat, and the whole staff, including secretaries and doormen, was no more than a hundred or so" (1978:241). This spirit of economy and circumspection was reflected even in the style of communication favored by his associates in the Planning Commissariat: "short sentences, numbered paragraphs marking the transition from one idea to the next without clumsy bridging passages, a limited number of concrete words, and few adjectives" (1978:243).[16]

Monnet and his associates transplanted virtually all the major traditions of French socialist modernism, with a few refinements from the French nation-state, to an evolving federal Europe. The European Commission and the European Council, counterparts to the Planning Commission and Planning Council under the French Plan, became the dominant executive and legislative institutions respectively of the European

Community, and now of the European Union. The European Parliament's role was minor, as a consultative body that conferred a modest democratic legitimacy on the project's actions. Over the past half century the legacy of middling modernism has become deeply ingrained in the fabric of the very lean institutional structures and practices of Europe. By the late 1990s there were fewer than twenty thousand Eurocrats practicing the method and "austere art" of convergent action to deal with the daunting complexities of an expanding polity stretching over fifteen member states. And, in the waning days of the twentieth century, these European middling modernists pondered a daring enlargement of their project deep into east central and southern Europe, including thirteen new states—official candidates for EU membership—under the jurisdiction of their technocratic universalism.

## SACRED MODERN

The founders of the European Union shared a common political philosophy and personal experience. "Robert Schuman, Konrad Adenauer, and Alcide de Gaspari, were three exemplary Catholics, three men who had lived near foreign borders and were themselves of divided nationality" (Bromberger and Bromberger 1969:84). They drew on Christian Democratic principles to delineate a federal architecture for the European Community, referred to in its early history wryly as "Vatican Europe."[17] Social Catholicism influenced by "neo-Thomist" writers, most notably Jacques Maritain and Emmanuel Mounier, became a dominant force in the European movement.[18] Their philosophy and political economy promoted a durable and wide-ranging politics oriented toward discriminating a "common good" upon which a broad societal consensus could be built.[19] This politics, in turn, fostered a style of political analysis, a tempo for institution building, and an ethical grounding for EU action.[20]

Social Catholicism, like French social modernism, has its roots in the emergence of industrial societies in the late nineteenth century. It addressed, however, the "social question" in a wholly different way. Rather than pursuing technocratic interventionism, the Catholic approach seeks to foster an intricate moral discourse through which conditions of individual autonomy and ties of social interdependence are subject to ongoing analysis and facilitation. Catholic political economy starts from a distinctive conception of the relationship between society and the individual:

> Man is a social person, who achieves his perfection only in society. The state exists to help the persons who live within the society. This is the meaning of the Latin word, subsidium, aid, help. Normally, this aid is indirect by the care of

the complex conditions that enable the subordinate [groups] . . . and individuals to care for their own needs. This complex of conditions is what has been traditionally called the "common good." (Mulcahy 1967:762)

The Catholic discourse is preoccupied with shifting patterns of interdependence encompassing virtually all groups in society. Its interventions are oriented toward sustaining dynamic bases of solidarity expressed in reciprocating ties of aid and stewardship. The peculiar power of Catholic social doctrine derives, however, as much from its activist outlook as its principled forbearance.

The activist dimension of the Catholic engagement with society is counterbalanced with a notable commitment to restraint. The autonomy and the "active agency of groups" are to be preserved and protected, thus requiring explicit limitations on governmental intervention, particularly as exercised by the state. This endows the Catholic discourse with what appears to be a conservative dynamic that fundamentally distinguishes it from the interventionist premises of French social modernism. To read this Catholic commitment to restraint as conservative, however, is misleading because it may in fact constitute the most radical elements of Catholic political economy. Restraint operates in a paradoxical way in this framework, since by preserving the autonomy of various groups Catholic political practice in effect sustains *diversity*. This commitment to pluralism in turn promotes ongoing societal differentiation and advancement of a "common good." Jacques Maritain (1950) formulated this philosophical approach to diversity as follows:

[A] sound application of the pluralist principle and the principle of the lesser evil would require from the State a juridical recognition of the moral codes peculiar to those minorities comprised in the body politic whose rules of morality, though defective in some regard with respect to perfect Christian morality, would prove to be a real asset in the heritage of the nation and its common trend toward good human life. Such recognition would not be grounded on a right, I know not what, of which any moral way of life whatsoever would be possessed with regard to civil law, but on the requirements of the political common good, which in democratic society demands on the one hand a particular respect for the inner forces of conscience of the human subject, and, on the other hand, a particular care not to impose by force of law rules of morality too heavy for the moral capacity of large groups of the population. (Maritain 1950, quoted in Sigmund 1988:175)

This approach also accounts for a deep suspicion within the Catholic movement of the unbridled operation of capitalist markets and, in the notable case of Emmanuel Mounier, misgivings about the influence of the liberal democratic state.[21] Both were understood to debase "moral diversity" and "spiritual autonomy" through the advance of pervasive materialism and insensate rationalism. The Catholic doctrine that has come to encompass this broad-based commitment to diversity and restraint is known as the principle of *subsidiarity*.[22]

The Catholic discourse opens onto a deep substratum of European social philosophy reaching back to the thirteenth-century writings of Thomas Aquinas, particularly his appropriation of Aristotelian philosophy to underpin a form of "Christian rationalism."[23] For those who embrace Catholic social doctrine, the EU embodies a series of fundamental political and ethical challenges first delineated by Aquinas in *Summa theologiae*. They engage the European project in terms of what might be understood as a "sacred modern" epistemology.[24] What they find in Aquinas, the "Angelic Doctor," as Pius V described him, is a sociology, a means to act within and upon the world. They find a conception of "civil society" that allows them to pursue disciplined political analyses and interventions, a Christian teleology.[25]

Aquinian philosophy was refined into a modern theory of social justice through a series of well-known papal encyclicals beginning with Leo XIII's *Rerum novarum* (1891), which sets out the basic tenets of Catholic social doctrine. Pius XI's encyclical, *Quadregesimo anno* (1931), reviewed the development of Catholic social teaching in the forty years after *Rerum novarum*, and this was further elaborated upon by John XXIII's *Mater et Magistra* (1961) and *Pacem in terris* (1963). What the neo-Thomists—above all Jacques Maritain (1891–1965)—added to this tradition of Catholic social teaching is a democratic legitimacy and practice, which became the foundation of the Christian Democratic political movement in Europe.[26] Again, the term subsidiarity has come to designate the philosophical and sociological architecture of this sacred modern tradition around which many of those who are designing the European Union align their intentions and articulate their visions.

By the 1990s subsidiarity had become a central defining concept in the broad-based political debate on European integration; it came to serve as a pivotal idea not just for those preoccupied with the Christian Democratic political economy.[27] The centrality of the concept was based on its suitability to serve as an axis in the struggle over the definition and the disposition of power within an emerging federal polity. The effort to define subsidiarity as a political instrument discloses not merely a single concept but a range of concepts and formulations, centrally concerned with sustaining diversity. Specifically, it serves as a principle for circumscribing domains of action for public authorities, for establishing formulas for allocating governmental powers, for defining norms of societal stewardship, and for setting the conditions of individual freedom. Most crucial, however, is the application of subsidiarity to the basic question of federalism—that is, what powers are to be retained by member states, regions, and localities and what powers shifted to the European Union by virtue of integration?[28] In other words, subsidiarity has been employed to mediate a debate on issues of "sovereignty." In the following section I have very briefly summarized how elements of Catholic social teaching have come to operate as a social and cultural grounding of European federalism.[29] I suggest that the authority of social Catholicism to serve as the second surrogate discourse of European federalism derives from its potential to sustain simultaneously "pluralism" and "solidarity" as principles guiding the creation of a distinctive social order and not just an integrated market or, for that matter, a technocratic polity.

## POLITICAL CONSENSUS

There are many ways to depict how the foundational principles of Catholic social theory made their way from papal encyclicals to the Maastricht Treaty on European Union.[30] For the purposes of this analysis, I sketch briefly the manner in which concepts central to Catholic social doctrine have become ingrained in the political discourse of the European Parliament. Leo Tindemans, initially in his role as Christian Democratic prime minister of Belgium and more recently in his capacity within the Parliament as president of the European People's Party, and the late Altiero Spinelli, an independent member of the Communist and Allies Group within the Parliament, are the principal figures in this very abridged account.[31] This discussion is important because it helps explain how and why subsidiarity gained currency among political groups that are not generally seen as sympathetic to Catholic political economy.

In 1974, at a time when European integration seemed stalled, Tindemans was asked by the European Council of which he was a member to define what he meant by the term "European Union," a concept he had been urging them to consider. Tindemans drafted an ambitious and far-reaching document that formally extended the European idea from that of "Community" to "Union." Known as the Tindemans Report, the document argued for a decisive shift from the mere coordination of policy to the creation of common policy over a broad range of competencies, including economic and monetary policy, defense, foreign relations, social policy, and citizenship.

Economic turmoil—"rates of inflation and unemployment the likes of which have never been seen by the present generation," provoked by the oil crisis of the early 1970s—served as a backdrop to the report. For Tindemans the crisis revealed the classic contradiction between the powers of the Community and its member states. The inability of Community institutions to formulate unified economic and foreign policies to deal with the oil and related crises yielded a resurgence of "purely national preoccupations." He diagnosed the threat to unity not on the level of the Community, where the weaknesses were expressed, but on the level of the member states. "The fragile nature of Europe must surely be a reflection of the powerlessness of our States" (Tindemans 1977:5). The retention of national control—largely devoid of power—exposed the political bankruptcy of the member states and thereby, in his view, doomed the development of the Community. He refers to it as the "two-fold spiral of powerlessness" (1977:91).

Tindemans's solution was itself in the classic mode, calling for an acceleration of the construction of Europe. By this means Tindemans sought to recapture the pragmatic foundation of the European project. His central argument was that political, economic, social, and perhaps even cultural problems that seem to be intractable within or between nation-states can be redefined when either raised to the European level or devolved to the level of regions or local authorities. The economies and politics of scale achieved by further integration would provide classic efficiencies that would recast the range and scope of institutional remedies. The less dramatic call for decentralization in his report was intended to improve governmental responsiveness, manageability, and democratic accountability. The simultaneous transfer of powers to the Community, regions, and local authorities held the promise of "a new type of society, a more democratic Europe with a greater sense of solidarity and humanity" (1977:9). It also constituted an assault on the powers of the nation-state from above and below.[32]

Tindemans had pulled together recurring themes drawn from visions of a European Union discussed as early as the League of Nations. What was novel about his report was that it drew together various strands of theorizing about Europe into an integrated plan. The transition from "Community" to "Union" was presented as a systematic course; the role of Catholic social doctrine was clear but tacit.

The term "solidarity" is used throughout Tindemans's text, but the use of "subsidiarity," he acknowledged, was implicit. Tindemans interpreted subsidiarity in an interview at the Parliament during the drafting of the Maastricht Treaty in 1991:

Subsidiarity is an old principle. You know people now-a-days refer back to Thomas Aquinas, other people say the principle is much older still. I do not know, I am not an historian. But certainly in Thomas you will find it. In Christian social doctrine . . . there are two principles for the organization of society.

The principle of subsidiarity on the one hand and the principle of solidarity on the other. Subsidiarity requires that what can be done in a satisfactory way by a lower authority must not be taken over by a higher one. So in the organization of a country, what a village commune is doing well must not be taken over by a province and what a province is doing well must not be taken over by a region, what a region is doing well must not be taken over by the state.

He explained to me his reluctance to use the term "subsidiarity" in the report noting that as a student one of his professors cautioned: "take care with the principle of subsidiarity . . . because reactionary people very often invoke it to justify doing nothing at the higher level." There is another "danger" that the concept might pose in the minds of "reactionary people." Subsidiarity establishes a social order in which pluralism is an absolutely fundamental condition. Rather than designing a polity, the Catholic doctrine that Tindemans invoked was concerned with creating a societal milieu within which a polity can be conceived and constructed. Whereas the design of the polity is ambiguous, the nature of the society and political economy advanced by the doctrine is more certain.

Michael P. Fogarty describes the operation of this Catholic political economy from which Tindemans drew:

> There is work to be done at every level of social organization from the individual to the international community, and the responsibility for what can be done at lower levels must not be allowed to gravitate to the top. Every social unit or group has a sphere of work which it can do efficiently in the interests not only of its members but of society as a whole, and this sphere must be defined and reserved for it. A higher authority may of course insist that some subordinate group live up to its responsibilities. It may call on the subordinate group to justify its independence by proving that there is indeed some sphere in which it can work efficiently on its own. It may check excesses or suggest new lines of development. It may "direct, watch, stimulate, and restrain." . . . But only in the last, extreme resort may it take over its subordinates' responsibilities and discharge them itself. (1957:41)

Centralization is appropriate in this framework only where economies of scale or the nature of a social task make it absolutely essential. In general, however, the principle demands the allocation of authority minimally necessary for groups and associations to fulfill their particular societal roles. The federative authority of subsidiarity also upholds domains of ideological pluralism and thereby the protection of minority positions:

> Different "spiritual families," in a common French phrase—Catholic, Protestant, Marxists, humanists, or whoever they may be—should . . . be permitted and enabled to follow their own way of life, even when they are in a minority in a nation or group as a whole. . . . [Ideological pluralism] reduces conflict

since it allows everyone, without discrimination . . . to build up a set of associations which fits his own ideals. (Fogarty 1957: 42)

By maintaining diversity of ideological perspectives, the terms of political engagement are also established. And, though it seems counterintuitive, the doctrine holds that it is precisely in the clash of these diverse orientations and their vigorous expression that solidarity is engendered:

> Since, in an imperfect world, some conflicts of ideals and loyalties are inevitable, the essential thing is that they should be fought out in a way which lets the truth eventually emerge and form the basis for a settlement. But this is likely to happen only if the parties in conflict hold firm, clear views which provide a solid basis for argument, and yet are open and sensitive to the views of others . . . everyone must sail "under his own flag." . . . And organizations have a right and duty to "sail under their own flag" in the same way as individuals; for association with others is needed even to reach a full understanding of one's own ideals, let alone to express them effectively in action. "Tolerance" is hardly the word for this attitude. . . . There is . . . a warmth of common humanity and common responsibility before God. But "the rigor of the game" is also part of its essence. (Fogarty 1957: 42–43)

Political discourse, under the terms of Catholic social theory, operates in such a way that issues are contextualized constantly within a wider interplay of interests and remedies. This concern for the "totality" creates a shifting consensus that can embrace, relativize, and transform a broad spectrum of beliefs and interests. This approach, by restraining partisanship and frustrating single issue agendas, is intended to achieve a "common good" in which shifting and unequal societal interests are linked through ties of cooperation and mutual aid to achieve social justice. The powerful sociological consequence of the political practice of subsidiarity is the promotion of a diversely constituted "civil society" and "social market."[33]

The Tindemans Report specified a comprehensive plan for the European Union and a program of reform necessary to build a federal polity. It reiterated the historical priorities upon which the European project was founded and employed a comprehensive political framework to give his plan theoretical and moral integrity. Although the report itself did not immediately ignite a program of change, it did set the terms of debate around which a broad-based political consensus could gradually be formed. It took the skill of Altiero Spinelli (1907–86) to demonstrate how this political consensus could be devised within the European Parliament.

In the early 1980s Altiero Spinelli, MEP, was an independent member of the Communist and Allies Group within the Parliament. Earlier he had served on the European Commission. His commitment to European unification was truly distinguished. Spinelli opposed Mussolini in the 1930s and had been imprisoned by the fascist regime on the island of Ventotene, where he composed his famous federalist manifesto for a "United States of Europe" (Lipgens 1985:471–92). Four decades later, as *rapporteur* for the Committee on Institutional Affairs, he drafted a report for the Parliament entitled, "Reform of Treaties and Achievement of European Union" (1982), which became the basis for the "Draft Treaty Establishing European Union" (1984)—essentially a federal constitution of Europe (Moravcsik 1998:357–58). Both documents followed closely the agenda set out by Tindemans. Notably, Spinelli employed the principle of subsidiarity specifically as a formula for the reallocation of competencies between the European Union and member states. This marked the first time that the Catholic nomenclature had been employed as a pivotal formula for conceptualizing European federalism (Spinelli 1983:210). The Draft Treaty, which was passed by the Parliament but never ratified by the member states, specified revisions of treaties to achieve a political union. Its most distinctive thrust was institutional reform that would have enhanced the democratic legitimacy of the Community by expanding the powers of the European Parliament.

By far Spinelli's greatest contribution, however, was his engineering of a broad and enduring coalition committed to union and embracing virtually all the political groups in the Parliament. Indeed, he established political union—within a federal structure mediated by subsidiarity—as the paramount agenda of the Parliament as a whole. Starting from essentially a left-wing position, he traced a rationale for unification that furthered social justice and democratic accountability. (We return to Spinelli's influence on the revamping of a European socialist agenda in chapter 6.) Political union would, he argued, create a powerful new framework to achieve democratic control over the economic forces unleashed by the Economic Community. The federal structure, governed by the principle of subsidiarity, would provide the context within which to revitalize European politics in general and those of the European left in particular. Spinelli demonstrated how one could, from the standpoint of all but the most nationalist political parties in the Parliament, make a compelling case for unification. Spinelli's leadership also established the Committee on Institutional Affairs as the focus for theorizing on constitutional issues within the Parliament. Drawing on senior political leaders and constitutional experts, the committee drafted a series of reports that stated the European Parliament's position on the specific architecture of the European Union, as it was taking form as the Maastricht Treaty (Colombo 1990a; Giscard d'Estaing 1990). These reports asserted a vision of a federal polity very much in the spirit of Spinelli.

Thus, Catholic social doctrine took root as a surrogate discourse on federalism, through the deliberations of the European Parliament, the insistence of the German Bundesrat (representing German regions), and the activism of the European Commission under Jacques Delors, and it came to define a critical provision of the Maastricht Treaty:[34]

> The Community shall act within the limits of the powers conferred upon it by this Treaty and of the objectives assigned to it therein. . . . In areas which do not fall within its exclusive competence, the Community shall take action in accordance with the principle of subsidiarity, only if and in so far as the objectives of the proposed action cannot be sufficiently achieved by Member States and can therefore, by reason of the scale or effects of the proposed action, be better achieved by the Community. . . . Any action by the Community shall not go beyond what is necessary to achieve the objectives of this Treaty. (1992 Treaty on European Union, Article 3b)

Again, the centrality of this constitutional provision rests on its ability to foster a diversely constituted federal union. It permits the integration of a wide range of member states with different political histories, legal traditions, economic systems, bureaucratic structures, taxation policies, trade practices, education institutions, linguistic conventions, and so on. It means such diverse entities as Sweden and Greece or Luxembourg and Britain can operate within an integrated political framework. The constitutional significance of subsidiarity rests on its ability to serve as a counterweight to the forces of "convergence" and "harmonization" promoted by the technocratic operation of the EU—as Nicholas Emiliou puts it, as a barrier against "the enterprises of ambition." Subsidiarity is specified as a fundamental constitutional principle: "This Treaty marks a new stage in the process of creating an ever closer union among the peoples of Europe, where decisions are taken as closely as possible to the citizens." For those who fear that unification will subvert the diversities and distinctions of Europe, Article 3b of the treaty stands as the constitutional bulwark for pluralism.

The reallocations of power orchestrated by European integration under the terms of subsidiarity are both profound and enigmatic. Federalists are adamant that European integration is not merely about the reallocation of competencies or sovereignty, but about the *creation* of power. This is a classic federalist position premised on a forceful acknowledgment of the waning power of the European nation-states. It holds that governmental jurisdiction exercised over areas such as trade, defense, or environmental policy is limited or negligible when exercised by small states like Ireland or Denmark. Yet, when these competencies are pooled among fifteen or more member states, they can acquire enormous power.

Although it is clear that a profound reallocation of sovereignty has taken place among the member states of the EU, the actual consequences of these transactions are very difficult to appraise. The reallocation of competencies cannot be understood in terms of the simple transfer of sovereign prerogatives, largely because the nature of sovereignty itself changes as a result of the process of integration. A notion of more or less stable and independent public authority exercised by territorially bounded European nation-states is increasingly implausible. What can be said is that the circumspect application of subsidiarity, engineered through a modernist technocratic practice, has over the past half century created entirely new, though deeply ambiguous, bases of political and economic authority. It is authority that does not conform to conventional notions of sovereignty rooted in the history of the nation-state.[35]

## CONUNDRUM

The technocratic practice of French socialist modernism and the mediational politics of social Catholicism arose in response to an era of accelerating capitalist development and its social repercussions at the end of the nineteenth century. They are both challenged at the close of the twentieth century by economic forces channeled through the center of the European project, though appearing to emanate from beyond its jurisdictions. The creation of the single European market and the advance of European Monetary Union are aligning the EU, albeit fitfully, with the supranational scope and pacing of fast-capitalism, yet the telos of this regime targets precisely those instrumentalities of solidarity and consensus that have endowed the EU's project of political union with its raison d'être. It is this contradiction, this flaw that integralists have grasped and drawn to the center of their political theorizing and implanted at the heart of their subterfuge.

At the outset of the twenty-first century the rhetoric of global competitiveness has replaced that of European modernization. The premise of statist economic planning is being drawn into question by those who seek to engage what are presumed to be dazzling material possibilities of expanding European and global markets. A fast-capitalism, antagonistic to the social order out of which the European social market and welfare state were wrested, is being untethered in the name, ironically, of "unification." Its advance—codified by the single market and monetary union—undermines the possibility of a science, political economy, and metaphysics of solidarity as business and political elites avow a newfound faith in the market as the arbiter of the human condition.[36] While political leaders, particularly on the left, embrace the provisions of the Social

Chapter of the Maastricht Treaty as an enduring basis of social justice, the economic provisions of the treaty create a very different set of dynamics. Specifically, the convergence process by which member states qualified for European Monetary Union in 1998 radically constrained statist control by limiting fiscal and monetary policies primarily by forcing the reduction of public deficits to a small percentage of GDP. In other words, purely "economic" criteria set out in the "stability and growth pact" of the treaty have disciplined taxation policies and social welfare benefits and, perhaps most painfully, restricted interventions to address unemployment. With monetary union this dynamic is gaining further momentum as these eleven economies continue their realignments for European and global competition on the one hand, and as they begin the difficult processes of "structural reform" on the other. What this latter entails is the further deregulation of markets, reining in the subventions dispersed under the Common Agricultural Policy and, in general, curtailing social welfare programs, most notably pension benefits. The fledgling European Central Bank is the new arbiter of monetary policy among the eleven and, to varying degrees, among the other four member states as well as those states seeking EU membership, with price stability its key concern for the new currency, the euro. The nature of the central bank's independence or accountability to the EU and its member states is and will continue to be a highly contested issue.

Fast-capitalism thus operates in a classic manner under advanced European economic and political integration: increasing market liberalization and structural reform erode the complex architecture of solidarity that has formed the distinctive substructure of modern European society. This in turn is reflected in the nature of European political decision making and control. Indeed, as federalists would have it, political power will be redefined and recreated by the process of unification, but it will emerge in a new way, increasingly outside of the scrutiny and management of political authorities. Most significantly, the forces of European-wide markets will increasingly have the potential to transform society, circumventing the political supervision of the EU or, for that matter, the attenuated control of its member states. As I argued in the preceding chapter, perhaps the most striking example of this is the creation of a vast multiracial and multicultural society that has to an important degree taken place independent of any formal political agenda in its own right. That is to say, the intricately legislated course to economic and political integration created a profoundly pluralist Europe as a derivative process largely outside the institutional jurisdiction of the EU and largely independent of its political planning and control.

This brief analysis by no means represents a thorough, let alone balanced, assessment of the trajectory of EU development; rather it permits scrutiny of the critique of contemporary Europe framed notably by Jean-Marie Le Pen and his followers from which they forge their political insurgency. In the face of the EU's faltering science, political economy, and metaphysics of solidarity, they cast "culture" and "tradition" as alternative idioms of solidarity and as a basis of authority. This approach reopens the field of society as a domain upon which European integralists can forcefully cast their populism, expressionism, and pluralism.

# Chapter Four

## CULTURAL PHYSICIAN

A TINY dissident movement emerged in France at the close of the nineteenth century that mounted a revisionist assault on Marxism; its nonconformist members were known as "revolutionary syndicalists." Conceived by Georges Sorel and developed by his followers within groups like the Cercle Proudhon, the movement proposed an implausible, if not bizarre, revision of virtually all the basic tenets of Marxism.[1] Indeed, "revisionism" hardly captures the thorough evisceration of Marxist doctrine accomplished by the Sorelians.[2] What started as revisionism, in fact, opened up an entirely new ideological path upon which a virulent synthesis of socialism and nationalism took form. This synthesis jettisoned virtually the entire intellectual tradition of the European Enlightenment and circumscribed a wholly novel terrain for modern political radicalism. In the process it liberated "new" forces to propel political insurgency: the power of the irrational, the unconscious, and the intuitive.[3]

Sorelian socialism followed a remarkable and unlikely course. Specifically, two radical "alterations" of Marxist theory, formulated on or about 1910, were crucial in casting a new revolutionary politics that ultimately set the course to fascism. On the one hand, the economics of capitalism was superseded in the Sorelian scheme by the psychology of myth as the driving force of class struggle and the catalyst for revolutionary action. On the other, the "proletariat" as agent of revolution was supplanted by the "nation," unified across classes, as the moral framework for radical action. This chapter touches briefly on the innovations represented by the Sorelian and fascist legacies as a way to introduce the politics of Jean-Marie Le Pen. Le Pen is neither a Sorelian nor a fascist, but in the late twentieth century he and his followers drew on these two traditions to define an integralist politics for Europe.

Revolutionary syndicalism, as formulated in Sorel's *Reflections on Violence* (originally published in 1907), espoused a radical laborism: workers organized in syndicates—essentially fighting units—would, once galvanized by the "general strike," lead the socialist struggle against the bourgeois order.[4] Sorel's faith in the working class, however, was disclaimed abruptly in the face of what he and his followers believed to be a monumental historical impasse, an impasse that led them to repudiate the proletariat as the agent of revolution:

> The proletariat of the great industrial centers of western Europe corresponded to the portrait [Gustave] Le Bon had painted of it: it too was only a crowd, and

a crowd is conservative. . . . This proletariat was no longer and would never again be, an agent of antibourgeois revolution. One had therefore either to follow it into its retirement or find an alternate revolutionary force capable of destroying liberal democracy and rescuing the world from decadence. . . . [T]he ineffective proletariat would be replaced by the great rising force of the modern world, born of modernization, wars of independence, and cultural integration—that is, the nation. The nation with all its classes [was thus] joined together in the great fight against bourgeois and democratic decadence. (Sternhell 1994:26–27)

Thus, during the first decade of the twentieth century Sorelian socialism migrated toward the nationalism of Charles Maurras and his followers affiliated with L'Action française.[5] The new alignment was clearly drawn in Maurras's famous pronouncement: "a socialism liberated from the democratic and cosmopolitan element fits nationalism as a well made glove fits a beautiful hand" (quoted in Weber 1991:264). These activists sought a socialism with a national character, drawing its inspiration from "the old French socialism of Fourier and Saint-Simon, Considerant and Louis Blac, Lamennais, and George Sand and Eugène Sue—not from German intoxicants like those produced by Marx and Engels" (Weber 1991:266).[6] The social order imparted by this socialism became, under the sway of nationalism, antimaterialist, illiberal, and resolutely authoritarian. "Where Charles Maurras differed from the Socialists was not in matters of social *concern*, but in matters of social *order*—denouncing their egalitarian myths and their belief that authority stems from the mass when, to him, authority is clearly established only by the natural hierarchy of competence and birth. Maurras, then, opposes socialist democracy; he also opposes socialist internationalism" (Weber 1991:264). Implied is a radical inversion of the Durkheimian telos of modern society, a "socialism" founded on an ersatz "mechanical solidarity" and predicated on renewed sentiments of rootedness (Noiriel 1996).

Through the intellectual work and activism of Maurice Barrès, George Valois, Pierre Drieu la Rochelle, Marcel Déat, and Robert Brasillach an incendiary course was set in the direction of this new order through a "national revolution," which culminated in Vichy.[7] The same underlying synthesis continues to animate the politics of contemporary European integralists:

Thus, it was quite natural that a synthesis would arise between this new socialism, which discovered the nation as a revolutionary agent and the nationalist movement, which also rebelled against the old world of conservatives, against the aristocrats and the bourgeois, and against social injustices and which believed that the nation would never be complete until it had integrated the proletariat. A socialism for the whole collectivity and a nationalism that,

severed from conservatism, proclaimed itself as being by definition the mes-
senger of unity and unanimity thus came together to form an unprecedented
weapon of war against the bourgeois order and liberal democracy. (Sternhell
1994:27–28)

Like social Catholicism and French social modernism discussed in the
previous chapter, the advocates of this national socialist synthesis addressed forcefully, if not obsessively, solidarity and the nature of human
collectivities. They did not focus their radical interventions solely on social or economic structures, however, but emphasized the potential of a
cultural assemblage to serve as the basis of collectivity. Their socialism,
unified across classes, dissolved "society" into the "nation," thus creating
a nationalism that could become not just an idiom of solidarity but a
vehicle for social justice. They sought to formulate a politics that could
circumvent a disintegrating "bourgeois public sphere," underpinning liberal democracy, and engage directly the human substance of an integral
lifeworld.[8] These are the dissident maneuvers that connect Jean-Marie Le
Pen to the Sorelian legacy and the fascist synthesis.[9]

Le Pen has defined a comprehensive integralist agenda for France. The
project yielded significant popular support, ranging as high as 15 percent
of the vote in the first round of the French presidential elections of 1997.[10]
On the local level the successes of the Front national (FN) were also impressive, yielding hundreds of elected representatives and outright control
over four towns in the southeast of France: Toulon, Orange, Marignane,
and Vitrolles. Winning Vitrolles from the Socialists, the FN for the first
time took an absolute majority of the vote in a local contest, marking
perhaps the apogee of the FN's electoral ascendancy in the late 1990s. In
late 1998 and early 1999 a spectacular crisis of leadership and a bitter
battle for succession split the FN. More than half of the FN's politburo
were either expelled or resigned as did three of the four FN mayors and
three MEPs. Le Pen's faction gleaned barely over 5.7 percent of the vote
in the European elections of June 1999, the minimum needed to retain
five seats in the Parliament—less than half the party gleaned in the 1994
European election (Atkinson 1999:17–19).[11] This chapter focuses on the
interventions, at times maladroit interventions, by which Le Pen crafted
in the early and mid 1990s a European profile for his political insurgency.
His innovations aim to reanimate the national socialist synthesis against
various registers of Europeanization.[12] Chapter 10 examines an excoriating polemic formulated by Le Pen that captures these innovations and
shows how they spawned, at the end of the decade, a fully formed integralist politics of Europe. Ironically, the volatility of this polemic may
have helped foment the ruinous schism within Le Pen's own leadership
cadre.

## THE EUROPEAN

Roger Johnston, parliamentary assistant to Le Pen, arranged a series of interviews with MEPs from the Front national during a plenary session of the European Parliament in Strasbourg during the spring of 1991. I met Johnston a month earlier in his office in Brussels and he provided an overview of the positions of the FN and he agreed to schedule meetings with members of the group the following month in Strasbourg.

After a day of interviews with four MEPs, two from the FN, I called to check if Johnston had scheduled appointments for the following day. He confirmed the time for an interview with Bruno Gollnisch, another MEP, and invited me to the suite of offices within the parliamentary complex occupied by their political group. He indicated that Le Pen wished to speak with me. Expecting little more than a brief introduction, I took one of the mirrored elevators to the seventh floor and entered the suite. Johnston greeted me and almost immediately ushered me in to meet Le Pen. A conversation that lasted over an hour followed. I had the impression during this early encounter with Le Pen in May 1991 that he had recently constructed and was trying out a new "European" persona and that I was a test audience. In other words, I sensed that we were not engaged in a dialogue, but that I was being led through a scripted set piece as he articulated the basic elements of his integralist outlook.[12]

Le Pen was born June 6, 1928, in La Trinité-sur-Mer in Morbihan, Brittany. He is a robust figure with a broad face and ruddy complexion. His mien is animated with an open smile, which tends to fold down into a sly frown. When I met him he was wearing a double-breasted navy blazer, white shirt, and a bright floral tie. His physical demeanor is expressive, exuding a taut energy that one might associate with a much younger man. He engages the listener with a curious mix of generosity, amiability, and cunning. Le Pen is an expert subject.[13]

The presence of Le Pen and his associates at the European Parliament itself poses important questions.[14] The purely cynical view—which I held initially—was that the Parliament provided the Front national with a forum within which to articulate its resolutely French political agenda. Lacking the electoral strength to secure seats in the National Assembly, the FN took advantage of the European Parliament's different electoral rules, and the propensity of the French electorate to view European elections as an opportunity to register protest votes, to win seats in the European Parliament and thereby gain a measure of political legitimacy. This assessment is, no doubt, correct. However, circumstances conspired to make Le Pen a far more consequential figure in European politics. One formulation was decisive in this transformation: by linking nationalism to the emergence of a multicultural and multiracial Europe, Le Pen and his associates defined acutely the terms of political contestation that have come to have broad relevance across Europe. Indeed, their inventory of political imperatives—most notably on immigration—has moved from the margins to the center of political struggle in western Europe.[15] I had a chance to observe this metamorphosis at close range. Karel Dillen, president of the Vlaams Blok, Franz Schönhuber, president of the Die Republikaner, and Ian Paisley, president of the Democratic Unionist Party, were also interviewed during this period. These three have formulated integralist positions, which have *not* in themselves achieved the kind of European-wide influence of Le Pen's insurgency; Dillen and Schönhuber, however, strongly affirmed the importance of Le Pen's political breakthrough. Similarly, the leaders of the British National Party whom I subsequently encountered in London also recognized the centrality of Le Pen's innovation, specifically how it allowed them to align their politics with various registers of Europeanization.[16] Thus, the interviews with leaders of the FN were pivotal because they established the conjunction of a staunchly French integralism and the prospect of European integration. Above all, the conversations disclosed how the conceptualizing of racial and cultural pluralism in Europe was being fashioned within an integralist framework. This insight allowed me to scrutinize the historically specific elements of contemporary formations of integralism as they were taking a deeply ironic form.

While maintaining a fervently French orientation, Le Pen seized opportunistically upon a series of attacks against him to expand his political purview. In part this shift was catalyzed unintentionally by the activities of antiracist and antifascist movements orchestrated from within the European Parliament itself.[17] This was made most plain, as suggested in the previous chapter, in a parliamentary report drafted by Glyn Ford. Again, the critical labor performed by the Ford Report was to position Le Pen's politics within the history of *European* fascism and racism. While aimed at identifying the serious "threat" posed by the emergence of a new wave of racism and anti-Semitism, the report also gave Le Pen and the politics he articulates a powerful European identity.

In a brief conversation I had with Glyn Ford about the impact of his report, he rejected out of hand this idea that the report may have inadvertently strengthened the agenda of the Front national. In retrospect my questioning of Ford about this issue may have been tactless; nevertheless, there was a sense of unease within the Socialist Group in the Parliament with respect to the unintentional repercussions of the Ford report.

Two outcomes were particularly troubling: first, it provided Le Pen with a distinctive European profile that, in fact, gave him a new and expanded audience; second, and more disturbing, it tethered the debate on a multiracial and multicultural Europe to the most noxious aspect of Le Pen's political agenda, its resonances with French fascism. The splicing of the discourse on racial and cultural pluralism in Europe to an antiracist and antifascist politics perversely concedes to Le Pen the power to set the terms and parameters of struggle.[18] Rather than marginalizing Le Pen and his associates, it may have in fact allowed aspects of their agenda to leach into mainstream politics. Moreover, these attacks on Le Pen missed a significantly more troubling dimension of his politics. Far more devastating than whether or not Le Pen is a "racist" is the fact that he is creating a discursive field within which "racism" is increasingly difficult to define, confront, or oppose, where a multicultural and multiracial France and Europe emerge as *alien* concepts.

There is another important reason why Jean-Marie Le Pen's presence in the European Parliament is of fundamental significance. If Jean Monnet and Jacques Delors were carriers of the French social modernist project from Paris to Brussels, Le Pen is the carrier of its most ardent political critique. Le Pen understands intimately the derelictions of French social modernism. He knows that its failures lurk materially in decaying urban centers. He has fashioned a political vision that follows the course of a faltering "science of solidarity" through the deterioration in public services, the persistence of intractably high levels of unemployment, and the proliferation of extravagant forms of corruption by politicians and public officials. For Le Pen, the populist, the European Union is a manifestation of this tyranny wherein "big business" and "big brother" conspire under the dissolute mantle of progress. He is convinced of the failure of the modernist ideal of progressivism and he recognizes the emergence of new domains of alienation inaccessible to technocratic interventions:

> *Le Pen*: If power at all levels is no longer fed by moral codes, even lay or Marxist morals, it becomes a power without any faith. It then amounts to a corruption, which opens the way for tyranny.

Durkheim's vision of a dynamic organic solidarity as the basis of modern society is utterly compromised in Le Pen's view, because the "rebirth" of France and Europe is only possible by invoking the mysterious registers of mechanical solidarity: blood, earth, devotion, hierarchy, rootedness. It is from these symbolic elements, these inner verities, that the essential moral distinctions necessary for a rebirth of society are derived. To legitimize this integralist construal of collectivity requires a fundamental assault on modernist constructions of "truth" (Noiriel 1996).

## TRUTH AND REALITY

In the face of what he believes is a proliferating estrangement, Le Pen has framed a radical critique of Europe for which he prescribes a familiar imaginary of rebirth. The critique recurs in FN publications:

> The socialist/communist left, void of energy and ideas, and the right-wing UDF [Union of French Democracy], and RPR [Rally for the Republic], which have betrayed our national values, now come together only to fight the Front national and defend their privileges and perks. Their corruption disgusts the youth and demoralizes the nation. The Front national, an assembly of patriotic, lucid and courageous men and women, embodies the fight against decadence. Today, it is the only hope for the French people. In a world full of danger that will see many unexpected changes, our country needs a government that, with the strength of the people behind it, will be capable of putting into action a true program for the rebirth of France and Europe. (http://www.front-nat.fr/ October 1997)

From this general analysis Le Pen defines a trajectory by which a diffuse populism is transmuted to an ardent integralism with overt fascist resonances.[19] Le Pen accordingly fashions himself as a visionary who can see the true contours of reality. He discerns looming global struggles, a state of war, in which profound demographic forces are determining the fate of humankind. He draws intuitively on Michel Foucault's pivotal concept of "biopower" as the new adjunctive technology of his political vision:

> *Le Pen:* For several decades I have been aware of the importance of demographic transformations converging at the end of the twentieth century. Unfortunately, I may be one of the few politicians who is aware of this phenomenon. There is a contradictory evolution of demographic forces between the North and the South: the North is becoming poorer and older, the evolution of the South explodes with a young population. Without a radical reversal of this evolution the nations of the North will disappear within fifty years. Demographic colonization is much closer to war than economic or cultural colonization as we knew it in past centuries.

He touts a theory of globalization that recapitulates the racialized anxieties of social Darwinism and broaches what Emily Martin (1994) calls a post-Darwinism, where culture can also operate as nature. The non-European immigrant is evidence, indeed the embodiment, of this unfolding conflagration. The cultural traditions of Europe, what he refers to as "natural structures," provide the only basis of resistance and refuge:

> *Le Pen*: We believe human beings can and must find their self-realization in natural structures such as the family, the workplace, the city, the nation. It is these entities that are the real safeguards of human freedom and prosperity.

These natural structures are the foundations that sustain his integral public. Order and harmony can only be achieved through the "rootedness" of family, religion, custom, language, and nation. He devises an epistemology, drawn from the authority of experience, that repudiates faith in progress:[20]

> *Le Pen*: The left, or leftist intellectuals, believe and claimed that scientific knowledge and technological advances would necessarily bring about human happiness. But that is not universally true! Progress may or may not bring human betterment. When this faith in progress was undermined, their dogma collapsed. Progress was the very foundation on which socialism, communism, and the left in general based its beliefs and convictions. There is now the profound realization that progress can kill humanity.
>
> *Holmes*: But you believe this scientific orientation also displaces human values?
>
> *Le Pen*: Yes, of course, but I want you to understand this clearly: it is the "idea" of progress that is at the heart of the ideology of the left. The left believed that technological and scientific progress could bring human betterment and happiness. It did not happen.

He extends this commentary to what he sees as the sordid fictions and misrepresentations propagated by the media. The media, as an appendage of the political status quo, forge counterfeit realities that mask the truth of his vision and his insight. He scorns intellectualized, elite discourse in favor of the authenticity of experience and the seductions of instinct:

> *Le Pen*: We do consider the eruption of mass media and its competition for public attention as powerful factors of social decline but, I want you to understand what was said before. If you are aware of the power of mass media and the demagogic challenge it poses to political power, you must also see how powerful it is in breaking up the foundations of society. . . .
>
> You must know that in real life these things [immigration, crime, and corruption] create a lot of suffering for citizens, especially the underprivileged. The problems of housing, family life, education, and unemployment are felt very harshly by people. They feel real anxiety for the future. Thus, these people believe our views to be right because they accurately reflect the dilemmas of real life. . . .
>
> Men perceive reality in two ways: either directly through lived experience of unemployment, poor housing, etc. or indirectly, thanks to the media. But, when the lived facts become overwhelming, far beyond what is told in the media, you don't need the media any more.

*Holmes*: The message of your presentations is that politics is not merely an intellectual discourse but an instinctual engagement.

*Le Pen*: Of course! Absolutely true! Human beings don't just communicate by their intellects alone, but also by their physical sensibilities, their emotions, and their gestures. Probably the worst sin of our time is to overvalue "intellectualism" and to limit humankind to their intelligence alone.

The authenticity of Le Pen's personal relations as well as his very humanity are challenged by the debate on race. Accusations of racism and fascism, he insists, are mere "devices" to silence him. He appeals to the listener to escape rarified ideological engagements and, instead, to reenter the sublime certainties of lived experience. He draws the listener into an intimate relationship in which kinship is conferred, not through rational disputation, but through enthrallments that can be read in daily life. He postures as if to say: "Look at me, I am just like you, I believe what you believe, I feel what you feel. These things do not make you a racist. How can they make me one?"[21]

## CULTURE AND POLITICAL ECONOMY

Le Pen casts his alternative epistemology around a specific permutation of "culture" that Raymond Williams, like Isaiah Berlin, has traced from Rousseau on through the romantic movement "as a process of 'inner' or 'spiritual' as distinct from 'external' development. The primary effect of this alternative was to associate culture with religion, art, the family and personal life, as distinct from or actually opposed to 'civilization' or 'society' in its new abstract and general sense" (Williams 1977:14). The interplay between the "inner" subjectivities of culture and the "external" abstractions of society punctuate the struggles that operate at the core of Le Pen's metaphysics: he seeks resolution by devising a national socialism. He presents himself as the "cultural physician," intervening against the alienating forces of fast-capitalism and the faltering science and political economy of statist solidarity, which threaten to separate human beings from those "natural structures" that define their community of values. The figure necessary to mediate symbolically and rhetorically the national socialist synthesis is the stranger, the outsider. Historically it was the Jew, more recently the immigrant. The "unassimilated" immigrant is an anathema to this construction of society predicated on shared moral precepts, sublime cultural distinctions, and dark historical fears and aspirations. The immigrant, like the Jew, is not merely the object of prejudice and disdain in this social imaginary, but a defining instrument of political action (Mosse 1978; 1999).

It has been widely noted that Le Pen has played a major role in the emergence of "culture" as a "key semantic terrain" within the politics of contemporary Europe.[22] Maurice Bardèche, fascist writer and brother-in-law of the notorious fascist collaborator Robert Brasillach, recognized immediately the historical significance of this semantic legerdemain: "this substitution of the idea of heredity [with the idea of culture] is the pivot on which the whole renewal of the right . . . is based. Thanks to this manouevre we can now recognize, even affirm, the diversity of races, which we prefer to call ethnic groups. . . . [T]he right thus transformed by the discovery of culture, will be able to call itself antiracist" (quoted in Wolfreys 1993:418).[23] Understandably, most attention has been on what Pierre-Andre Taguieff (1991b) refers to as the doctrine of "cultural incommensurability":

> [This doctrine] exalts the essential and irreducible cultural difference of non-European immigrant communities whose presence is condemned for threatening the "host" country's original identity. . . . [R]ather than inferiorizing the "other" it exalts the absolute, irreducible *difference* of the "self" and the incommensurability of different cultural identities. . . . Collective identity is increasingly conceived in terms of ethnicity, culture, heritage, tradition, memory, and difference, with only occasional reference to "blood" and "race." (Stolcke 1995:4)

Adherence to this doctrine of *cultural* incommensurability distances Le Pen from the tradition of fanatical bigotry traceable to the writings of Arthur Joseph de Gobineau, while permitting the extreme right to remain true to elements of Gobineau's crude sociobiology and impassioned fatalism.[24] What this doctrine promotes is "clandestine racism" or "differential racism" (Stolcke 1995:4; Taguieff 1991b:330–37). But mere bigotry is not the goal of Le Pen's insurgency; rather, it is a means by which he reinvigorates the national socialist insurgency. These "new" forms of prejudice, directed primarily against non-European immigrants, are cast as a rhetoric of social justice and an instrument for calibrating a wide-ranging political economy. This approach has been formalized in the FN's policy of "national preference."[25]

Jonathan Marcus is emphatic: "Opposition to immigration is the central mobilising tenet of Le Pen's movement, occupying a similar position to the role performed by 'the class struggle' in an orthodox Marxist party" (1995:105). National preference gives priority to those deemed to be French in almost every aspect of economic and social life eradicating virtually any political rights for immigrants (Wolfreys 1993:424). What Le Pen and his associates have shrewdly discerned is that national socialism is deeply inlaid within the fabric of the modern European nation-state. It resides in the restrictive policies and practices of welfarism. The challenge for integralists is to reradicalize welfarism, and the non-European immigrant provides the key.[26] The provisioning by the state of housing, education, health, and social security has always been restricted by status. The intent of exclusionary immigration policies, as institutionalized particularly in wealthier northern Europe, has been to protect the fiscal and the national integrity of the welfare state. By establishing "national preference" at the center of his insurgency, Le Pen can refurbish social welfarism with a radical cultural hygiene. Placing the state in the service of an overarching policy of "national preference" establishes the distinctive workings of an integralist political economy within a national socialist framework. This intervention, moreover, provides an incendiary rejoinder to the ethical and moral subversions of fast-capitalism. The immigrant is the agent, the embodiment of this occult neoliberalism that threatens France and Europe—hence, the absolute necessity to resist.

Thus, Le Pen was crafting, at the time of our first encounters, a story about Europe premised on an unsettling formulation of cultural hygiene. He and his associates embraced "culture" as an instrument of radical critique, an idiom of solidarity, and the crucible of an exclusionary "social justice." He goes on to assert that the emerging forms of alienation and estrangement that signal the retreat of a bourgeois public are precisely those which enable him to engage an integral public.

## INTEGRAL PUBLIC

Jean-Marie Le Pen claims special knowledge, knowledge that few politicians grasp or fathom. He can see beyond France to the global forces shaping history. He also gives voice to the anxieties and anguish of segments of the French public who feel their struggles are ignored. For many the struggle is material, played out within declining sectors of urban industrial France, but for many others, whose economic status is less threatened, a moral or spiritual estrangement looms, imperiling their sense of social order and cultural coherence. The modernist science of solidarity has failed both. The dogmas of leftist intellectualism claimed that scientific knowledge and technological advances would bring happiness. Faith in progress was the foundation of socialist modernism and at the heart of the ideology of the left. The profound realization of the twentieth century according to Le Pen is that progress can destroy and kill. Thus Le Pen operates on alienation that is manifold: recapitulating the classic modern conditions of social discontent but bound to and intensified by the failure of modernist programs of amelioration and reform to sustain faith in social interventionism. This disillusionment erodes, if not annuls, the progressive underpinnings of a bourgeois public, ceding ground on which Le Pen fashions the sensibilities and outlooks of an integral public.[27] Le Pen does this through an intimate artifice by which latent idioms of solidarity are made manifest.[28]

"What are the objectives of human societies?" Le Pen asks rhetorically. His answer is order and harmony. The "national factor" is fundamental, forged in a primordial past by people who chose to live together and whose association over time spawned well-harmonized groups. Cultural incommensurability dictates that populations should live within their own territories within their own historical borders:

> *Le Pen* conceives of national populations as quasi-races, the attitudes and behavior of which are determined by mental or cultural forms which are fixed and unvarying, separating peoples forever, each enclosed in their specificity. Cultural identities refer to human natures. Differentialist and cultural racism does not deny the zoological unity of man (given the criteria of inter-fertility); it confirms the essential division of humanity into quasi historico-cultural species, separated by mental barriers which can never be crossed. (Taguieff 1991a:61)

"Order" is achieved through the fusion of national tradition and individual identity. "The *nation* is the community of language, interest, race, memories, and culture in which man develops harmoniously. He is attached to it by his roots, his dead, the past, heredity and heritage. Everything transmitted to him by the nation at birth is already of inestimable value."[29] This, in Le Pen's view, is an irrefutable basis of legitimacy.[30] "True transcendency comes from biological continuity and from it alone. It is therefore essential, in this perspective of bio-material mysticism, to safeguard the trans-individual continuity at two levels: family and nation. The integrity of the territory, the purity of identity and the integrality of the heritage must be simultaneously defended" (Taguieff 1991a:44–45). If these domains of integrality are breached and racial mixing is permitted discord will inevitably ensue:

> *Le Pen*: In France there are laws that promote social egalitarianism and, as such, are responsible for the arrival of millions of immigrants from the Third World. As a general rule, we believe populations should live in their own territories, within their own historical borders. When cultural and ethnic identities are mixed, it makes for an explosive combination.

Images of the civil war in the former Yugoslavia and urban violence in the United States are held out as vindication, if not proof, of Le Pen's cultural analysis. Again, according to Le Pen, these violent outbursts are expressions of a global struggle driven by profound demographic and economic

imbalances between North and South. Le Pen posits apocalyptic consequences—ethnocide—for those who do not heed the implications of the
global contestation of the emergence of biopower.

He postulates emerging cultural rifts—a "new metaphysics"—displacing ideologies of class struggle.[31] He casts tainted forms of egalitarianism
against a vision of human freedom rooted in hierarchy. "The egalitarian
movement which consists of leveling age groups, the sexes and peoples, is
to be criticized in my view because it masks reality, which is based on
inequality. . . .The theme of equality strikes us as decadent."[32] Indeed, Le
Pen argues that the egalitarian principles espoused by the left led to the
extension of precisely those rights and privileges to immigrants, which in
turn "created the objective conditions" for racialized conflict. Again, the
traditions of Europe provide the only refuge. Humans must find their
self-realization in "natural structures"—the family, the workplace, the
city, the nation. These are the real safeguards of freedom and prosperity
and the substructure of an integral public:

> *Le Pen*: By allowing the national structures to be attacked or weakened,
> human freedom is reduced.

New immigrants in limited numbers can be assimilated by the French
nation only on the basis of reciprocated "love":

> *Le Pen*: We understand and accept that foreigners may want to come stay
> here for a while, to work, to study and then go home. Or, because of their love
> of France—provided it is reciprocated—may want to assimilate and become
> French. We have no problem with this; but it is only possible when small num-
> bers of individuals are involved, not large groups.

This does not, for Le Pen, imply a racist position:

> *Holmes*: How do you respond to the attacks that you are racist?
> *Le Pen*: I know lies are part of any political struggle. It doesn't trouble me
> because I know we're at war. It *is* war and I try to fight it in my own way by
> saying, "Look at me. Come to my house, see the people who live with me.
> Come to our meetings. There are black, yellow and other [minority] men and
> women who attend. We never have fights there. Never, never—"
> *Holmes*: Nevertheless, various groups in French society are sensitive to your
> positions.
> *Le Pen*: The establishment thinks Le Pen is hated by émigrés but that's not
> true. I have friends in all countries of the world. I am godfather to a *métis* [a
> "mixed-blood"] child from Reunion Island, I have black men and women in
> my house. All these people, I think, like Jean-Marie Le Pen. Many, many times
> I have encountered friends, people in the street, in restaurants, [presumably
> emigrants] who smile and call, "M. Le Pen, M. Le Pen!" It is not true that we

hate foreigners. No, it is not real. We do prefer the French, the Europeans, but that doesn't mean we hate the others.[33]

He ended his defense with the kind of defiant remark that for many listeners confirms his racism: "I won't marry a black woman just to prove that I am not a racist!" This rhetorical maneuver—for which Le Pen is famous—has a deeply disturbing aim. It is not intended merely as a denial of racism, but as a calculated effort to obscure the meaning and the moral force of the notion of "racism" itself. This is part of a broader strategy of broaching "the unspeakable," a hallmark of his populist subversions, which he acknowledges unabashedly:[34]

> *Holmes*: Is your appeal based on your willingness to say things that other politicians dare not say?
> *Le Pen*: That's it. Exactly. It is even one of our slogans. "Le Pen says in a loud voice what people think in a low voice."

What is unsettling about this tactic, which Le Pen practices brazenly, is that it provides a dissonant means to legitimize what are the most opprobrious aspects of an integralist politics. He does this through an intimate artifice that draws on the authority of experience and instinct in the face of what he insists is a corrupted public sphere.

## INTIMATE ARTIFICE

I doubt that Le Pen has read much of Antonio Gramsci, Jürgen Habermas, Raymond Williams or Max Weber, but he has diagnosed fundamental distortions and contradictions infiltrating the public sphere in Europe at the close of twentieth century.[35] He seeks to act upon this disorder and glean power from it. In the process he has delineated an alternative political imaginary. His analysis cleaves toward the axioms of identity politics, but his intervention goes much further. Le Pen argues that mainstream political discourse—framed by elite representations of "social reality"—conflicts with the lived experience of an increasingly alienated public. He labors, as the cultural physician, to create the basis of a public constituted paradoxically by the authority of "inner truths."

Le Pen champions a politics that is removed from what he sees as a debased and corrupted operation of the public sphere substituting, instead, "direct experience." Civil society, as an enduring framework mediating between the individual and collectivity, is bypassed. His social construction of "truth" is not susceptible to vigorous public scrutiny but is conveyed, as it were, on faith. Unmediated by the interplay of rational discourse, the message that he conjures achieves a powerful immediacy.

Thus, though Le Pen deplores the "untruths" conveyed by those who control the media; he is adept at composing alternative communications, which easily and persuasively travel across this same circuitry and enter the lifeworlds of his followers.[36] Again what is devastating about these communications is not their "racist" character per se but the fact that Le Pen has created a discursive field—resistant to critical scrutiny—within which "racism" is increasingly difficult to define, confront, or oppose.[37]

It is the accusation that Le Pen is a "fascist," however, that has the most curious resonances within a weakened public sphere. To the extent that fascism has come to encompass an ultimate evil, it has served as a powerful, though surprisingly vulnerable, moral standard. By merely fashioning himself as something less than a paragon of evil, Le Pen achieves his unsettling purpose.[38] He evades the fascist stigma and thereby discredits the left's overall critique, which is premised on the association of Le Pen's integralism with defining elements of European fascism. Le Pen's endeavor marks out an intimate political imaginary where there is no easy position, no outside position, from which to frame an oppositional stance. Indeed, as the left tries to thwart Le Pen's agenda via an elite discourse—a discourse that he believes is no longer preoccupied with the authenticity of experience—it is disabled. Le Pen insists that the left too is now burdened with a history; its program can no longer be cloaked in an unassailable faith in progressivism but must come to terms with its own wavering science, political economy, and metaphysics of solidarity. At the same time, he offers an alternative "socialism," denuded of technocratic pretensions, that derives a social justice from the "reality" and "truth" offered by "tradition," by hierarchy, by the "natural structures" of Europe.

This brings us back to the European project, which draws its moral legitimacy from a historical critique centrally and inexorably opposed to fascism. Le Pen's rhetorical strategies erode the clarity of this moral stance by obscuring the peculiar status of fascism as a transcendent evil.[39] "Fascism," like "racism," is masked within this kind of political imaginary, which focuses directly on the substance of lifeworlds, the verisimilitude of experience. It is through this artifice that Le Pen has fashioned a contentious European integralism.

In sum, the basic elements of Le Pen's integralism go to the core of the Western liberal tradition. In Isaiah Berlin's terminology, his "populism" avows the authority of experience and the power of instincts as the basis of political engagement. It allows him to assault constructions of "reality" and claims of "truth" based on reason and rational appraisal. His "pluralism" insists on the absolute nature of cultural difference—the doctrine of incommensurability—and the explosive potential posed by the "cultural mixing" and the "rootlessness" that lurk at the heart of cosmopolitanism. His "expressionism" is founded on the creative power of European cultural traditions. Most notably, it resides in what he calls Europe's "natural structures": family, community, nation. These structures serve as consummate instruments of solidarity, their creative power imparted through the intuitive and the unconscious. These are the basic elements at the center of Le Pen's effort to align society with the spirit and trajectory of the Counter-Enlightenment, opening the way for a new nationalist socialist synthesis. Superficially, it yields, as Pol Vandromme puts it in reference to an earlier generation of integralists, not policy but "a sort of morality of style" (quoted in Weber 1991:271). But, let there be no doubt, there is a "theory" or, perhaps better, a "system" or an "epistemology" that informs Le Pen's stratagems and subterfuge, one committed to a vision of society that seeks to thwart the emergence of an integrated, cosmopolitan Europe. In the next chapter we consider how these elements are interpreted by Le Pen's colleagues.

## Chapter Five

## AN ESSENTIAL SOCIOLOGY

THE PUBLICATION of Charles Péguy's *The Mystery of the Charity of Joan of Arc*, along with Georges Sorel's review of the text in *Action française*, April 1910, established a cultic foundation for a refurbished national myth (Weber 1991:264). The aim of this peculiar historical intervention was explicit: to divorce French Catholicism from Catholic universalism as an essential prerequisite for distilling the mythic element for a national socialist synthesis. By 1919 "the Bloc National government proceeded to wrap itself in the Tricolor. Symbolically it made the feast day of Joan of Arc into a public holiday and turned the memory of the Maid of Orléans into a cult" (Eatwell 1996:195). The socialist element of this symbolic maneuver was wrested in the 1930s by Jacques Doriot, leader of the Parti populaire français (PPF), who joined the image of Joan of Arc with allusions to the Paris Commune, the "key defining acts of left-wing rebellion" (1996:207). The heirs to this tradition at the close of the century have linked Sorelian theory to the work of Antonio Gramsci and, by so doing, foster the coexistence of a thoroughgoing radicalism with a fervent conventionality.

In early May 1993 I attended a Front national rally, the Fête de Jeannne d'Arc. It was a drizzly Sunday morning for the march through Paris in honor of Saint Joan. I bumped into a number of sashed FN-dignitaries lining up with representatives from each region of France, many clad in regional costumes. Also taking part were FN-affiliated groups of women, youths, and veterans, as well as representatives of conservative religious organizations and hunting associations. Le Pen arrived at the head of the procession along with the FN leadership bureau, their close family members, and an actress on horseback outfitted as Saint Joan. A line of FN security personnel, in blue blazers and grey slacks led the march. The parade quietly wove through Paris along a route tightly controlled by the police. There were periodic stops for Le Pen and his retinue to pose for photographers. A lone heckler with a small child followed for a few blocks. The only disruptions that I observed resulted as members of the media rushed to photograph fifteen or twenty cheering skinheads positioned on a cordoned off street corner.[1] The march ended at a small square in central Paris encircled by food vendors and concessionaires hawking assorted nationalist texts, political literature, buttons, posters, bumper stickers, and the like. Le Pen delivered a well-staged speech covering familiar themes, which the audience of a few thousand acknowledged enthusiastically. These followers of Le Pen who traveled from across France to participate in an uneventful parade were distinguished by their conventionality, an ardent French conventionality.[2]

This chapter is based on excerpts of conversations with three activists: Bruno Gollnisch, Yvan Blot, and Roger Johnston. They each elaborate on fundamental elements of Le Pen's epistemology, demonstrating how the mandates of integralism can be connected syncretically to other agendas. Gollnisch's account is perhaps the most formidable. By vigorously confronting the antiracist agenda of the left, he, like Le Pen, creates a renewed basis for an integralist synthesis. He surveys the retreat of left-wing politics from its traditional engagement with society and the possibilities this creates for the politics of the Front national. Blot, by contrast, is interested in legitimizing Le Pen's integralism via an account of French history. His analysis circumvents the Enlightenment to find intellectual and stylistic precursors to Le Pen in the baroque philosophy of the early eighteenth century. Blot's account is part of a more general effort by supporters of Le Pen to skirt the legacy of fascism and embed their integralism within a broader and deeper national history of France. Roger Johnston has very different preoccupations. He tries to convey a sense of the seductions (and aversions) of French identity—its mythic essence—as rendered by Le Pen. Specifically, he seeks to articulate the powerful aesthetic force evoked by French identity, a Catholic identity, and the fundamental truths it conveys.[3] These three accounts taken together trace an integralist sociology in which acute cultural representations serve as instruments of political power.

In the previous chapter I argued that the ideological confrontation between Le Pen and the forces of the left in the European Parliament catalyzed the reconstitution of the FN's integralist politics as a European and not merely a French phenomenon. This dialectical interplay echoes an earlier historical episode, an earlier confrontation with the left, that had shaped and defined the FN's political identity in France. Indeed, it was within the rancorous crosscurrents of the post-1968 period that the FN was founded. The FN became a formidable insurgent movement, first through the organizational tactics inherited from the Ordre nouveau (ON), followed by the far more important ideological innovations conferred by the Nouvelle droite (ND). The ideas that were taking shape in the accounts of the leaders of the FN that I interviewed were formulated in at times bitter defiance of the program of the French Socialist Party during the close of the presidential reign of François Mitterrand. In chapter 10, we will see how Le Pen in the same vein defines a scathing critique of the "rightist" or "Gaullist" program of Jacques Chirac.

## FROM ORDRE NOUVEAU TO NOUVELLE DROITE

The peculiar innovation pursued by those who founded the FN in 1972 was the translation of integralist aspirations into a "frontist" organization.[4] The frontist structure of the FN can be traced to its founding by the leaders of the Ordre nouveau, an organization whose members were deeply committed to nationalist ideals, both fascist and nonfascist, as well as the extreme right's tradition of street fighting.[5] The leadership of the ON made a definitive analysis of the French political landscape in the early 1970s that led it to embrace a distinctive institutional strategy: "the modern French State, a technocratic regime with control of an enormous administrative network exerting its influence over politics and economics alike, could not be defeated by a small group of revolutionary nationalists. The newly formed Front would therefore have to win a broad popular base, prove itself capable of running a modern state and take part in elections" (Wolfreys 1993:416). The leadership also embraced a new vehicle for its populism: a democratic participationism that emerged in the *absence* of a principled commitment to democratic ideals:

> ON leaders like [François] Duprat and [François] Brigneau came to accept that to attract a significant electoral following they needed to set up another organization that was totally separate. The resulting group was formed in 1972 and took the name Front National (FN); its title was an indication that it brought together a coalition of forces on the extremist and nationalist right: genuine fascists, monarchists, Catholic fundamentalists, nostalgics for *Algéria française*, and others. They wanted a party driven by a clearer sense of ideological purpose, even if there was some disagreement over exactly what this ideology was. But when it came to choosing a leader for the FN, they agreed to accept another of the notables they had so suspected in 1969–70, Jean-Marie Le Pen. (Eatwell 1996:316–17)

Duprat put the frontist aim of the FN rather more crassly, calling for it to become a "receptacle for all discontents" (quoted in Wolfreys 1993:416). Jonathan Marcus adds the crucial point that the FN was also "frontist" in the sense that its overt political programs were a cover—a front—for a veiled agenda that would not stand up easily to open public scrutiny (1995:12). On a practical level, a frontist structure also has significant liabilities insofar as it can give license to various forms of opportunistic behavior, behavior unrestricted by overt ideological rigor or clear-cut organizational discipline. The ruinous struggles that enveloped the FN's leadership cadre in late 1998 and early 1999 revealed these divisive potentials.[6]

The new generation of FN leaders has more or less successfully evaded the disgrace and stigma that adhere to the history of the French extreme right in the popular imagination. The work of a movement that came to be known as Nouvelle Droite was crucial in allowing young right-leaning intellectuals to gain legitimacy and to distance themselves from groups with disreputable histories of the sort that adhere to Ordre nouveau. But what may well have been intended as merely a cosmetic shift in tactics yielded far-reaching substantive change in ideology and practice. This change can be said to characterize a new formulation of integralism. The intellectual, philosophical, and tactical foundations of this transformation were conceived within an intellectual milieu that defined itself in response to the events of 1968. The ND was

> essentially a group of intellectuals who eschewed the rough and tumble of conventional politics in favor of "metapolitics," an oblique strategy seeking to achieve victory for their ideas through the patient infiltration of the media and the educational system. By the turn of the 1980s they had achieved influential positions on the mass-circulation weekly *Figaro* magazine and a number of lesser journals, as well as public support from a galaxy of distinguished academics. (Fysh and Wolfreys 1992:316)

The main organizational expression of the Nouvelle Droite was the Groupement de recherche et d'études pour une civilization européenne (GRECE), founded in 1968 by Alain de Benoist.[7]

Benoist became a major theorist and intellectual leader of the ND. He and his associates at GRECE forcefully reappraised the entire intellectual heritage of the extreme right, even questioning if "right wing" accurately located them on the political spectrum. Indeed, they reached well beyond traditional right-wing intellectual circles drawing on the works of "cultural Marxists," most notably Antonio Gramsci, and gaining support from intellectual luminaries like Louis Rougier, Julien Freund, Mircea Eliade, and Hans Eysenck. The iconoclastic influence of Julius Evola was central:

> Seminal influences on New Right thought were Nietzsche and Julius Evola. Their ideas can be seen in the starting point of its philosophy, which held that the root of Europe's problems was its adoption of "Judeo-Christian" values rather than indigenous pagan ones. The Judeo-Christian tradition was seen as stressing monotheism and monoculturalism, which for the ND marked the origins of totalitarianism. The Judeo-Christian culture was also attacked for its egalitarianism, which was seen as spawning secular ethics like Marxism. In its place, the New Right sought to substitute a more hierarchical philosophy, pointing to scientific evidence that people were not equal. But such was the power of this Judeo-Christian conditioning, according to the

ND, that it would be necessary to build "man" again from scratch. (Eatwell 1996:313–14)

At the base of this philosophy was the effort to destroy the foundations of secular as well as religious humanism—the universalistic values of the European Enlightenment—which, in their highly idiosyncratic view, are the pillars of totalitarianism. In place of the humanistic framework, Benoist and his followers in GRECE adduced a "right to difference" based on a "scientific" appraisal that demonstrated for them the "biological facts" of inequality and hierarchy (Simmons 1996:212–13). As noted in the previous chapter, this yielded a "differentialist" doctrine based on cultural "incommensurability." This doctrine was refined into an influential theory of practice through an unlikely engagement with the work of Antonio Gramsci:

> Deeply impressed by the sophistication of Marxist theories and moved by the idealism of the 1968 student revolutionaries, these mainly Parisian-based intellectuals sought to adapt Marxism, and particularly the work of Antonio Gramsci, to the project of renewing right-wing ideology. They accepted Gramsci's argument that the route to political power did not lie in winning elections or in fighting in the streets . . . but rather in changing people's ideas. Gramsci observed that state power depended less on structures such as the army, the police, or the government and more on the state's ability to determine people's concepts, ideas, and even the kind of language they used. The true instruments of power were the media . . . and education. Those who were able to shape social consensus, to achieve ideological hegemony, possess more power than all the politicians, soldiers, policemen, and judges combined. The ability to determine the "taken for granted" beliefs of the ordinary citizen was the ability to control society itself. (Simmons 1996:209–10)

The hegemonic orientation became part of the FN's strategy, joining a new sophisticated ideological presentation with the older language of affiliation and consent. This allowed not just a powerful new iteration of the nationalist socialist synthesis, but the delineation of a "new" mainstream within which integralist politics can operate.[8]

My three interlocutors included in this chapter all joined the FN after its electoral "breakthrough" in the early 1980s.[9] The breakthrough was engineered by the late Jean-Pierre Stirbois, who represented the so-called *solidaristes* faction within the party.[10] Stirbois, as Le Pen's most powerful lieutenant, was responsible for establishing the centrality of the anti-immigration stance in the FN program; he stressed the need for local level political organization and helped marginalize fascist elements within the FN's leadership as a means to establish the party's credibility as a new electoral force. Bruno Mégret and Carl Lang completed the work of Stirbois to fashion the FN as an efficient political organization (Marcus 1995:36–51; Simmons 1996:187, 202). Thus, the accounts that follow are drawn from the "new generation" of the FN leadership, removed at least generationally from the more unsavory collaborationist and fascist legacy of the party's early history. What their accounts reveal are the important sources of radicalism and conventionality with which integralism is imbued.

## EVISCERATION

Bruno Gollnisch, MEP, spoke of the Front national with wit and vehemence. He candidly analyzed the strategic aims and shortcomings of its integralist politics. Gollnisch was born in Neuilly-sur-Seine in January 1950. On the occasions when I spoke to him in 1991 and 1993, he was seeking a traditionalist position that tied his personal experience to a radical critique. He is a former professor of Japanese literature and law and dean of the faculty at the University of Lyon III. He represented the FN as an elected deputy to the National Assembly. Since the mid-1980s he has represented the FN as a member of the regional council of Rhône-Alpes. In 1989 Gollnisch was elected a deputy to the European Parliament. In June 1995 he also won election to the municipal council of Lyon and in October of 1995 he became the FN's general secretary.[11] During the struggles that rent the movement in 1998–99, he remained one of Le Pen's most loyal supporters.

Like the Sorelians before them, those in the FN leadership endeavor to strip socialism of its rationalism, materialism, and cosmopolitanism and replace them with a radically parochial substance.[12] Gollnisch and his associates summon a nativist socialism that begets a conception of society within which Le Pen can speak for the "aborigines" of France:

*Holmes*: Let me get back to the issue of race. Technically you can say that M. Le Pen is racist because he advocates policies based on racial distinctions.

*Gollnisch*: Well, even this I wouldn't say. This could be the view of people in France but it's not the policy of the FN. Our policies are based on *nationality*. For example, there are Jews and Arabs in favor of France. There are Arabs in the ranks of the FN. If a black person comes to a meeting of the FN, there will be absolutely no problem. So, although "race" is not [the basis of our policy], we do acknowledge that race exists. There are some differences between the Bantu and the Swede; differences of mentality, culture, habits, and so on. Obviously, France will not be the same if, thirty years from now, two-thirds of the population has African origins.

*Holmes*: But the implication of M. Le Pen's policies can lead to discriminations based on race?

*Gollnisch*: Yes, but it depends on the way you take the word "racism." Our adversaries try to say it's a racist policy to retain some form of national identity. Obviously, it is easier for people to assimilate if they are from the same race, culture, religion and so on than if they are from a completely different race, culture, and religion from the majority of the people in the country.

I don't know if Le Pen told you when you met him, but he was interviewed by a university professor when he went to America. I don't remember which university. Among the questions put to Le Pen was, "Why are you against immigration, because you see a country like America built entirely upon immigration?" Le Pen responded, "Yes, I know this but remember in France I am the representative of the aborigines." American immigration policy may have been good for the melting pot, but certainly not for the Sioux, Navajo, and so on.

Central to Gollnisch's analysis is his argument that the discourse on "race" is, in fact, a means for the left to maintain its moral ascendance in the face of a broad ideological crisis.[13] He believes the technical achievement of social equity, through public control of social and economic life, has failed. Yet the ethical impulses for social justice persist, shorn of a strategy for social implementation. The left attempts, in Gollnisch's view, to reclaim its moral position by substituting an antiracist agenda. For him, however, this is a crude ploy, constructed to obscure an epic historical failure:[14]

*Gollnisch*: As a system [socialism] has failed. It is discredited. As a moral, ethical aim it has been corrupted. So what is left? Nothing. Except to be antiracist! This is the only thing left which gives them a sense of generous spirit [a sense of moral ascendance]. . . . Socialism failed as a technical means to achieve social justice through public property and public management of the economy and social life. Socialism is also discredited, especially in countries such as France, where it is supposed to be in favor of the poor, the workers. Even for the workers the [national] identity problem is prominent and a lot have turned to us [the FN]. Scandals and corruption have discredited the left's moral position and socialists absolutely need this upper moral position. You have to understand this in European politics. . . . they [the Socialists] have the absolute need for moral superiority. . . . With the failure of their social and economic system, they need an ideology of substitution. In most cases, this ideology takes the form of antiracism—even if it's [imposed] in an artificial way, even in a totalitarian way.

A taunt punctuates Gollnisch's commentary: lurking within the controversy over race he sees an effort by the left to contrive immunities from racism rather than to eliminate or combat it. In other words, the issue of race as posed by the left has become for him a vacuous ideology stripped of the requisite programs of social reform. While there is a vibrant moral underpinning to the socialist political economy, Gollnisch argues that what endows the traditional moral agenda of the left with its abiding integrity is a theory of social action, an intricate engagement with the material and social conditions that constitute human society. In his view the lapsed or ineffectual state of this kind of social practice, its inability to engage contemporary social predicaments, disables the wide-ranging moral authority exercised by the left. Shorn of the technical means to pursue social justice, the left is forced to embrace other ideological or ethical agendas, in this case an antiracist agenda, which hinges on an alternative rendering of the social realm. Gollnisch insists that this shift obliges the left to embrace essentially *his* rendering of "society," wherein society is conceived of as principally a "moral system," rather than the conceptualization of society as a "material realm" susceptible to "scientific" interventionism.

Nothing more effectively confirms Gollnisch's analysis than repeated denunciation by the left of the FN's bigotry without an alternative program of social action to address meaningfully the underlying conditions that engender racism. It allows Gollnisch to identify a "politics of substitution" contrived by the left within which Le Pen emerges as a demon in a parable of good and evil. Their antiracist discourse is merely, he believes, a cover for an abject failure on the part of the left to delineate a meaningful oppositional framework drawn from its traditional ideological inventory and its commitment to social action. It is vindication for his own moral delineation of society in the tradition of Sorel, Barrés, and Maurras.

Notwithstanding Gollnisch's chagrin at what he regards as false accusations and defamations, there is a deep sense of vindication. Socialism—as a materialist project—has failed. Its goal of social equity, through public control of social and economic life, is, he insists, discredited as a moral and ethical aim. The epochal collapse of communism is proof. Social democracy and communism differ only in degree and not in nature as he sees it. Hence, a "doctrinal vacuum" was created. The left responded with a "politics of substitution" oriented toward gaining moral and ideological superiority via what the FN leadership refers to as "soft totalitarianism." For Bruno Gollnisch and his associates this is a cynical cover by which the left disguises its inability to formulate and sustain a meaningful program of social democratic action.[15]

But there are for Gollnisch also lingering problems with history that restrain his integralist aspirations. The history of the Second World War, the Holocaust, and the Resistance impair the patriotic claims of the FN; they persist as a source of disgrace. He confides, however, that there are signs of deliverance. Contemporary political scandals by the political establishment take on an important significance in what he sees as the moral struggle for recuperation. Corruption is not merely evidence of personal malfeasance for him and his colleagues; rather it stands as proof of ongoing traitorous betrayals of the nation by mainstream political parties of the right and left. They are acts of treason. Each new expression of political corruption by those opposed to the FN is thus subject to a spurious historical appraisal whereby contemporary political "affairs" serve to erode the calumny of Vichy.

## VEIL OF APPEARANCE

Yvan Blot has been described as the *maître-à-penser* of Jean-Marie Le Pen.[16] Born June 26, 1948, in Saint-Mande he was elected to the European Parliament as a member of the Front national in 1989. He was one of the founders of another important institutional manifestation of the Nouvelle Droite, the Club de l'horloge, which he established in 1974 along with a group of graduates of the École nationale d'administration and the Polytechnique.[17] While GRECE provided a broad cultural agenda, the Club de l'horloge provided a comprehensive political program from which Le Pen and others have drawn. The Club de l'horloge was as intellectually formidable as GRECE but more oriented toward policy issues, drawing its membership from "high civil servants linked through personal ties rather than formal structure" (Eatwell 1996:313). The club, organized along the lines of a "think tank," published a lengthy series of books, position papers, and the review *Contrepoint* and journal *Eléments*.[18] Its members worked directly in various right-wing campaigns, though the club claimed no single party affiliation. According to Blot the club "chose to present its project under the auspices of the republic," thereby establishing a new basis of legitimacy for the extreme right.[19] "The Revolution and its values, hitherto associated with the left, were relocated in a lineage which saw 1789 as the reassertion of the pure origins of Indo-Europeanism" (Wolfreys 1993: 419). The Club harnessed right-wing iconoclasm to a pragmatic agenda of "cultural infiltration" and political activism.[20]

Blot described his conversion to the congregation of the Front national. It begins with ideological betrayal of the principles of nationalism on the part of Jacques Chirac, which was resolved for Blot in a personal meeting with Le Pen:

> *Blot*: I was a member of the Gaullist Party in France, the RPR.[21] I was the personal assistant of two general secretaries of the Gaullist movement and I was a member of the Central Committee of the Gaullist Movement. I was also a member of parliament for the Gaullist Party. However, I was very distressed and deceived by the evolution of this party. The former generation of

this party was people drawn from the Resistance and it was very attached to the idea of the nation and the idea of freedom. The new generation has abandoned these commitments and I think responsibility for this lies with Jacques Chirac.

His first meeting with Le Pen contradicts Blot's preconceptions and confirms in his mind suspicions of media distortion of M. Le Pen:

> *Blot*: I was introduced to Le Pen and I was very impressed by his personality. That was surprising because, like other French people, I knew him only through the media. I knew it [the media portrayal of Le Pen] wasn't an accurate portrayal of reality but I was still surprised. I decided to follow him and work for him.

Blot recognizes Le Pen as a singular figure whose vision goes against the grain. He ascribes Le Pen's uniqueness to cultural resonances that *predate* the French Revolution—the philosophical harmonics of the baroque.[22] He recognized how Le Pen's "contrastive" epistemology is capable of penetrating the illusions of history fostered by the Enlightenment. He believes this penetration allows Le Pen to array experience against the social aspect of things and destroys the "veil of appearance." A new social order is revealed, one in which the state must serve as guardian of natural structures and the traditions they encompass:

> *Blot*: I've always been more interested in political *ideas*. I'm a member of the academic society for political sciences. I am working on a book about Le Pen and my thesis concerns M. Le Pen's reintroduction of baroque philosophy and baroque ideas into French political life. He expresses himself in a baroque style. He doesn't speak or write like a technocrat, like all my friends from École nationale d'administration, but has a special manner which uses a lot of imagery and paradox. His rhetorical style is *contrastive*. He pits reality against the social aspects of things, particularly those developed by the media or by officials. I had the occasion to study baroque writers and these writers had a similar manner of expression. They tried to explain the truth to the public by shocking them a bit, in order to destroy the veil of appearance. M. Le Pen does the same and thus is very different from the classical political right influenced by the Enlightenment.
>
> Not only is his [rhetorical] form baroque, his philosophy is too. The seventeenth and the first part of the eighteenth century is an especially interesting period because the philosophy of this time attempts a tentative synthesis between tradition and the progressive sciences. One idea, drawn from [Gottfried] Leibniz, was very important: there are laws of harmony in the universe and the action of the individual must develop within this harmonic framework; otherwise you disrupt reality. It is a view that insists on the power of reason and the limits of reason.

Although this philosophy was attacked by the ideals of the French Revolution, [France was] founded on the belief that, by his will and by his reason, man can be the lord of the world. I discovered in M. Le Pen this [harmonic] vision. . . .You *can* do something, but you must be modest. For that reason, M. Le Pen is always respectful of tradition, but he also believes it's possible to manage progress.

The idea of the book was to show mankind's overconfidence in reason—the power of revolutionary change had enormous costs in human life and still didn't improve the human condition.[23] Because communism has failed, because the ideals of the French Revolution have failed, the illusions of history created by the Enlightenment have vanished. I think now is the time to possibly recapture the thoughts and ideas of the early eighteenth century, the idea of natural communities like nations and so on.

It is incumbent on the state to respect tradition because traditions contain historical understanding and experience by way of custom. We have to alter our thinking and avoid a constructivist attitude like that of the socialists. We think this is the case for Europe too! This effort to build Europe is a radically constructivist one. The early eighteenth century has a lot to teach us; it is now possible to develop a new baroque outlook, new baroque policies.

Blot makes a small but important addition that grounds the integralist imaginary in a French and European history, not just cultic mythology, that predates the Revolution. He contends that Le Pen embraces a distinctive philosophical tradition, a way of knowing, that confers intellectual credence and historical legitimacy on his politics. Blot aligns Le Pen's integralism with the metaphysics of the baroque. Leibniz's harmonics bequeathed to Le Pen a contrastive epistemology within which experience is arrayed against the social aspect of things. It is an intellectual model that aims to shock the public in order to strip away the veil of appearances and supplant the illusions of history fostered by the Enlightenment. The authority of reason is abridged, if not superseded, by the use of contrastive imagery and paradox, opening the way for alternative criteria to confer truth.[24]

Thus, Blot envisions a new order in which the state serves as the guardian of natural communities and the traditions they encompass. From this vision he derives the basic postulates of a theory of action that is emphatically circumstantial. The authority of cultural traditions, he insists, must be orchestrated to constrain and manage progress. Social action must develop in a harmonic framework that protects the reality of human existence from the ruptures of revolutionary upheavals or constructivist programs of the European Union.

Blot played a curious part in the upheavals of 1998–99. He was viewed as one of the closest advisors to Bruno Mégret, his old friend from the

Club de l'horloge. In fact he was seen as the main ideologist of the Mégretist faction of the party. He participated in the challenge to Le Pen's leadership and openly sided with the Mégretists in December 1998, but by early February 1999 he had deserted Mégret's FN-Mouvement national and applied for readmission to Le Pen's organization (Raymond 1999:33). Soon thereafter Blot was restored by Le Pen to the party's leadership Bureau politique.

## THE ASSISTANT

Roger Johnston shadows Le Pen at public rallies and conferences. Officially, he was one of three secrétaires généraux adjoints of the Technical Group of the European Right. He is soft-spoken and during our first meeting he called attention—unprompted—to his dark complexion and his Asian ancestry.[25] When speaking about Le Pen, Johnston undergoes a transformation. He assumes an animation, inflection, and laughter reminiscent of his mentor:

> *Holmes*: How does M. Le Pen describe himself if he is against both the right and the left?
>
> *Johnston*: As the [representative of the] nationalist right. He is tired of the labels of extreme right or far right, which don't correspond to that which we are defending. We are advocating something in which we believe. It's not about right or left, it's more about what is right and not wrong. However, these values are more recognized [as belonging] on the right of the political spectrum.[26]
>
> *Holmes*: Le Pen speaks about problems, which the establishment [left or right] won't touch?
>
> *Johnston*: Le Pen says loudly what everyone is speaking softly. He is also, as you may know, the best orator in French politics—a very strong speaker. He speaks so well. He has such a wide-ranging vocabulary. Did you know he is a jurist by background?
>
> *Holmes*: Can you tell me more about his background?
>
> *Johnston*: He lost his father when he was fourteen and was in the French Resistance when he was sixteen. He had a hard time. He was a student president [at university]. He has done really great things, really important things. For example, during the Algerian War, he was twenty-seven years old and the youngest deputy in the National Assembly. Then the war broke out and he said, "My duty is to my country" and left his seat and enlisted to fight. People say he did it to torture Algerians [laughter] but it's just the kind of person he is. His word always matches his deed and you have to admire that. He is a very consistent person. You don't have to like him but you have to admire the way he

stands his ground on his beliefs. He is from Brittany and the French say people from Brittany are strong-willed and stubborn, but have beautiful hearts. Whenever Le Pen does something, he stands by it. Le Pen's oratory can put a strong stand in a beautiful way and that's why he has been banned from the media.

Roger Johnston's insights appear more modest than those of Gollnisch and Blot, but are no less emblematic of key integralist tropes. He is preoccupied with the power of French identity, which he embraces through the charismatic persona of J.-M. Le Pen. He believes that Le Pen sees the lucid surfaces of reality and recognizes historical processes, which are misunderstood or distorted by the establishment. Above all, he defends tradition. For Le Pen, custom stands as the repository of centuries of cultural experience and knowledge, the endowment of national identity:

> *Johnston*: I hope you get to see our Joan of Arc celebration. You'll see we are defending a vision of France that has its roots in a Judeo-Christian tradition. You will see a pride in the French manner that's not evident in other political parties. It's said France is the elder daughter of the church. Judeo-Christian values are the moral fiber of France and we're trying to resurrect that vision and restore French pride.
>
> Yes. We have to restore a quality of life in which morality plays a greater role. Most of our people are of a Catholic or a Christian background.[27] And although we don't make that a political platform, it nourishes our vision. We definitely want more morality; we want to reestablish a sense of values which come from both the French and especially the Christian tradition. We want to purify and nourish the thinking in political life.
>
> *Holmes*: Unassimilated immigrants constitute a menace?
>
> *Johnston*: The growing immigration that comes from outside of Europe is a threat to our culture and our employment situation. I think the immigration situation is catalytic and makes our problems more obvious. It even raises questions of national security. The children of immigrants, who are born on French soil, are French, but they tend to be loyal to their Muslim traditions and practices. This is contrary to [our understanding of national] loyalty.
>
> The solution—close off the flood by changing the laws for what Le Pen calls "national preference." We are against open borders because the flood will be uncontrollable. We also want to limit immigrant rights to social welfare benefits and cooperate with those countries [from which immigrants come] to make development possible there so they'll not have to leave [for France and Europe].
>
> *Holmes*: So the basis of M. Le Pen's politics is immigration?
>
> *Johnston*: Without any doubt.

The presence of these foreign bodies is symptomatic for Johnston of metaphysical peril, the enemy within.[28] Their loyalties are inevitably suspect.

They may be born in France, but they retain their fidelity, it is imagined, to Islam. "Catholic France" must resist.

Johnston makes the simple, but absolutely crucial point: integralism is not just a political imaginary, it is a framework for action:

> *Johnston*: M. Le Pen has the incredible power to discriminate right from wrong. He is *not* a man from the past. He is fresh, a visionary. He has a consistent vision of mankind. Everything, [every criticism] you can imagine has been thrown against him; he's even been accused of murder and torture. He went to Algeria for two years and put his life on the line for his beliefs. He's an unusual politician, which gets him in trouble, because he's too outspoken. That is his strength, but sometimes I wish he would be a bit more subdued.

Le Pen, it is asserted, knows how to act, he can fight for what he believes, he has courage. This means that Le Pen can live and act in the present. What those beguiled by the power of the national socialist synthesis—however disastrous and fraught that vision might be—have been drawn to historically is this resolute insistence on action and to see action as the direct expression of will. In the face of what the FN leadership sees as a waning materialist political economy, the cultural idioms of nationalism frame an alternative metaphysics of solidarity and calculus of social justice. The socialist project, by joining the moral imperatives of class struggle with scientific analysis, generated a symbolic system capable of translating thought into action with speed and power. It awakened, bridled, and focused the interplay of intensely felt experience and rational analysis on the material conditions of human existence. This *materialist* rendering of socialism is what integralism seeks to eviscerate.

## An Essential Sociology

Gollnisch, Blot, and Johnston draw on a language, more Gramscian than Sorelian, by which to gain access to preexisting consenses and bases of solidarity, a hegemonic language that operates easily on the "natural structures" surveyed by Le Pen. What they conjure is a patois of the social and the national that stands in sharp counterpoint to elite technocratic political discourse.[29] Yvan Blot has noted: "A language can be effective in communication and action only if it is 'rooted'" (quoted in Simmons 1996:224). Again, by "rootedness" Blot refers to a vernacular that is congruent with everyday experience, such that it can enter the lifeworlds of an integral public without the mediation of liberal democratic principles and practices. What appears to be merely a cloying nostalgia in Le Pen's and his associates' accounts is, in fact, far more significant. It is their figurative "vocabulary of battle."[30] They have refurbished the language of "nation," which allows them to engage latent cultural consenses and tacit idioms of solidarity. In other words, their political vision gains legitimacy not merely through sophisticated political disputation, but through a pseudo-intimacy that penetrates persuasively the lifeworlds of a new French and now a European public. What they understand is that the strategic deployment of cultural idioms can confer a seamless conventionality on a radical politics; this artifice is fundamental to the practices of integralism.

These three accounts demark an essential sociology, a means not just of representing society but entering and acting upon it. It begins with a fundamental critique that can be cast against the French state or the European Union. The corrosive power of fast-capitalism, liberal democracy, and socialism in its materialist guise has obscured and rendered remote the enthrallments of populism, expression, and pluralism. Integralist sociology posits forms of alienation and estrangement in which "society" itself becomes increasingly opaque for the individual, as an inauthentic cosmopolitanism and a crass consumerism obscure real human values, true social distinctions, and, above all, abiding bases of collectivity. The politician, the leader, plays a vital role in the face of these historical circumstances. The core struggle is fundamentally rhetorical: to devise a contemporary language of association and affiliation that affirms collective practices of belonging and thereby restores the authority of populism, expressionism, and pluralism as principles of political economy. Again, to achieve this demands a method, an intimate artifice, by which deeply sedimented cultural idioms are recaptured and rendered as bases of public authority and social order. An acute orchestration of symbolic forms generates not just a compelling representation of society but also a distinctive basis of power.

## Chapter Six

## SOCIETY AND ITS VICISSITUDES

WHEN, in the early spring of 1845, Marx took up residence with his family on rue d'Alliance, not far from where the Madou stop of the Brussels Metro now stands, he began experimenting with the ideas that ultimately framed a wide-ranging politics of Europe. By the time Engels arrived in April, Marx had worked out the main elements of a materialist theory of history. Their collaboration began with an effort to clarify the differences between them and a German Hegelian, Ludwig Feuerbach, resulting in the famous *Theses on Feuerbach*. The exercise, however, led to a more comprehensive statement of their overall theoretical project—what Marx demurely called an effort at "self-clarification." The document, now known as *The German Ideology*, chronicled the development of the basic tenets of their revolutionary theory, a theory born out of the struggles unfolding at the center of an industrializing Europe. Through their "scientific inquiry" they established themselves as the arbiters of the "illusory" and the "real." The analysis ranged from the nature of personhood to a critical theory of the state. They uncovered a political geography encompassing all of Europe by emphasizing the borderless nature of capitalism, and hence the contingent character of the nation-state (see McLellan 1974:140, 151).[1]

Central to their theorizing was a disquisition on the most enigmatic cultural creation—"society."[2] Marx and Engels endowed society with a form that was both imagined and enacted, its workings etched across the expanse of material existence. Through it they rendered intelligible a fundamentally secular view of the relationship between the individual and the collectivity. They conjured a dynamic vision of history regulated by an austere calculus inlaid in the urgencies of capitalist production. Society was construed as the outcome of human agency, but a creation not always or necessarily consonant with human will. Marx and Engels believed their theory of society allowed them to enter history, to formulate "conscious participation in the historical process." Their forceful interpretation of the human condition using key societal abstractions represented an imposing cultural breakthrough.

Brussels was not merely a locale where Marx and Engels formulated grand theory; it was a site from which they began actively to shape the history and engage the politics of Europe. From very modest organizational beginnings, in the form of the Brussels Correspondence Committee, they began to translate theory into action:

> We published at the same time a series of pamphlets, partly printed, partly lithographed, in which we subjected to a merciless criticism the mixture of French-English socialism or communism and German philosophy, which at the time constituted the secret doctrine of the League [of the Just]. We established in its place the scientific understanding of the economic structure of bourgeois society as the only tenable theoretical foundation. We also explained in popular form that our task was not the fulfillment of some utopian system but the conscious participation in the historical process of social revolution that was taking place before our eyes. (Marx, quoted in McLellan 1974:158–59)

The committee linked correspondents in Paris, London, and Cologne (the most important communist center at the time) with members across Germany. The reports of these correspondents chronicled diverse "revolutionary" developments, which Marx analyzed within an overarching historical scheme. He drew on these locally situated accounts and commentaries and wove them into a supranational narrative on which he constructed a revolutionary politics. The theoretical and propagandistic work in Brussels culminated in the drafting of an emphatic little text, *The Communist Manifesto*.

The Brussels Correspondence Committee was also the means by which Marx established wide-ranging personal contacts, in particular, with the League of the Just, the best-organized of the exiled German workers groups, with approximately one thousand members. In June 1847 a league meeting in London decided to reorganize and to change its name to the Communist League; it adopted the slogan "Proletarians of All Countries—Unite." The June conference in London inspired Marx "in early August to turn the Brussels Correspondence Committee into the branch of the Communist League with himself as president. It had thirty-seven members to begin with" (McLellan 1974: 173). The following year, 1848, revolutionary upheavals were engulfing Europe and Marx's work in Brussels came to an abrupt halt with an expulsion order from the king of Belgium. On the same day, Marx received a document from France, signed by a member of the provisional government, allowing his return to Paris.[3]

## Lapsed Vision

The legacy left by Marx and Engels was a multilayered, modernist politics interleaving "scientific" assertions and moral invectives. It imparted a vision of society, fashioned from acute empirical analysis, revealing an epic contest lurking within the most mundane details of everyday existence. It generated a master narrative—the class struggle—inlaid through the exigencies of human labor

> to the extent that history moves forward and with it the struggle of the proletariat assumes clear outlines, they no longer need to seek solutions by drawing on their imagination; they have only to take note of what is happening before their eyes and to become its mouthpiece. So long as they look for knowledge by merely constructing systems, so long as they are at the beginning of the struggle, they see in poverty nothing but poverty—without seeing in it the revolutionary, subversive aspect which will overthrow the old society. From this moment, knowledge which is a product of historical process will have associated itself consciously with it, ceased to be doctrinaire and become revolutionary. (Marx, quoted in McLellan 1974: 164)

The intimate dilemmas of proletarian life were divorced from ethnic, religious, or national idioms and universalized. "Science"—political economy—was employed to translate countless parochial conflicts into a boundless, *secular* epic: "The history of all hitherto existing society is the history of class struggle." They created a societal screen against which the workings of industrial capitalism were projected and rendered meaningful and from which an encompassing political program was derived. It constituted, at least for some, a demystification of the enigmas of human experience by way of practical reason.

Why this legacy has faltered is the core dilemma facing most particularly those committed to social democratic and socialist programs, but many others as well. At the close of the twentieth century, they face not only the apparent defeat of grand designs based on centralized planning and public ownership but the retreat of a much broader societal ethic manifest in various political formulations of social justice. In its place they confront the advance of an individualistic ethic expressed in a shrill rhetoric of personal responsibility. In this manner the ethos of fast-capitalism, in which the abstract principles of market exchange are rendered as *ethical* imperatives, assaults or supersedes other socially derived moral frameworks. The retreat of socialist agendas—focused on the historical role of the working class—is examined in this chapter from three perspectives: first, in terms of a brief reflection on the circumstances that precipitated the collapse of the Italian Communist Party, the PCI; second, from the standpoint of a reconstitution of a leftist activism cast from the vantagepoint of the EU; and, third, in relationship to the retreat of British working-class politics in the wake of Thatcherism and Blairism. The narrow aim of this discussion is to link tentatively these political transformations to lived experience of "new" ill-defined groupings, remnants of the industrial working class and segments of a marginalized middle class, whose integration into postindustrial European society is increasingly precarious. The broader aim is to show how this might open possibilities for radical integralist cultural agendas.

## RESIDUES

In interviews during the early 1990s, I encountered politicians who represented parties with strong Marxist traditions and who were struggling with the significance of the post-1989 Europe for their personal convictions and political commitments. Their accounts tended to emerge as reflections on the past rather than as partisan engagements with the present. Their recourse to memory framed conceptualizations of society as an analytical and moral tableau against which they traced their own biographies, their own careers of militancy. Perhaps most clear in this regard was an exchange I had with Luciana Castellina, MEP, who grappled with these questions by recounting her own stormy relationship with the old Partito comunista italiano. She emphasized in her account the vibrant commitment of the PCI to the creative potentials of civil society.[4]

For Luciana Castellina the traditions and practices of the PCI encompassed an ethical medium—one with which she did not always agree—within which ideas and social action were given coherence.[5] Its history as a popular party and a nationalist party, born out of the Italian Resistance with its heroic founding figures, had deep personal significance for her. Marxist ideals as interpreted by Antonio Gramsci were wed with Palmiro Togliatti's democratic pragmatism to establish the party's commitment to a vibrant rendering of civil society. Civil society was conceived in her view as the critical field of action from which the PCI derived its characteristic forms of political power. The daily fight for people's rights and claims emerged as the "passion" of the party and the basis of its legitimacy. Civil society was the creative milieu within which what she understood as the PCI's dynamic form of political authority was forged and its spheres of jurisdiction demarcated.[6]

The PCI ruled on the local level. According to Castellina it instituted the social prerequisites for small business enterprises to flourish in Italy. The PCI promoted a culture in which initiative and enterprise thrived. It was Togliatti's genius to assimilate a distinctive type of democratic rule that alleviated any pressures to impose a single philosophical or ideological agenda. Yet, this program was somehow compromised or betrayed. The PCI did not understand the new social movements of students and young workers in the 1970s and 1980s. The party did not embrace the issues and the culture of these new radical elements; rather, it embarked on a doomed course of cooperation with the Italian governing parties, without being in the government itself. The preoccupation with power and governing impeded fresh analyses.

Castellina asserted that the predicaments of left-wing parties in Europe were the outcome of intricate crises tied to the national histories of each party.[7] The divisive crosscurrents spawned by Reaganism and Thatcherism provoked, in her view, a general crisis for which the left across Europe offered no fresh appraisal and, hence, little in the way of political response. The metamorphosis of the working classes, exemplified by the rise of the "contingent worker" in western Europe, was the most prominent symptom of these changes. More broadly, the escalating internationalization of the economy rendered the spectrum of *national* policies of the left ineffectual.

In the European arena the left in her view was completely defeated. Capitalism was granted free circulation by the EU—indeed, it became the driving force of the European project. Commodities and labor crossed borders freely and Europeanization came to be directed by the interests of capital and not the social needs of human beings. Political instruments to control the distribution of wealth were lost, and social justice was undermined. One insight haunts her analysis: the mantle of social change was lost by the left. Those radical political programs that had succeeded in transforming western Europe since the 1970s were formulated by the right. The radical programs of the right were calculated to fragment society and collapse social space, defeating the left's project of social integration.

## In The Spirit of Spinelli

By mid-decade I began to encounter approaches based on recasting traditional leftist preoccupations across a transnational mapping of European society. This effort was pursued very much in the spirit of Altiero Spinelli's socially progressive federalist conception of Europe. Central to Spinelli's partisan vision was the conviction that the European Parliament provided a powerful new context from which to generate new agendas for the left. He was convinced that Europe would created new constituencies, new critical perspectives for radical analysis, and new bases for pursuing social justice. What this demanded in Spinelli's (1986) view was that the left not merely respond to axes of struggle surfacing with European integration; rather, the left had to be an "avant garde," at the forefront in the institutional construction of a European Union.

I heard this legacy articulated by Kratis Kyriazis, who was general secretary of one of the two communist coalitions within the European Parliament. His effort to conceptualize a supranational political context was rudimentary; his application of socialist principles framed a leftist mini-malism. Though attenuated, his approach not only retained a conceptual continuity with the traditions of Marxism, but it was based explicitly on a European field of political activism as surveyed by Spinelli. He formu-lated a position rooted not on a sophisticated Marxist analysis but on adherence to basic socialist principles. Even in February 1991, when I first met him and the fate of European communist parties seemed bleak-est, he expressed the conviction that the historical situation would turn. The stance allowed him to engage in serious criticism and candid reflec-tion with disarming good humor.

His assessments were similar to those of Castellina. He recognized the extent of the internationalization of capital while acknowledging that the forces of the left, particularly the trade-union movement, remained trapped in the apparatus of the nation-state. A frayed social fabric with spreading unemployment and poverty together with the reemergence of the extreme right blighted his view of Europe, but they also opened the possibility of a new basis of struggle. By our last meeting in mid-decade he had distilled a deceptively simple solution based on the restoration of social solidarity. He believed that through a commitment to democratic practice new possibilities for solidarity would take shape allowing the mantle of social justice to be reclaimed by the left.

He asked rhetorically, What is social solidarity? For him it requires a "new" conceptualization of society in supranational terms, anticipating the rifts and struggles around which new human interests will coalesce. Solidarity can be pursued along tangents of discord, ones that traverse, for example, Albania and Greece or Germany and Turkey. For Kyriazis, these new axes of struggle intersect in Brussels. The European Parliament, in his view, is the focal point for the generation of new configurations of solidarity. He understands his role, not in some dissident action or theo-retical breakthrough, but in the practical tasks of parliamentary practice: meeting, debating, and voting. By recourse to a leftist minimalism, Kyr-iazis hoped to rework the terms of political struggle and, if not reenter, at least conceptualize the supranational Europe that Marx and Engels sur-veyed more than a century and a half earlier. In a maneuver reminiscent of social Catholicism, he envisions an insurgent form of democratic activ-ism by which feelings can be structured, passions aligned, and solidarity mediated.

But his account also betrayed a degree of ambivalence kindled by an old militancy. Even as he laid out his moderate tactics, Kyriazis broached the possibility of more radical alternatives. With each new conflict the forces of the left can stake out unified positions, consistent with their traditional reckoning of social justice based on class interest. They can seek to represent the sentiments of new European constituencies who are exploited, marginalized, or victimized by the incursions of contemporary regimes of power. In other words, for Kryriazis, the role of the left is to retrieve for the newly disadvantaged and alienated a languishing politics of struggle, perhaps even class struggle, against an increasingly elusive and powerful establishment. These aspirations were, however, muted. In the aftermath of 1989, the traditional leftist agenda, however intellectually compelling, cannot inspire brash self-confidence even for Kyriazis. He seemed content to harbor a quiet faith that history was still on his side.

Thus, while Castellina recounted the dilemmas confronting the left, Kyriazis reasserted the classic, albeit adumbrated, leftist solution. As new social strife emerged across Europe, he believed the left would seek oppositional positions from which to redefine its progressive agenda. He maintained a steadfast faith in the ability of the left to sustain new domains of solidarity through both its traditional theory and its traditional practice. Yet it is precisely this conviction that is challenged by the onslaught of fast-capitalism and the subversions of reflexive modernization. The looming questions are far reaching. Are formations of alienation being created in Europe that are politically inaccessible? Are the progressivist politics, from social democratic to Marxist-Leninist, particularly in the guise of a technocratic managerialism, not just discredited, but as Le Pen suggests, responsible for the legacy of alienation? The historical circumstances taking hold at the close of the century are reigniting the social question in new and perhaps unprecedented ways. The most far-reaching provocation in this regard was posed initially by Thatcherism: has a politics rooted in traditional notions of solidarity been superseded by a politics in the service of the individual and the market, a politics in the service of fast-capitalism (Strathern 1992:168–69)?

The social question has also undergone a fundamental reanalysis by the leadership of the German SPD, the French Socialist Party, and the British New Labour Party. The outcome of this analysis, by contrast, is a shared confidence in what is believed to be a comprehensive renewal of European social democracy. These parties have not always, however, conveyed such an optimistic vision. They have, during earlier episodes of revisionism, seen fit to jettison a vision of society rent by class struggle, and they now face the continuing challenge of creating a new moral predicate upon which to refine their vision of a humane and democratic social order (Sassoon 1999).

## SOCIAL DEMOCRACY AND ITS CONTRADICTIONS

The impressive reconstruction of the social democratic left in Germany, France, and Britain at the end of the 1990s reflects important tactical and theoretical innovations that intersect with many of the questions posed thus far in this chapter. The leaders of these parties, Gerhard Schröder, Lionel Jospin, and Tony Blair, have shrewdly identified four major domains of political mediation—rather than fixed ideological positions or governing philosophies—that can impel the center-left toward a continual modernization. They have engaged each of these domains of activism with different substantive emphases and with different stylistic presentations, depending on their party's history and their appraisal of its contemporary challenges. The first of these domains is marked by a commitment to what Lionel Jospin calls *la gauche plurielle*, which is designed to appeal to the widest catchment of left and center-left constituencies and seeks to address their divergent interests. The second domain is expressed in the revival of the rhetoric of solidarity that has been refocused on middle-class rather than working-class values, subtly in France and Germany, and not so subtly in the case of Tony Blair's "one nation Britain." The third is denoted by a commitment to a socially progressive Europeanization that is pursued around a national framework of interests and aspirations. The fourth domain is the recognition of the vitality of the market economy in stimulating individual initiative and the generation of national wealth and prosperity. It is acknowledged, however, that various forms of statist control and regulation are required to achieve what they define as preeminent societal values. This new activist framework, articulated by relatively young and energetic leaders, has created a politics of the "neue Mitte" or "radical center" that is the basis of an impressive electoral resurgence. It also provides a conceptual context within which to debate the shifting nature of relationships—and the values that inform them—among individuals, governmental agencies, business enterprises, and civil society in response to various registers of globalization (Blair 1999; Jospin 1999; Meyer 1999).

This new social democratic framework, like social Catholicism, creates broad latitude for political maneuver, yet each of its elements also contains, in the old language of the left, contradictions and impasses. Can diverse center-left orientations be successfully mediated over time within this new pluralist and inclusive social democratic framework? Can political solidarity, derived from middle-class preoccupations, address deep-rooted problems of social justice while accommodating the demands of economic restructuring and welfare reform? At what point do the requirements of Europeanization clash ineluctably with the interests of national agendas and national identity? Can the state successfully manage a vibrant market economy that furthers fundamental social values and cultural distinction?

In the second and third parts of the text, I examine what is perhaps the most radical and far reaching of these social democratic alternatives, Tony Blair's New Labour. I look at how Blair redefined the project of solidarity by rendering the values of social justice congruent with the logic of the market and how this creates stark contradictions in postindustrial Britain. Within the urban districts of Britain crosscut by these contradictions, integralism can operate both as an overt politics and, more elusively, as cultural practice and style of life. To begin this discussion we turn first to the peculiar subversions instigated by Margaret Thatcher that opened the way for Blair's "one nation Britain."

## DEFERENCE AND SUBORDINATION

Margaret Thatcher formulated a remarkable populist attack on the science, political economy, and metaphysics of solidarity that opened a particularly devastating assault on the social question: one that challenged the entire project of social justice in the face of widening inequality. Her attack emerged initially as a radical critique of British political culture, but its implications extend well beyond mainstream British politics to what she saw as the "corporatist structure" of European politics in general. Conceptually, Thatcher's analysis was based on a rather simple insight: she recognized a profound flaw in the politics of solidarity as practiced by the left—its reliance on "deference." This was an arresting observation, particularly for a Conservative politician, insofar as elements of the extreme left in Britain have long held that "deference," as a form of hegemonic control, had to be eradicated as a first step in the struggle to eliminate class distinctions. In this view, these traditional practices of deference served as the ultimate social cement by which the establishment kept its power.

The implications of Baroness Thatcher's attack on deference was described for me by Edward Newman, who was at the time a British Labour Party member of the European Socialist Group. He asserted that the subversions of deference have ongoing consequences for the social fabric of Britain—above all, for the presumptions of virtually all forms of traditional authority. He believes the allure of neofascism, the fervor of racism, the loss of communal values, and the cultural demeanor of the underclass are all animated by the retreat of this moral idiom by which pivotal aspects of social difference have been historically mediated in Britain.[8]

Thatcherism's populist appeal to sections of the middle and working classes was based on the insinuation of a wide-ranging ambivalence about authority. Elaborating on Thatcher's insight, Newman points out that loyalty to the Labour Party and the labor movement was in fact deeply marked historically by deference. He described how it could still be observed in the way Labour politicians of different generations comported themselves in public:

> The deference which marked loyalty to the Labour Party, loyalty to a traditional position in society, is much less than it used to be. But similarly, so are positive things like solidarity. Everyday deference declines. You can see this difference even in the way a politician of my generation in a Labour area will talk to a private or public meeting of constituents as compared with the generation of MPs who are twenty or twenty-five years older. One can see it in the way they [older MPs] respond on a doorstep or work a crowd in a shopping precinct; you see these active politicians in their late fifties and early sixties who can only reach out to older voters. They cannot relate. In fact, they are laughed at by younger people. Their speaking manner, their patronizing style. They expect that, as a Labour MP, people must listen to them, that they will give them the lead, they know best and all the rest of it. Younger constituents don't want to be talked to like that.

Under the sway of Thatcherism deference increasingly came to be understood as subordination. This had direct electoral appeal to a new generation of working-class voters. These younger working-class people who voted Conservative were people who, according to Newman, "didn't see why they should do what they were told any more. . . . Mrs. Thatcher's 'Get rich quick, I'm alright Jack, look after yourself, there is no such thing as society,' amounted to a rejection of a lot of those conservative social values which put people in their place and helped them know their place." The project of trade unionism had in a fundamental way depended on inordinate deference to authority; Thatcher understood this and, most famously, in her attack on the coal miners' union made it a pivotal axis of her political insurgency. It was a shrewd insight. The Labour Party's agenda of social reformism and progressivism, intended to protect the interests of the working class, also in her view ratified their subaltern position.

The incisive formula by which underlying social assumptions of industrial Britain were usurped by the political rationale of fast-capitalism was decoded by Margaret Thatcher. She understood how the notion of "society" as a domain of interleaved moral responsibilities can be superseded by the idea of "society" in the service of an abstract market. To accomplish this, however, she was moved to pursue an unusual populist subversion. Her eradication of key values and practices of British political culture amounted to a supremely Machiavellian maneuver aimed at the foundations of the socialist project of the Labour Party.

Thatcher portrayed deference as intrinsic to socialism, as an oppressive form of authority that was inherently elitist, exercised by a cadre of leaders who defined the terms of class-based solidarity and sought, thereby, to discipline what people thought and how they acted. Specifically, by attacking deference Thatcherism ventured to impugn the moral claims, social distinctions, and material dispensations underpinning welfarism. Her canny sabotage inspired a populism that defeated repeatedly and then transformed the Labour Party. She relentlessly equated welfarism with dependency. Her ardent advocacy of individual enterprise and contempt for the moral presumptions of socialism subverted precisely those social values that, she believed, put people in their place. Thatcher had found a way to become the champion of a compelling type of "agency." This is what the modernizers of New Labour had most brilliantly and perhaps most ruthlessly exploited in the lead-up to the general election of 1997 and the victory of Tony Blair:

> Both Toryism and socialism brought sentiments and values from a distant past into contemporary politics. The Tory tradition showed traces of the deference and *noblesse oblige* of premodern hierarchy. Likewise the sense of solidarity among socialists drew on values of an older organic society. It makes sense, therefore, to use the term "modernization," much fancied by Tony Blair, to describe the disappearance of these vestiges of a more traditional society. (Beer 1998:24)

The legacy of the Thatcherite "revolution," based on the eradication of traditional social grounding of British politics, whether predicated on solidarity, deference, or noblesse oblige, ultimately cleared the way for the modernization of the Labour Party. At its base this formulation of "modernization" instills a very specific image of society, one that provokes anxieties in Europe. Within the EU this alternative modernization is seen as anathema to the social modernist project of integration. What federalists fear, only slightly less than fascism, is the political effort to define society in the interest of an abstract market and under the moral jurisdiction of individualization. They dread the dissonant fast-capitalism personified by Margaret Thatcher and now Tony Blair, but, in fact, given life by their own institutional project of economic integration through the provisions of the Single European Act and European Monetary Union. This defining characteristic of fast-capitalism, whereby market forces, once freed of institutional control, operate increasingly outside the supervision of political authorities, directly threatens European social modernism. Blair goes further: he equates the technocratic project of solidarity manifest in welfarism as an instrument of social injustice.

## UNDERCLASS

Newman, like Kyriazis, holds out the hope that politics rooted in class interests and collective values can be retrieved to impede the advance of a fierce individualization. Yet he also sees societal breakdown typified by the emergence of an underclass that is increasingly difficult to reach politically, as its members have become an entrenched and brutalized presence in postindustrial Britain. The character of their alienation coincides with that of the "new poor" described by Bauman:

> *Newman*: The other change is in the growth of the "underclass," what we used to call the "lumpen-proletariat": a segment of society alienated from everything. It's all about getting by at the "I'm alright Jack" level. In other words, you try to avoid paying taxes, you don't bother about voting because politicians are all the same, you register for [un]employment if you can get benefits but that's usually too much aggravation and you can get more working on the black market anyway. It's what we call in Britain "doing a little bit of this and a little bit of that."
>
> *Holmes*: Ten or twenty years ago, these people would have formed more stable working-class families.
>
> *Newman*: Twenty years ago they would have been in work, low paid perhaps, but they would have been paying taxes and officially employed. They would have been taking part in society. They are now living in a semilegal existence where the borderlines with criminal involvements become blurred.

The development of their marginalization and subjugation follows, in Newman's view, a clear historical route: as governmental responsibilities for social welfare are curtailed or removed, the underclass emerges. The making of the British underclass is the consequence of the systematic unmaking of the British working class. There are tens of thousands of these people in blighted urban districts; twenty years ago they formed a more or less stalwart section of working-class society. Now they live lives that are crosscut by criminality, their social integration increasingly precarious. Newman is also puzzled by the strange migration of Thatcherite values stressing radical individualism, which once only permeated the thinking of middle-class business people and the like, and which now contour the thinking of marginal sections of the working class who are not regularly employed. These values surface unexpectedly among the new poor, who have utter disdain for the insipid trappings of English respectability and whose contempt for authority is visceral. "There is a lot of aggression, a lot of hostility, a lot of alienation. It's a general grievance against the status quo. Clearly, there is a lot of racism but it's more covert than overt. Racism is still not seen as respectable. That, of course, is the problem with the underclass. They are not bothered with being respectable." These people harbor aggression which New Labour is neither interested in nor capable of directing against the establishment. Thatcher is right; an all encompassing conception of society is difficult, if not impossible, to sustain.

Newman's account opened the question of society as it is manifest in a postindustrial Britain, in the lives and circumstances of an "underclass." He surveyed what has become an increasingly obscure landscape on which formations of alienation are being created, alienation that is inaccessible to mainstream political scrutiny or bureaucratic intervention. These are the same locales in which the British working class was made, where its social identity was forged. Now, within these decaying industrial districts the working class is being unmade and undone, as the relationship between the individual and the collectivity mutates in new and unpredictable ways.

In shifting the research to the East End of London I sought guides to some of the more nettlesome and distasteful features of this landscape. The leadership of the British National Party (BNP) provided this guidance. This macabre political grouping champions the prejudices of the socially alienated and the culturally estranged. Its leaders have formulated an integralist politics that mingles easily with an overt fascism. They are shameless racists and, on occasion, proficient street fighters. Their integralist fears and aspirations, even when politically muted, gain expression as a fugitive style of life.

# PART TWO
EAST END

## Chapter Seven

## CALL IT FASCISM

THE EAST END of London is a locale swept by the full force of late modern fast-capitalism. Within its council housing reside "new" arrivals dislocated by the insensate force of global markets and pressed against "indigenous" residents who themselves struggle with novel forms of alienation and exile. An enfeebled welfare state mediates the material conditions of a multiracial and multicultural Europe. In this kind of milieu, where the newly defined contours of European society are being contested, an incendiary politics has materialized with race and nation at its core. The inability of political leaders to render the transformation to a multiracial and multicultural Europe meaningful, let alone intervene and regulate it, risks shifting the struggle into the hands of thugs. These vexing issues, which conventionally oriented political actors will not or cannot address, have the potential to breed violent action, a potential that has been realized on the streets of the East End of London. The results of failed or inept democratic politics are visceral, split heads and battered bodies.

There are two profound ways that fast-capitalism has insinuated itself into the fabric of social life and cultural experience on the Isle of Dogs. First, its workings are manifest in the physical displacement of human beings, most recently from South Asia (specifically the Sylhet district of Bangladesh) into the urban wards of Tower Hamlets. Second, its dissonant operation is detectable in the radical "flattening," to use Marilyn Strathern's terminology, of social distinctions underpinning British industrial society. The most conspicuous outcome of these processes is the creation of a multiracial and multicultural Britain. Less visible is the formation of "new" ill-defined groupings, remnants of the industrial working class and segments of a marginalized middle class, whose integration into postindustrial British society is increasingly precarious. On the one hand, these "indigenous" inhabitants—faced with what they believe to be a burgeoning immigrant population—struggle with a rupture in their sense of belonging interleaved with fears that their way of life is doomed. On the other, they experience acutely the "flattening" of social distinctions as the moral claims and the material dispensations of class are eroded. How these experiences gain expression within a virulent integralist politics is the primary subject of this and the next two chapters. Thus, the focus of the analysis in this part of the text shifts to an examination of the East End as a site of a flagrant mutation of integralism; it is where integralism is joined to a racialized political economy to yield fascism.

The incident that opens this second part of the text is the by-election victory in September 1993 and subsequent electoral loss in the spring of 1994 of an obscure East Ender, Derek Beackon, to the Tower Hamlets's Borough Council as a representative of the Millwall ward on the Isle of Dogs.[1] What makes this an unusual circumstance is that Mr. Beackon ran as a candidate of the British National Party.[2] His election represented the first significant achievement for a nationalist and defiantly racist party in Britain in the 1990s.[3]

Chapter 8, "Factual Racism," and chapter 9, "Authoritarianism," encompass the stories of four leaders of the BNP: Richard Edmonds, Michael Newland, Derek Beackon, and John Tyndall. They are unbalanced and idiosyncratic tales, which trace the obsession of each of these figures with national integration. The leaders of this truculent party have reclaimed a decisive ideological position. They have identified the instrumentalities of the welfare state as the contemporary social embodiment of "community" and "nation." Fast-capitalism, with its ideological rationale in neoliberalism, is the dark force they seek to combat. They revile Margaret Thatcher. They delineate grim cultural critiques of Britain from which a mendacious political program is derived. Their assessments are lurid. The cultural critiques they conjure take form as candid self-portraits revealing all four as besieged exiles in their own homeland. Inlaid in these critical accounts is a vivid narration of a nation, an illicit Britain.

In chapter 10, "Radical Symmetry," we will see how Tony Blair, shortly after he became prime minister, took up the project of national integration in a way that confirms many of the BNP leaders' darkest suspicions. Blair proposes a British nationhood that is unified across classes. Moral claims based on class are rebuffed in his "one nation Britain," while the project of social justice as it has come to be institutionalized within the welfare state is disavowed. Much as the leadership of the BNP suspected, Blair seeks a virtual elimination of socialism from the Labour Party's doctrine. By forcefully articulating his agenda of individual duty and personal responsibility, Blair clears a political space where the traditional project of British socialism no longer has a conspicuous mainstream claimant.

This part of the text closes on a familiar note. Like their counterparts in France, during the last month of the decade the BNP's leadership cadre slipped into crisis, pitting the "modernizers," who sought to appeal to a new and broader public, against the party's old guard (King and Raymond 1999). In September 1999 Nick Griffin, backed by Michael Newland, usurped John Tyndall's long-standing leadership at a party conference. Their insurgency was orchestrated on the BNP's website which provided the communicative and representational means to ply their form of intimate artifice (King 1999; Lowles 2000).

## ISLE OF DOGS

There are few more incongruous places in Europe in the last decade of the twentieth century than the Isle of Dogs. On the northern end is the Canary Wharf Project with twelve million square feet of new offices, hotels, and shops as well as the tallest building in Britain, Canary Wharf Tower designed by Cesar Pelli. It is the focus of the enormous Docklands Redevelopment Scheme, the most extravagant expression of the real-estate construction and speculation that swept London during the late 1980s and 1990s. The project aimed at attracting the burgeoning financial services industry from the City of London as well as newspaper publishing from Fleet Street to new facilities in and around the Docklands. The *Times*, *Guardian*, *Financial Times*, *Daily Mail*, and *Daily Telegraph* have relocated all or part of their operations here.

In the south of the Isle of Dogs is Mudchute Park, with a small working farm; Island Gardens with a pleasant view of the Thames and entrance to the Footway Tunnel under the river to Greenwich; Cubitt Town, an old industrial area with housing built for workers ringing now abandoned factories, shipyards, and docks. Across the Thames to the East the twelve protruding poles that support the newly constructed Millennium Dome are in clear view. Crisscrossing the island are the great basins, slipways, and channels of the West India and Millwall Docks, monuments to the area's maritime past. An elevated light railway stretches two and half miles or so from north to south. A linkroad connecting the island with Limehouse and the rest of the East End was recently completed. It is reputed to be one of the most costly roadways in Europe. Renovation and conversion of the old warehouses that line the waterways and docks have created new outposts for London's new elites.

The Isle of Dogs in the nineteenth and early twentieth centuries was the center of shipbuilding and related industries along the Thames. In 1857 the *Great Eastern*, the largest vessel of its time (630 feet in length) was launched here by Isambard Kingdom Brunel. The Millwall iron works alone employed four thousand men and boys in the 1860s. Labor activism made the island an important setting in the founding of British trade unionism. It was also an area in which Oswald Mosley found sympathetic listeners in the 1930s. The Docklands were bombed intensively during the Second World War. In early 1996, the Irish Republican Army chose Canary Wharf as the site to recommence a bombing campaign in Britain after an extended cease-fire.

The end of British maritime dominance after the Second World War led to the close of the docks and the end of the island's industrial base. The displaced workers and their offspring still inhabit the poor council estates. They identify themselves as "islanders." Since the late 1950s new waves of immigrants from Asia and the Caribbean arrived creating a sense among islanders of competition for limited public housing and jobs.[4] Millwall was, however, one of the least affected areas of the borough. By the 1990s, the minority character of the ward was 13.5 percent "Asian" and 6 percent "Black." This compares with the overall distribution of 27 percent "Asian" and 7 percent "Black" for the Borough of Tower Hamlets with a total population of 161,000. Official unemployment in the borough was over 26 percent. Tower Hamlets has one of the highest percentage of residents living in council-owned housing in Britain. Of 67,581 dwellings under the borough's housing authority, 45,475 were judged as "unfit" or "in need of repair."[5]

## POLYETHNIC LONDON

Gerd Baumann with a group of collaborators has pursued an ambitious ethnographic survey of the polyethnic suburb of Southall in the Borough of Ealing in West London that provides a complementary perspective on the material presented in this and the next two chapters. Within this suburban district of sixty thousand residents, approximately eighteen miles west of the Isle of Dogs, Baumann probes the way cultural affinities and differences among ethnic and religious communities are negotiated and contested within a single social field (Baumann 1996:37–71).[6] By problematizing "community" and "culture," he can examine the distinctive strategies that Southallians devise to engage what he calls "the dominant discourse of ethno-cultural communities."[7] Although the overall aims of Baumann's challenging research are quite different from those pursued herein, his depiction of the dilemmas facing "white Southallians" has direct relevance for this study. Notably, he and his colleagues find little in the way of a "nationalist discourse" among white Southallians.[8] "Those English people who did not join the white exodus, remain in Southall largely by choice, and they have redefined their place in town. Neither [Barbara] Hawkes nor [Teresa] McGarry nor I have encountered much rhetorical emphasis on a white status as 'nationals' when others are members of ethnic communities" (Baumann 1996:138). Rather, he suggests, white Southallians appropriate an English "minority" identity:

> The position of white Southallians amidst the local *communities* is ambiguous and often equivocal. While Irish *culture* is recognized as a distinct heritage, an Irish *community* is seldom acknowledged either from the inside or the outside.

An English *culture*, by contrast, is hard to define not only for locals, but for the ethnographer, too; and while there were local *communities* of English people until they dispersed, an English cultural *community* is not seen to exist. To call the entire white population one *community*, again, is far more plausible from the outside than from the inside. The word that most white Southallians most readily use themselves is that they are a "minority." (Baumann 1996:134)

He goes on to identify a series of strategies by which the white English and Irish, who effectively "lack community," define themselves and operate pragmatically within a "multi-ethnic social field":

> To deal with this "minority" position among *communities*, three strategies can be discerned. A political option open to Irish Southallians is to seek recognition as an ethnic minority or ethnic community in accordance with the dominant discourse of ethno-cultural communities. A second option, open to all white Southallians, is a cognitive strategy. It consists in cultivating a shared minority consciousness, and it is achieved most easily by stressing white Southallians' exclusion from public services distributed by ethnic targeting. A third option consists in a pragmatic strategy, and is the one that best avoids subjective alienation: it involves the creative forging of affinities and alliances across *community* boundaries. (Baumann 1996:134–35)

Nevertheless, Baumann finds among white Southallians precisely the submerged sensibilities that ignite an integralist politics in the East End. "The fear of being branded racist keeps many white Southallians from spelling out in public that, in a widely used phrase, 'things have gone too far the other way': 'I'm not a racist,' explains a middle-aged, locally born Englishwoman, 'but there are things that I want to complain about. Except I can't. Because I would be labeled a racist, and I'm not' (1996:139). One of Barbara Hawkes's informants is far more explicit: "An English [presumably white] employee of the [Ealing Borough] council itself expressed most blatantly what probably most white Southallians would have endorsed at the time: 'According to Ealing Council, if you're white, you're a racist'" (1990:64, cited in Baumann 1996:139).

Baumann summarizes the council's assessment of those white residents who remained in Southall, who did not participate in the "white exodus" during the last two decades:

> The resentment was further incensed by the council's declaration of 1988 as "Anti-Racism Year." . . . Of the dozen or so conferences and workshops targeted at ethnic minorities, political activists, and council employees, white Southallians heard little. . . . To "join with all ordinary people . . . [and] to fight the disadvantages common to them all" is one thing; to join with politicians avowing that "racism runs through all aspects of life in the borough" is another, even to those who do not wish to ignore or condone it. It was felt . . . by many white Southallians I questioned on the subject [to be an insult]. It is

not hard to see why, since it makes no allowance for people who, after all, had not moved out; and it blatantly stereotypes the white, or perhaps only the English, cultural heritage as a consistently racist form of life. (1996:139)

Thus, Baumann's text can be juxtaposed to the analysis presented in this part of the study. Whereas Baumann traces the merging alignments of a multiracial and multicultural Britain, I observed a contrary phenomenon; what I address is an integralist politics that seeks precisely to resist and thwart these transformations.

## DELINQUENT AURA

"As the most distinctive new radicalism" of the twentieth century, fascism is also its most discredited (Payne 1995:496). Since the Second World War neofascist and neo-Nazi groups have often taken great pains to fashion themselves in a manner that has cast them as political absurdities.[9] This is, of course, a source of significant public fascination with them. Bill Buford recognized this delinquent aura in his encounter with British neo-Nazis among the membership of the British National Front, the immediate forerunner of the British National Party:

> The fact is I think I was different. I wasn't hostile to the National Front. I couldn't take it seriously: I really did regard it as a convocation of loons, although I probably didn't know enough to justify making such a judgment. When I came to England as a student, everyone took the National Front very seriously: opposing it was a popular cause, a rallying point at the college bar for articulate, intelligent, liberal-thinking people animated by their distaste for what the National Front represented. Intelligent, liberal-thinking people are meant to show tolerance for dissent, but the National Front was fascist and so intolerable that it made liberals behave as if they weren't liberals. This, I felt, was a tribute to the National Front. It was an evil of such an order that many of my friends believed that its members should be banished from society— imprisoned at the least; some wanted to see them maimed. Their feelings were that strong. This too was a tribute to the National Front. . . . For my friends, it would have been inconceivable that one might actually talk to a member of the National Front, let alone have a conversation. And that was why I was trying to have one. I was curious. I had a chance to meet the devil, and I wanted to find out if he deserved his bad reputation. (1992:139–40)

The argument, which culminates my analysis, is that a shift is taking place not in the nature of fascism in Britain, but in its social expression and apprehension. Rather than inspiring self-marginalizing groups or grouplets, fascist sensibilities are generating integralist convictions that coincide with the definitive experience of an unnamed and unintegrated social formation encompassing disenfranchised remnants of industrial working and middle classes. The character of this social milieu resists conventional analysis; perhaps its most distinguishing feature is the intoxication of its participants with violence. Consummate hostility to elite portrayals of reality and an abiding contempt for the emerging practice of multiculturalism bind their anomie.

In other words, the enthrallments generally associated with "fascism" are gradually being reconfigured by a "new" public in a postindustrial Britain. Members of this public are not—nor are they likely to become—BNP supporters. Indeed, it is doubtful that their obsessions and aversions will coalesce within any formal political context.[10] What the leaders of the BNP recognize among members of this rancorous public is the very literal character of their alienation, an alienation in which relatedness among persons is itself obscured, perspective is lost, and personhood infringed. Strathern sees this kind of English alienation arising among those who experience a distinctive form of impoverishment, who lack the (private) material means to "exercise choice," who are bereft of a class-based perspectivism to orient themselves socially:

> For the nature of the enabling technology—financial flexibility—suggests that the perspectives are constituted merely by the choices that resources afford. Those without means to exercise choice are somehow without a perspective, without a communicable view on events.
>
> Loss should be understood in a strictly relative sense. All the English have lost is what they once had, which was the facility for drawing partial analogies between different domains of social life. Referring to one class from the perspective of another went along with the ability to compare different domains of activity—to talk of individual responsibility toward the general public, or to assume that the welfare of the family meant the welfare of the community. (Strathern 1992:142)

In this framework the flattening of social distinctions and deletion of perspective can create domains of particularly fierce alienation wherein anomic and brutalized styles of life are liberated and endowed with perverse meaning. The BNP leaders interviewed in the following chapters know well this milieu and give a persuasive rendering of the struggles that operate within and upon it. They pride themselves on having access to domains of alienation beyond the reach of conventional politics.

## NOMADS

The East End is the setting of one of the most courageous early experiments in European ethnography, Henry Mayhew's 1851 *London Labour and the London Poor*. Mayhew's relevance for this study resides in his assessment of an urban alienation. In the first part of the text I argued that Johann Herder had formulated a powerful and highly influential conception of alienation based on loss or denial of cultural rootedness in pastoral, preindustrial settings. Mayhew's monumental depiction of the wretched condition of the poor of Victorian London reformulated precisely this issue of "rootlessness" in perhaps the most urbanized districts of nineteenth-century Europe. In this maelstrom of a nascent fast-capitalism these "nomads" underwent physical deracination and material degradation that converged with precipitous decomposition of conventional forms of meaning and morality. Yet he finds among the urban dispossessed of the East End cultural aspirations similar to those noted by Herder and configured theoretically by Berlin. Christopher Herbert comments on Mayhew's portrayal of a populist expressionism that emerged among these street folk. "What Mayhew comes to discover is that it is precisely such ordinary pleasures, morally disreputable though many of them may be in the case of street people, which 'bind them to existence' in society, the binding filaments being . . . networks of stylistic effects charged with cryptically expressed meaning" (1991:249). These networks of style—Mayhew focuses specifically on dialect, fashion, and taste—serve as the basis for generating radical markers of difference. "Its fundamental principle . . . is their fierce antagonism toward the respectable 'settled' society amid which they live as persecuted aliens" (1991:236). Estrangement itself, in Mayhew's analysis, becomes a means of engendering pluralism based on an emotionally charged system of incommensurable values dividing rich and poor, rooted and uprooted.

There is a third figure, Oswald Spengler, who recognized that the type of alienation characterized by Herder in a pastoral Europe and the figure of the "urban nomad" depicted by Mayhew in the East End presaged a specific type of modern political order. Theodor Adorno, in an otherwise critical if not scathing analysis of Oswald Spengler's *Decline of the West*, nevertheless finds a compelling depiction of urbanites in the transformed cities of the future. Adorno comments specifically on Spengler's description of the creation of a "new primitive man" or "intellectual nomad," a portrayal with eerie significance for this study:

> The image of the latter-day city-dweller as a second nomad deserves special emphasis. It expresses not only anxiety and estrangement but also the dawning ahistorical character of a condition in which men experience themselves as objects of opaque processes and, torn between sudden shock and sudden forgetfulness, are no longer capable of a sense of temporal continuity. Spengler, who sees the connection between atomization and the regressive type of man which revealed itself fully only with the onslaught of totalitarianism, states:

"Each of these splendid mass cities harbors horrendous poverty, a brutalization of all customs which even now, in the attics and garrets, the cellars and backyards, is breeding a new primitive man." (Adorno 1967:55)

In a section entitled, "The Physiognomy of the Modern Metropolis," Spengler (1922) describes, almost lyrically, the inhuman urban landscape upon which the "intellectual nomad" is created:

> They no longer have anything in common with the houses in which Vesta and Janus, the Lares and Penates resided: rather, they are mere shells, fashioned not by blood but by utility, not by feeling but by the spirit of commercialism. As long as the hearth remains the real, meaningful center of the family the pious soul, the last bond to the country has not disappeared. But when that, too, is lost and the mass of tenants and overnight guests in this sea of houses lead a vagrant existence from shelter to shelter, like the hunters and shepherds of primeval time, the intellectual nomad is fully formed. This is a world, the world. (quoted in Adorno 1967:55)

The interlocutors who are the subject of this part of the text not only embody Spengler's prediction, they invoke him as their prophet. They fashion themselves as harbingers and agents of an authoritarian order.

Mayhew and Spengler, thus, trace two very different paths that these "urban nomads" can potentially take: in the first instance, toward a proliferation of populist values and expressionist styles as "an organized struggle of consciousness against its antithetical principle, the degeneration of meaning" (Herbert 1991:222); in the second instance, toward a stark authoritarism—under the sway of a seamless "will to dominate"— as the only way to act upon a pluralistic world bereft of mediating forms of democratic consensus (Adorno 1967:55). The fascist synthesis, which the BNP leadership seeks to pursue in the contemporary multiracial and multicultural wards of inner London, allows them to embrace simultaneously Mayhew's expressionist and Spengler's authoritarian prescriptions. Indeed, the generational schism within the party at the close of the century runs along this axis.

## AUTHORITARIAN ORDER

The single most important political question posed by globalization is how its transformative dynamics will be resisted and where they will be contested. The great metaphors and stratagems by which the left conceptualized its confrontation with industrial capitalism no longer sustain meaning or action. The factory floor no longer circumscribes the critical field of struggle for an accelerating transnational fast-capitalism. Nationalism has reemerged as the dominant idiom of opposition and the language in which integralist political imperatives are asserted. Its extremes are marked by a tactical repertoire of racialized confrontation and thuggery.

Ultimately, this theoretical imperative compelled me to relocate the study to the impoverished urban precincts of the East End. It meant loitering with neofascists and recording their world view, a tableau tinged with the paranoid and the delusional. But let there be no doubt, these marginal political actors have conjured elements of an acute reading of the historical moment and their integralist politics go beyond the mere refinement of strategic cultural idioms to establish domains of solidarity and frameworks for action. They have formulated a *national socialism* based on a critique of the moral economy of multiculturalism, with a bisecting critique of the political economy of an impaired welfare state. Their assessment forcefully attacks what they believe to be the symptoms and the agents of globalization.

The BNP is electorally insignificant, its prospects dismal.[11] Yet its leadership has drawn together a virulent analysis that speaks to the defining experience of a deeply rancorous public. This group of activists harbors fascist aspirations, which they bind to a wrenching experience of present-day Britain. By reinvoking *society* as an analytical framework and moral tableau, they confer an unsettling conventionality on their world view. Their vision assumes a distinctly *un*radical appearance. Their ideas appear less and less as the deranged brooding of "thugs" and more and more as familiar—though by no means reasonable—dogma.[12] Above all, they seek ideological syntheses at a moment when social consensus is elusive.[13]

These interlocutors also trespass the lapsed boundaries demarking the political left and right. The retreat of Marxism and the general decline of left-wing politics in post-Cold War Europe allows for a disquieting accretion of BNP positions. Denied its great historical nemesis—international communism—anticapitalism and antiliberalism assume a paramount position in party doctrine.[14] Concurrently, the traditional commitment of British fascism to social welfare legitimizes the BNP's claim to areas of social policy relinquished by New Labour. A radical critique of fast-capitalism joined to an ardent defense of social welfare principles allows the BNP to insinuate its ultranationalism within a program of "social justice."

It is improbable that activists, like those at the core of the BNP, will glean any direct benefit or influence from their militant insights. What is vastly more troublesome is the potential for their *ideas*, in one political guise or another, to be leached and naturalized within a mainstream political discourse and reappear, as Primo Levi puts it, "walking on tiptoe and calling itself by other names" (1987:397, quoted in Griffin 1995:392).[15]

The individuals portrayed in the following chapters are recognizable and not entirely unsympathetic characters. Their dilemmas are plausible. Their resentments are "real." Drawing on prosaic ideological ingredients, they plot a course to an authoritarian order, a *Volksgemeinschaft*. I have been asked repeatedly why I would be interested in these people. For what it is worth, this is the most precise answer I can give: if Bill Buford sought out members of the British National Front to take the measure of the devil, I was drawn to leaders of the BNP as guides through precincts of abject alienation. It was here that I found the telltale evidence, as read through their wayward political discourse, of how fast-capitalism moves through the East End of London and how it can redefine social and cultural struggles across Europe.

## Chapter Eight

## FACTUAL RACISM

PORTRAYALS of Richard Edmonds, the national organizer of the British National Party, and Derek Beackon, a former member of the Tower Hamlets Borough Council, reveal how the cultural predicaments of a besieged white working class can inflame an integralist politics. They, like their mates, are preoccupied with the changed authority of class within British society; that is to say, they are outraged that the moral claims and the material dispensations of the working class have been deposed in postindustrial Britain. They are appalled that the programs of the welfare state—erected to reproduce a stable working-class community—now serve the needs of "immigrants" who embody a new, multicultural Britain. This vexing reality imbues their racist politics. Edmonds and Beackon place welfarism at the center of their national socialist struggle.[1]

The decisive shift in political discourse in Britain from the waning struggles of a white working class to the emerging predicaments of a multicultural society incite what Edmonds calls a "factual racism":[2]

> Now, we use that term ["racist"], not in a pejorative sense as do our opponents but in a positive, indeed, factual sense. Thirty years ago an "Englishman" was taken to be a white man. He was neither a Jamaican, an Asian, a Chinese, a hottentot, nor a bushman from the Kalahari desert. We use the term racist in a factual, what we would say a positive, sense. We describe a racist as someone who attempts to maintain Britain as racially white.

Beackon is more circumspect:

> If I talked about immigration [at work] and said, "This immigration has become a bit too much, let's call a halt to it now"—harmless words really, I mean, we have to face up to it, don't we? But anyway, they would call me a "racist," a "Nazi." Now a lot of British people are still afraid of that word, so the BNP have retaliated and say, "Yeah we are racists. So what?" It was like these people had a club or something. They call you a "racist" and then expect you to shut up! But we don't. We just say, "Yeah okay, we're racists because we want to live with our own kind."

What these two characters pose is not a question of mere "cultural incommensurability," as articulated by Le Pen and his associates, but an arrogant and unadulterated racism. They embrace a defiant rendering of "pluralism" that asserts the cogency of racial distinctions as a supervening societal principle. They are convinced that racial differences are immutable and insurmountable, and, thus, the invidious discriminations these men advocate are essential for the "authentic" collectivity they seek to preserve and protect. What is profoundly disconcerting about their scurrilous populism is that it is premised on rather conventional political ideas and aspirations. These two figures advocate a prosaic "socialism" oriented toward economic redistribution by which community benevolence and compassion is institutionally expressed. They avow unremarkable "cultural values" of respect, generosity, duty, and deference as central to their populist agenda. They decry violence perpetrated against law-abiding citizens. Yet, when their construal of these British "virtues" is crosscut by a delegitimization of traditional class-based prerogatives and a rupture in a sense of belonging, they breed, among partisans like Edmonds and Beackon, an incandescent bigotry.

Thus, what these two accounts reveal is a crucial potential of integralism to take familiar outlooks and sensibilities and render them as an egregious politics. Again, as I suggest in chapter 1, one of my primary purposes for employing the notion of integralism is to provide an analytical space within which various atavistic political formations—most notably fascism—are rendered as a phenomenon that is disconcertingly familiar rather than alien. What the accounts in this section of the text demonstrate is that despite their illicit character, inherent in these ideas is a precarious proximity to conventional political values, and hence their true danger and our abiding vulnerability to them.

The other important aspect of these accounts is that they begin to broach the social milieu of Zygmunt Bauman's "new poor," of Spengler's "new primitive man," and of Mayhew's "urban nomads," where integralism is expressed not merely as a formal political stance but as a brutalized style of life. In an inversion of Zeev Sternhell's insight noted earlier, fascism emerged initially as cultural tradition before it became a political phenomenon. In the East End the sensibilities that we associate with neofascism as they lose their overt political expression are transformed into the austere styles, attitudes, and predispositions of the "underclass" or, as we will see in chapter 10, what Tony Blair calls the "workless class," whose integration into the nation is increasingly tenuous.

As the entitlements and subventions of the welfare state are withdrawn and as social integration in the "one nation Britain" is increasingly predicated on gainful employment, these figures, the human remnants of the British industrial era, slip into an ambiguous moral status unworthy, as Bauman suggests, of benevolence and compassion. Their fate is only traced superficially as homelessness, unemployment, drug addiction, criminality, and the like. The truth is they have become the unsavory and unwanted "other," the dispossessed. As Newman suggested, they care little about respectability and flaunt their contempt for authority. They refuse conventional forms of assimilation. Ironically, some of their most dissident stylistic innovations—fashioned originally by skinheads—along with their thuggish attitudes, and their predispositions to violence have moved out of the East End and gained currency across Britain and Europe. For a new generation of Europeans the latent cultural message that inheres in these fierce stylistic forms is once again widespread, if not persuasive.

## PALE BLUE BUNKER

Edmonds and Beackon were interviewed on separate occasions at the BNP's former "bookstore" or "headquarters" in Welling, southeast London. It is a pale blue, steel-clad row house along a nondescript street of small retail stores and residences. Edmonds is the owner of the building. Not surprisingly, neighbors were rather inhospitable to visitors seeking directions to this curious edifice. One enters the structure through a heavily bolted door. The interior has the subterranean feel of a fortified bunker. The Metropolitan Police were, according to Edmonds, consulted on the renovation and the fortification of the structure to insure the safety of its denizens.[3] Publications of the BNP lined the walls of the main, windowless room.

Architecturally, the building expresses the contradictions of an extreme integralist politics. Its walls enclose a stark inner space that is cut off from the richly textured multicultural neighborhoods of London. Those who work and loiter within adamantly resist any externalities that might violate the structures of feeling upon which their political assertions depend. They hold fiercely to a cloying vision of Britain that no longer exists, and perhaps never did. They counter the dynamic cultural transformation unfolding around them with their "factual racism," which can be invoked violently. The cultural landscapes, which are portrayed by these two BNP activists, encompass domains of alienation, which—as George Simmel acutely observed—create a paradoxical basis of solidarity. They are entrapped in a predicament of their own making where the hostile means by which they can act upon the world incite responses that confirm their sense of injustice, marginality, and vulnerability. They wrestle with what Isaiah Berlin calls their experience of "collective humiliation" (1997: 245). Hence, these are not pleasant portrayals; they are austere and troubled depictions, which are not always easy to decipher. I have tried to render them intelligible while being true to their jarring and at times contradictory character; the power of these messages is contingent neither on their coherence nor their consistency.

## GRIEVOUS BODILY HARM

Edmonds is tall, intense, and articulate. He speaks with a driving cadence. He has the habit, while answering questions, of making extended pauses during which he thrusts his face very close to the listener's, extending his lower lip and glowering. He paced and circled around me as we talked.

The crucial labor Edmonds performs is to translate integralist fears and aspirations into the vernacular of an urban landscape. His métier is tactical thuggery. What is at stake in his account is the social reproduction of white working-class household and community. What is resisted is the assumption of a pluralistic nation that aligns the polyethnic boroughs of London.[4] He embraces a theory of exclusionary welfarism as the grounding for his racialized populism, a theory derived from a highly local politics of experience. Although Edmonds and his fellow activists characterize their politics as "nationalist," the scope of its purview is claustrophobic, barely penetrating beyond the boundaries of impoverished urban districts of inner London. His politics coalesces at street level. He discriminates the geographies of racial inclusion and exclusion of the city.[5] He is inspired to confront physically those who embody the contradictions of his Britain—those who transgress its racial hygiene, its moral economy. Edmonds is an organic intellectual, with a taste for street fighting, whose vision skirts the paranoid and the delusional.[6] His actions splice the political and the criminal.

There were a series of violent skirmishes in the East End just before and immediately after the election of Derek Beackon on September 16, 1993. In a number of these confrontations Richard Edmonds appears to have been a participant, in one case a principal.[7]

On the evening of September 8 during a football match between England and Poland, a grievous assault on a 17-year-old student, Quaddus Ali, took place. Quaddus Ali was brutally attacked by seven men and one woman—alleged to be members or supporters of the BNP—while returning a video rental with three of his friends. The attackers pounced on Quaddus as he left the video store and dragged him into a nearby pub where he was beaten repeatedly. His mates escaped. Quaddus sustained severe injuries to the head, which left him in a deep coma at the Royal London Hospital. A series of clashes among antifascist groups, local

Asian residents, and the police ensued in the area along Brick Lane and Bethnal Green Road.[8]

A vigil by a large, peaceful crowd on September 10 in sympathy with Quaddus Ali turned violent and nine Bengali youths were arrested. The police were accused by supporters of Quaddus Ali of provoking the fracas. This was followed on September 11 by an incident in which "fifty BNP supporters" rampaged down Brick Lane breaking windows, damaging retail stalls, and terrorizing residents. Hundreds of "Asians" marched down to Cable Street in response, protesting the inadequacy of police protection and the lack of arrests.

The clashes culminated in a protest organized by the Anti Nazi League (ANL) on the morning of September 18, the Sunday after Derek Beackon's election.[9] Members of the ANL and local residents attempted to dislodge BNP members trying to sell their nationalist broadsheet from their usual corner location on Brick Lane. This spot on Brick Lane was considered the BNP's "pitch." Since the 1930s fascists had regularly congregated on Sundays at that same location to peddle their publications.[10] On this particular Sunday an unusually large number of BNP supporters were in attendance to celebrate Beackon's election. The confrontation was bloody with the BNP denied access to its traditional territory by local residents and ANL activists.

There was one more serious incident that took place subsequent to the confrontation on Brick Lane. Shortly after BNP supporters were dislodged, an attack took place on a "black and white couple" outside the "Ship" pub on Bethnal Green Road, an establishment regularly frequented by BNP followers. Four men attacked the couple, roughing up the woman and brutally cutting the man's face "to the bone" with a broken beer bottle. This sadistic form of assault is known as "glassing." Due to the significant police presence in the area because of the earlier fracas, officers were on the scene quickly, capturing the alleged attackers in the pub. One was Richard Edmonds. The four assailants were identified by the woman, arrested, and the next day all were charged with violent disorder. In addition, one of the attackers, Simon Briggs, was further charged with causing "grievous bodily harm." Edmonds was subsequently convicted of violent disorder and sentenced to prison for three months.[11] Questioned about the judgment he vehemently denounced the conviction, blaming it in part on the media and the image it projects of the BNP:

> Listen, if you want to talk about me, then yes, I have been charged and found guilty of a very serious offense of which I will go to my grave absolutely denying. I know I am 100 percent innocent! It is to my misfortune that I was charged with an offense that I did not commit and the jury chose to believe the prosecu-

tion. I have no doubt the jury was influenced, in part, by the portrayal [of the BNP in the press]. It's a vicious circle.

He insists the BNP's image has been tarnished by the media, "which are in the hands of the internationalists, in the hands of the one world order [people], in the hands of the liberals. . . .They use their power through the media, to blacken our [the BNP's] good name. . . . It's black propaganda. It's all a pack of lies." This tarnished image, he claims, was responsible for his conviction. I noted that the BNP often actively undercuts its own public image:

> *Holmes*: The Britain you seek is, above all, respectable. Yet you let your-selves be portrayed as thuggish.[12]
>
> *Edmonds*: I understand your question entirely. But, you see, no newspaper will give us friendly coverage, no TV studio will invite us in for a nice friendly interview. We have to campaign ourselves. We have to put our leaflets into mailboxes, go out and sell our newspapers and march in the streets. When we campaign we are physically attacked by our political opponents, confronted and attacked. In this last election, one of our candidates lost an eye. [He was] knocked to the ground and kicked in the face with a steel boot and blinded in one eye. That received a little bit of publicity but had it been a Labour, Liberal, or Conservative candidate who was blinded, you would still be hearing about it now.
>
> So, in practice, we find that we have to physically protect ourselves if we are to survive. So, we have to be robust in our manner of campaigning. But we always stay within the law. We always attempt to maintain discipline.
>
> *Holmes*: But sometimes the discipline breaks down?
>
> *Edmonds*: Nothing is perfect.

In this imperfect world Edmonds at times finds it hard to discipline his own impulses, his own propensities to violence. When he finds himself face to face with what he identifies as "foreign bodies," it ignites the sense of collective humiliation that sustains his and his mates' obsessive rage.

### Exclusionary Welfarism

Edmonds made a series of crucial assertions during our conversations that suggest how a core agenda of integralism is coalescing across Europe, not just in Britain. He invokes again a fusion of nationalism and socialism to thwart what he sees as invidious transformations of his world. He starts with a classic assertion of a primal "community" or "nation" without which "men go mad." This indivisible, racially homogeneous community, existing in memory and integral to "identity," he values above everything else. What gives his vision of community incendiary power is its linkage to the social apparatus of the state. He predicates regimes of "community" and "nation" on the political economy of the welfare state—regulated by a racialized delimitation of citizenship—to yield an exclusionary welfarism.[13] His pursuit of a radically discriminatory social contract establishes the basis for a resurgent British national socialism.

Public housing in particular encompasses the ambiguities of this rendering of community. It has become a setting where social justice is contested, where the social reproduction of the white working-class family is in jeopardy. For the white East Enders the local council housing belongs to them as a community manifesting their sense of belonging. In Edmonds's equation estate housing is "owned" by the council, so it is "owned" by the community. The right of newly arrived immigrants to England to petition for public housing, in his view, disrupts the moral economy of the white working-class estate, violating its traditional practices of succession. Under these customary arrangements flats were transmitted within families from one generation to the next, or preference was granted to young couples seeking housing in close proximity to their parents. The administrative priority given to housing homeless, immigrant families with numerous members, newly arrived to Britain, pits their legal claims against the traditional moral claims of "indigenous" families on the Isle of Dogs. These struggles over the integrity of the community, however, are not new. In the mid-1950s the practices of family succession were already under threat as a result of "white English residents" from outlying boroughs being allotted housing on the Isle of Dogs. This was the source of significant outrage. As one London tenant association declared in 1954: "We are in opposition . . . to the idea that people are simply units to be moved about the face of the earth in line with the impersonal schemes of some 'Big Brother'" (quoted in Young and Willmot 1957:168).

The "defects" in the legal application of citizenship create the mechanism by which a multiracial and multicultural Britain was created and Edmonds's deep sense of estrangement was instilled. The great partisan in the immigration debate, Enoch Powell, summarizes succinctly his rendering of the history of these deformations of citizenship in the wake of the empire. His analysis is consistent with the BNP's conviction that a multicultural and multiracial Britain is illegitimate. Powell's comments appeared in the *Sunday Times*, August 7, 1994, under the heading "Blame Complacency, Not Churchill":

> In his extract from *Eminent Churchillians* (News Review, last week) Andrew Roberts loads on to Churchill the responsibility for the group of problems which goes by the name "immigration."

I would like to set out briefly what did happen and who consequently, was to blame. What actually happened was the British Nationality Act 1948. That was legislation of the Attlee Labour government, though it had the support of the Conservative opposition. So both sides in politics were responsible.

When the war came to an end in 1945 two things took place. First, the Canadians passed a law defining a Canadian citizen. Secondly, it became plain that before long every part of the British Empire would be an independent self-governing country.

Until then all the inhabitants of the Empire had been subjects of the British Crown, and thus all possessed, though very few exercised the right to enter the United Kingdom and live there. If they became independent countries, and especially if they became independent republics as Burma did in 1946, that would stop.

The prospect horrified the British parties and the British public, who at the time were being persuaded to contemplate with great complacency the transformation of the British Empire into the British Commonwealth of self-governing independent nations—a piece of contradictory nonsense indeed, but a splendid salve for dented British pride. So what we did was to make a list of Commonwealth Countries and say that all their citizens were to be equivalent to British subjects, no matter whether they became republics or not.

Air travel and private enterprise did the rest. Through the open door, a door which always had been open, there now surged a great mass of citizens of independent nations, India and Pakistan in particular.

Shocked by what was happening, the Conservative government in 1962, against frantic Labour opposition, passed the Commonwealth Immigration Act, which gave Britain for the first time what all other countries take for granted—a definition of its own citizens—and confined to them the rights of entry and residence here. But it was already too late. An ethnic minority had come into existence, of which the age structure decrees that it must increase steadily in relation to the rest of the population.

So when we contemplate the consequences of what we call "immigration," we are contemplating the consequences of our own determination to take refuge from reality in pretence. So great a catastrophe does not happen unless a whole people wills it upon itself. That is what we did.

Again, for Edmonds public housing is the crucible of this misbegotten history. If you live somewhere, he observed, you get on the electoral rolls. Immigrants have a legal right to an abode, even if they are "illegal," and once housed they are put automatically on the electoral rolls conferring on them a basic right of citizenship. The fact that they are voting in numbers sufficient to win local elections, "wearing yashmacs," and "not speaking a word of English" is intolerable to Edmonds and confirms his portrayal of an embattled "white" community whose economic and social reproduction is threatened. It is a story which he believes power brokers in Britain, committed to neoliberalism and multiculturalism will not allow to be told. From his plausible account of an encroaching exile in his homeland Edmonds goes on, through cascading paranoia, to envision a plot to exterminate the "white man." Such a perspective provides the rationale for his lurid bigotry.

## Extermination

There is a tyranny to Edmonds's memory that juxtaposes a childlike vision of London in the 1950s as a happy city within a law-abiding society, against a middle-age vision of the present rife with invidious differences, cultural clashes, and societal decay.[14] These same reveries oblige him to project cataclysms into the future. Despite gross distortions in his analyses, in one important way he engages in an acute assessment of contemporary circumstances. He is willing to frame his local predicament in global terms, within a wider critique of political economy.

Edmonds sees motive in the drive and the power of transnational fast-capitalism: "to sack the white man." Its mechanism is obvious to him; jobs are exported to the Third World, to zones of cheap labor. Chronic unemployment is the permanent outcome of this system for segments of white British society. But the external threat is matched by an internal moral vulnerability: greed, stupidity, selfishness, and weakness, all manifest in a bankrupt political establishment whose members have opened the nation to the destructive force of immigration. The solution for these challenges is nationalism, a nationalism mediated through authoritarianism and corporatism. This means "putting white people before the power of money": "stop the export of technology," "stop immigration, stop the export of capital," "stop the importation of goods manufactured in the Third World." Edmonds has "no rancor" for businessmen. He would let them use their energies, talents, experience, and capital but "community values" must be supreme in his corporatist scheme:

> The sort of society we want is racially homogeneous, a society free of class conflict, a society where all members are catered for and looked after—and I hope this is not too shocking for your American ears—with a degree of socialism, whereby you have a national health service, a national education service so the poorer members of society have a decent basic level of life. If a young chap is intelligent but of poor parents he will be able to go to the best universities in the land, even if his parents can't afford to send him there.
>
> Our solution, summed up in one word, is "nationalism." We value the community above everything else. We see man as a social creature who needs a

community. Without a community, literally to be alone, most men would go mad. . . . Men need community in all senses of the word. They need to be needed. They need to play a useful role, which certainly must include having a job, having useful employment. This particularly applies to young people. We see young people going "off the rails," . . . I mean, degenerating. We see chronic unemployment leads to drug addiction, which is quite a problem here. Young people feel unwanted by society, abandoned by society, so they turn inward and start killing themselves with drugs.

Edmonds asserts that the program of the left, promoting multicultural-ism, destroys the traditional social consensus that made Britain, as he describes it, a sort of socialist state, in which "life was quite stable and pleasant," where the police were unarmed. He is preoccupied with street violence as a glaring and repugnant outcome of racial pluralism. He re-marks specifically on the importation of a new term from the street lexi-con of New York: "I remember the word 'mugging' only coming into London vocabulary in 1974 or 1975." There is more than a measure of bad faith in his aside. Edmonds's view of the history of this term is, per-haps, definitive given that the leadership of the British National Front—the forerunner to the BNP—played, as Paul Gilroy notes, a direct role in the first alarm over "mugging" and its linkage to the discourse on race in Britain:

> The neo-fascists had organized a "March Against Mugging" in September of 1975 under the slogan "Stop the Muggers. 80 percent of muggers are black. 85 percent of victims are white." This was significant not simply for its open defiance of the laws on incitement to racial hatred and the new tactic of provoc-ative marches through black areas but for the convergence it represented be-tween the respectable politics of race signalled by the authoritative official crime statistics and the street level appeal of the neo-fascist groups who had seized the issue of black crime and begun to refine it into a populist weapon which could prove the wisdom of their distinctive solution to Britain's race problem—repatriation. (Gilroy 1991:120)

Edmonds argues that the path to multiculturalism annihilates the social contract that sustained his memorialized Britain. Few, he insists, are will-ing to describe this ruinous progression. For Edmonds the proliferation of crime, the murder of police officers, the turning of young people to drug addiction are the consequence of a pluralist society that subverts the tra-ditional social order. Threats to the reproduction of the white working-class family and community posed by immigrants are a "life-and-death matter." He is disgusted that militant Muslims can make direct threats against the lives of British Jews with impunity. His outrage even extended to the fatwa against "the British citizen Salman Rushdie." It exemplifies "a whole society falling apart." He sees the problems of the Western world accelerating at an enormous rate as multicultural principles come to dominate. He predicts cultures will succumb to clashes that are impossible to resolve. The "alien-wedge" of nonwhite immigrants threatens the existence of the white race in Britain.[15] Edmonds "knows" that if you raise these views they call you "a Nazi" and you risk attack without warning. The scar running down the back of his head, inflicted during his participation at a BNP rally, is for him proof of these perils.

## Foreign Bodies

What poisons Edmonds's critique of neoliberalism is its identification of nonwhite immigrants as the agents, indeed, the embodiment of global capitalism. Each aspect of their difference—skin color, language, religion, dress—conjures the grim battle with "dark" global forces igniting Edmonds's racist fury. Each encounter with these differences ratifies his sense of exile, his sense of collective humiliation of the white working class. The elites of post–World War II Britain, Edmonds insists, conspired to disguise the struggle, through a "veil of silence." Politicians lied while the press reported that the presence of nonwhite immigrants was temporary:

> I remember the whole history of this from A to Z; except, of course, I was four years of age when the Nationalities Act was passed. I remember the first immigrants and the practical consequences. I remember the West Indians coming to London in the 1950s. I was a schoolboy, and we wondered what it all meant. The English working class, of which I am a part, had to live and work with these newcomers and, at the time, we didn't understand it. What are they doing here? we wanted to know. I remember clearly, as a young teenager maybe thirteen years old, 1956, 1957 maybe, discussing with my parents what all this meant. Our newspapers would tell us not to worry about immigration. The immigrants would only be here for a short time. They were just learning a trade and then they would be going home.

He added sarcastically, "I might say, for your interest, 'officially,' immigration stopped in 1961. I remember the newspaper headlines: 'Immigration Stopped.' . . . We were utterly, completely and absolutely lied to!"[16] Only Enoch Powell, he believes, depicted the confrontation "truthfully," in a virulently nationalist idiom:

> Look, anyone can talk pretty, meaningless words but the way to judge a man is by the price he paid. Nietzsche said, "Something is only good if written in blood." I don't know if you've read Nietzsche. A dramatic phrase. In other words, unless you have suffered, [what you say] is meaningless. Now, Powell

spoke out about immigration. Until then, nothing had been said. He broke the veil of silence, the conspiracy of silence and for that, he paid the price. He was immediately thrown into the political wilderness. All his chances and ambitions of being a government minister, possibly the prime minister of Britain, went out the window. He was treated as a total outcast. [17]

Edmonds's sense of betrayal and outrage have been rendered illicit, his claims have no "respectable" means of societal redress. He is left in a world largely stripped of mediating forms of political expression. His only recourse is to tactical thuggery, to street fighting. The South Asians he confronts are not the victims of a transnational capitalism, they are, in his view, its physical incarnation, its substance. His racism is factual and militant. Repatriation is for him the only answer.

## WHITE WORKING CLASS

The BNP is by any standard a tiny, fractious, secretive political movement.[18] Within this small circle, there are few more hapless figures than Derek Beackon. In his prior foray into electoral politics, before his election to the Millwall position, Beackon stood for a similar position in the Red Coat Ward in Stepney in May 1990. He received 93 votes; it would be hard to imagine a more marginal political aspirant in Britain. Yet, by gleaning 1,480 votes in a by-election for a minor council position in East London, his scabrous tale leached into a transnational discourse.[19] Edmonds was appalled at the speed with which the British establishment formulated what he sees as a defamatory rejoinder to his colleague's election:

> Don't think [I am] . . . blowing this out of proportion. We had one of our candidates, Derek Beackon, elected as councillor last September and within forty-eight hours, on the television, the prime minister, the home secretary who is responsible for law and order, the archbishop of Canterbury who is the head churchman in England, and the head of the metropolitan police condemned the electorate for voting for the BNP. Now, for this to come from the prime minister and the home secretary is very, very bad because they, as politicians, only hold their position because they were elected in. So, who are they to criticize the electorate? What right do any of these four gentlemen have to criticize a legal, law-abiding party like the BNP? They have no moral right to criticize us.

The BBC and other global media beamed these denunciations worldwide. The rendering of Beackon as the Nazi, as the "unsavory other," dissociates the disquietingly familiar aspects of his outlook and sensibilities as if they were alien. The delegitimization of Beackon's story allowed it to be recounted only in terms of its illicit character and yet, in so doing, it conferred on the tale a fugitive, symbolic capital.

A key aspect of globalization is its potential to spawn parochial milieus within which radical formations of cultural meaning gain expression. This alone is an argument for rigorous ethnography—multisited or otherwise—as perhaps the most suitable means to gain access to tightly circumscribed arenas of transnational cultural production. The interplay of the global and the parochial can yield a perverse bind that the election of Derek Beackon as a BNP candidate exemplifies. In its struggle to thwart the encroachments of racial and cultural pluralism as well as the forces of neoliberalism, the BNP is reciprocally defined by them. By resisting globalization, its leaders conspire to enhance their own estrangement, endowing their world view with a brutal inflection and rendering their organizational arrangements prone to internal strife and factionalism. Yet, under certain conditions, their "local knowledge," precisely because of its parochial character, can crystallize as a global discourse.

Derek Beackon was also interviewed in the BNP's "bookstore" in Welling a few weeks after the interview with Edmonds. On the day we met there was quite a bit of noise and commotion as party workers bundled and prepared for distribution the BNP's broadsheet, *Spearhead*. To escape the noise we went to a small second-floor room. It was a cluttered loft with the ambience of the disheveled bedroom of a careless adolescent boy. In one corner on a desk was a small portrait of Adolf Hitler. Beackon offered me tea.

If nineteenth-century print capital gave rise to new forms of "imagined communities," the electronic media of the late twentieth century has created new global circuits for fashioning affinity and difference (Anderson 1991). In his blatantly untheorized apprehension of Britain, Beackon has discovered just such meaning, which easily traverses this circuitry. Coverage of his election by the major media in Britain was thorough. Beackon, more than anyone else, was dazzled by it, despite the fact that his public performances were often ludicrous, and the reportage was uniformly negative, save for the BNP's own publications:

> *Beackon*: Well, when I won, it took two or three weeks for it to sink in. That's when you look back on these things and realize how important they were. I was shocked at the time as well. Gradually, the media attention from all over the world, from Europe, Germany, France, America sunk in. And, actually, it was quite enjoyable. I really enjoyed it.
>
> It wasn't until a week before the election that I had my first interview; with the *Evening Standard*, I think it was. I suppose the media thought we had a good chance of winning, perhaps more so than we did. In that week I must have had a dozen interviews. I got quite good at it, you know, especially with television. I enjoyed that most of all.

*Holmes*: I saw you on the ITV documentary.

*Beackon*: You mean the one called "Councillor Beackon, the Battle for Mill-wall?"

*Holmes*: Yes. I saw it about two or three weeks ago.

*Beackon*: Yeah, the "London Program." But that wasn't really an interview; it was more of the "fly on the wall" sort of thing. They were actually filming everything we done. Even when I was having interviews with other media, they was just there, filming. That was quite good. They was with us for about four weeks, so they got loads of footage. I quite enjoyed it afterwards even though it was nerve-racking at first.

*Holmes*: But some of the interviews must have been hard?

*Beackon*: Oh, they was. In a couple of them, obviously I didn't come over as well as I did in others. I didn't quite like the interviews where you're in a room with all these cameras and lights around you and you're just sitting there. I preferred the ones in the street, when activities were taking place. They were a lot easier for me.

*Holmes*: The interviews in which you sat in front of the camera and under the lights must have made you feel they were trying to make you out as a Nazi or a racist.

*Beackon*: Yeah, yeah, or make me look incompetent or edit it to make me look bad. But, in the end, I quite enjoyed them.

The more specialized coverage in the antifascist journal *Searchlight* was particularly distinguished and by no means flattering to Beackon. Indeed, after the arrest and imprisonment of Edmonds, *Searchlight* noted that Beackon was bereft of his handler and characterized him merely as a "limp puppet." In his peculiarly guileless fashion, when Beackon had trouble recalling details about his election, he referred me to *Searchlight*.

Nevertheless, Beackon concocted a deeply unsettling message, which he was able to communicate: everyone is undergoing exile, everyone's sense of belonging is growing tenuous. Ann Stoler notes an earlier figuration of this message in the account by Mayhew:

> When Mayhew wrote that "hearth and rootedness," those "sacred symbols to all civilized races" . . . were lacking in London's poor, he was not only claiming that the unmanaged mobility of society's subalterns was a threat to colonial and metropolitan authority. He was identifying what was distinctively part of the bourgeoisie's conception of itself: one that embraced property ownership, rootedness, and an orderly family life as attributes that at once distinguished the middle class and explained why they were inherently and socially superior. (1995:128)

What makes Beackon's insight so devastating and gives it global significance is his insistence that "hearth and rootedness" are being denied to everyone, stripping us all of our "sacred symbols." This predica-

*[margin handwriting: because sense of belonging]*

ment, which as Edmonds noted can render notions like "citizenship" meaningless, represents a powerful challenge to the social order. In Beackon's portrayal we have profound estrangement, a radical transformation of place, and a rupture in a sense of belonging that breeds bigotry.

Beackon is by no means an intellectual, organic or otherwise. He does not theorize. Yet his racism may be more penetrating and profound than Edmonds's "factual racism." Edmonds's bigotry is inflamed by the presence of "foreign bodies." Beackon's racism originates prior to the conditions of a multiracial and multicultural Britain in the fabric of the class-based moral code, sealed by the bourgeois nationalism of the nineteenth century. It draws on a social consensus fabricated during a much different era of globalization, one underwritten by Britannic imperialism. That is why, Beackon tells us, he hates white liberals:

> I must admit we never had any trouble with the blacks. They would ignore us or laugh at us and tell us it was not our country anymore; that we were old-fashioned with our Union Jacks and stuff. They wouldn't bother with us. Same with the Asians, no trouble at all. Not at all, even though we were on this corner [on Brick Lane selling the BNP newspaper], and they would be down the sides [of the street] with their [retail] stalls! . . . To be honest, it's not the blacks or the Asians I hate; it's the whites. I hate the [liberal] whites to be honest.

Political elites have abandoned those "exclusionary cultural principles" of nationalism that defined rights to citizenship, property, and public welfare (Stoler 1995:7–8). By their derelictions the elites of Britain, both of the old Conservative and New Labour parties, have forsaken those national imperatives which conferred a perverse worthiness on white working-class racism:

> *Beackon*: The Labour Party don't represent the white working class. These are the people with which I'm concerned.
> *Holmes*: So, you speak for the white working class?
> *Beackon*: Yes, because I am white working class myself and I know what it's like.
> *Holmes*: How do you make a living?
> *Beackon*: I'm an unemployed driver and I've been out of work since 1992. There's no jobs for anyone, and it's aggravated by bringing in more immigrants. If there are jobs going, it is the immigrants who get them. Still, there are a lot of them unemployed because they don't really want to work. Why should they when they can live for free on the dole? But still, there isn't work for the rest of us.

Beackon and his friends have not read *Reflections on Violence*. But they understand, like Sorel, how and why the seething subjectivities of nationalism coalesce as violence. What seems mindless rage is in fact consummate hostility to elite portrayals of reality.

### Nationalist Minded

Reminiscence for Beackon, as for Richard Edmonds, is an implicit critique of the present from which his integralist tale derives. He reflected on the East End in the 1950s, which is reimagined as a place of ethnic and racial innocence. His memory renders place a naive fiction. There were the poor streets of Stepney, where Derek was born and where he still lives, that made him working class. "I remember 1953 and the queen's coronation. I remember being a kid, standing on Mile End Road, waving the Union Jack and watching the queen drive past. We were very patriotic and very loyal to the royal family. Every street had a street party with Union Jacks and bunting strung across the streets. Our whole street, Bancroft Road, was white. . . . It was all white. Every street, white. It was a white community." The idyllic tale is rent by the appearance of someone different. He recalls as a child walking down Mile End Road and seeing a "black man" for the first time and running away—not because he hated him, but just because he didn't know what a black man was.[20] It was something strange for the eight-year-old boy. The few "blacks" who followed were assimilated as mates. In those bygone days they shared the culture, the style of life of the East End. Now everything has changed. Beackon has become "nationalist minded," as he too, like other working-class whites, undergoes exile in his homeland:

> When I went to school there was only one or two [Afro-Caribbeans] and that was acceptable. Basically, they followed our culture. You know they sort of mixed in. I don't believe in race mixing now. At that time there were a few blacks and we got on and all that but now, with the way things are going in this country, they are going their own way. Things are polarizing, aren't they? I can't accept them now even though I used to. Back then, they had basically the same culture as us.
>
> Now the Asians they have their own religion, their own culture, which is fine. Everybody has to have their own culture. We got ours, they got theirs. I don't want to change theirs and they don't want to change ours. But, regardless, ours is being changed anyway. I resent that. So, I can't get on with them and don't like living next door to them as I have to do in East London. I still live about a mile from where I was born. I've never actually moved out of the one square mile.

Faced with alienation Beackon becomes a cryptoethnographer of the familiar and the different. His rendering of distinctions begets the consciousness of a racist. During his brief tenure as councillor he went from house to house, drinking at the local pubs on the Isle of Dogs. He saw his people, had cups of tea with them, and became a friend rather than just a councillor. Derek had more in common with the local people because he was "a local man," one of them:

> *Holmes*: But the people who you think feel these problems—?
>
> *Beackon*: Are the white working class. These are the people I'm concerned with 'cause I'm one of them. That's why I stood as a candidate. That's why I talk about these things. I live there, I am from there. Gradually people are waking up. Maybe it's too late, I don't know. It could be.

His ethnography turns more choleric as he identifies the threat. Muslims, he believes, want to "take over the world":

> You know, on White Chapel Road. There's this big mosque there, the biggest in London. It's a very imposing, really big building. You hear it there. I have to check what times of the day they pray but you hear it, bellowing out, day in and day out. Especially if you live around there. I've often driven through there and I hear it.
>
> There were complaints [about the prayers], it was getting on people's nerves and all that. So, they [the Muslims] start saying the church bells on Sunday mornings get on their nerves! They didn't say "getting on our nerves," but, "they offend us." The church bells on a Sunday morning in a white Christian country offend them! In some Muslim countries abroad, Christianity is outlawed.

## Putting Asians First

Derek Beackon's election was, at the very least, an unlikely story. In his crude efforts to preserve his white working-class culture, he confronted a displaced Bengali community. He is emphatic that these immigrants are increasingly defining life in Britain. New Labour sees the immigrant population as the source of sustained electoral powers, a strategic part of their new core constituency. I asked what this commitment to multiculturalism meant. Beackon responded: "Now [multiculturalism means] putting the Asians first, putting their culture over ours. They say we must live in a peaceful, multicultural society but who are the ones getting pushed out?" The "alien wedge" has now usurped "his people" and taken control. What makes Beackon's discourse so intensely illicit is not its affinities to Nazism per se but his insistence that race and culture occupy a central, if unacknowledged, position in the politics of Britain. His transgression, ironically, is very much along the lines of Asian and Afro-Caribbean activists who argue that the white establishment is incapable of seriously addressing the politics of race in Britain (Gilroy 1991; 1992).

That this incapacity remains for the most part unacknowledged compromises the legitimacy of democratic institutions to mediate emerging power relations based on cultural difference:

*Holmes*: As a councillor, didn't you want to address the housing problem [on the Isle of Dogs]?

*Beackon*: Ah, I believe the housing problem is primarily a racial problem. Stepney, where I'm from, is predominantly Asian now. So the Isle of Dogs is about the best part of the East End now, except for some parts of Bethnal Green. It has been only in the last five years that the Isle of Dogs has had a housing problem and it's because of the growing number of Asians. So, the housing problem is really a racial problem in my opinion. It's just that a lot of people probably won't admit to that. If a young couple can't get a house, they say it's a housing problem, a housing shortage and all that. But, I blame the immigrants; or at least the Labour and Liberal parties for housing Asians and bringing them into these neighborhoods. As far as I can see, if they weren't here, there wouldn't be a housing problem in the first place. I'm not saying there isn't a shortage of housing, but I do think it's aggravated by the local council building houses and moving Asians into them.

*Holmes*: But isn't it caused by the Docklands Project, which razed a number of council housing estates and thus rendered residents [many of whom are "Asians"] who had housing in Tower Hamlets homeless? They had to be given housing in another part of the borough.

*Beackon*: Yes, I suppose that project is a problem as well. You've been around Canary Wharf, you've seen empty office buildings, why don't they build housing? Speaking from the point of view of the working-class man who has always lived in council [housing], I think the local council should build houses for the local people.

Beackon prefers to be thought of as "Derek." He has a sense of humor, albeit at times inadvertent. He seems a diffident racist and little more than a petty opportunist. One is struck, however, by the peculiar character of his bigotry. His anger emerges from an acute sense of betrayal by political elites, particularly those who claim to speak for the working class. He forces the question, Who is being pushed out?

## Racial Covenant

Derek was slow to learn intolerance for those "blacks" displaced to the recesses of the East End in the 1950s. His prejudice has a very different origin. He distrusts the Asians, but it is the whites he hates. What fires his rage is the abrogation by a generation of British elites of a grim social contract formulated in the imperial past. He understands, like Edmonds, that racism is integral to his nationalism, essential to his class identity. It is not a mere aberration of patriotism but is central to a British social order. Racism, incubated in the colonial practices of the nineteenth century, served as a fulcrum for what amounted to "class collaboration." This racial covenant underpinned not just British nationalism, but it cast the terms of class obligation and entitlement. It simultaneously defined Derek's subaltern status and imbued it with cultural meaning.

Ann Stoler has analyzed how the European colonial project was contingent on a racial discourse that contoured the frontiers of nation and infused the substructure of class:

> By bringing the discursive anxieties and practical struggles over citizenship and national identities in the nineteenth century back more squarely within Foucault's frame, bourgeois identities in both metropole and colony emerge tacitly and emphatically coded by race. . . . [I]n identifying marginal members of the body politic, they [the bourgeoisie] . . . mapped the moral parameters of European nations. These deeply sedimented discourses . . . could redraw the "interior frontiers" of national communities, frontiers that were secured through—and sometimes in collision with—boundaries of race. These nationalist discourses were predicated on exclusionary cultural principles that did more than divide the middle class from the poor. They marked out those whose claims to property rights, citizenship, and public relief were worthy of recognition and whose were not. (Stoler 1995:7–8)

Beackon is right. The usurpation of this racialized status quo in the late twentieth century sealed the fate of the white working class. Political leaders transgressed the old social compact that orchestrated class collaboration and integrated an industrial Britain. It is no accident that the place where he remembers waving the Union Jack for a newly crowned monarch is the same place where Derek remembers first encountering a black man. The logic of Derek's racism surfaces as he tries to uphold the moral economy of a vestigial working class in a postindustrial, multicultural London.

In Derek's mind there is a series of impacted treacheries. The need for an industrial work force has been curtailed, if not eliminated. There is little work for the skilled or unskilled hands of a white working class. Jobs have been exported by those who manage or mismanage the British economy. At the same time, the social protections and benefits, which working people have fought for over the course of the twentieth century, have become their undoing. The programs of the welfare state, erected to reproduce a stable working-class community, now serve the needs of immigrants who embody the new, multicultural Britain. White working-class East Enders are "pushed out." New Labour has abandoned them. Asians are on top because New Labour is for them and them alone. Council housing is decaying after years of Thatcherite neglect. The integrity of the Metropolitan Police has been compromised by racial politics. The vast wealth represented by Canary Wharf looms above all of this as vindication of a transnational fast-capitalism, upon which few if any social claims can be made. As the grievances of Derek and his cohort are delegitimized, they can surface as a vicious burlesque in places like Brick Lane.

## Jurisdictions of Style

Beackon's message at the end of the twentieth century begins to capture, if not fully articulate, a caustic cultural critique. His radically populist story mutates beyond "nationalism" to the jurisdiction of style. Transformation of place and estrangement within one's homeland are pan-European: everyone is undergoing exile, everyone's sense of belonging is eroding. This message speaks to the defining experience of an unintegrated social formation, populated not just by remnants of the working class but, as we will see in the next chapter, sections of the middle class— these are Spengler's regressive "intellectual nomads." The character of the social milieu that Beackon and his mates inhabit is refractory to conventional analyses; it is a domain beyond the purview of a science, political economy, and metaphysics of solidarity. These people understand themselves through the cultural imperatives of individualization—that is to say, the norms of alienation. Only a fascination of its adherents with violence, consummate hostility to elite portrayals of reality, and an abiding contempt for the moral codes of bourgeois society bind their anomie. Among the violent lads with whom he fraternized, Bill Buford observed these anomic predispositions. As the constitution of the "working class"—as something to believe in and belong to—is eclipsed, what remains, he contends, is volatile style and self-absorbed compulsion: "working-class habits, like those manifest by Tom Melody's East London lads, have simply become more exaggerated, ornate versions of an ancient style, more extreme because now without substance. But it is only a style. Nothing substantive is there; there is nothing to belong to." Buford sees this dispossessed group "stripped of culture and sophistication and living only for its affectation: a bloated code of maleness, an exaggerated, embarrassing patriotism, a violent nationalism, an array of bankrupt antisocial habits" (1992:262). Yet these stark stylistic devices by fusing, in Berlin's terminology, populism and expressionism can gain a cultural significance that extends beyond the narrow social confines in which they were first elicited.

Since the 1960s the disenchantments of Derek and his mates consolidated gradually, not merely as an ideology or doctrine, but as a distinctive style of life. As he puts it:

I remember skinheads from years ago: burly sort of thugs, shaven heads and wore swastika badges. They looked fine, didn't they? . . . Yes, the early sixties.

I remember, because I had just left school and it was just starting then—1961 or 1962. Yeah. It's all over Europe now but it did start in the East End. But, when it started it wasn't political at all, it was just a little cult. Now, it's really political. You just have to say "skinhead" now [and] you immediately think "nationalist."

British nationalists had to act tough in Derek's view because the newspapers ignored them. They tried "to kick their way into the headlines," as they used to say in the old British National Front. Denied access to networks of the conventional media, they sought expressionism in a radically different symbolic form, one that was communicable over an alternative, perhaps more powerful, global circuitry. The fashion accoutrements of skinheads, spawned and nurtured in the East End, penetrated taste across Europe. Leather vestments, shaved heads, pierced body parts, macabre talismans, extravagant alcohol and drug consumption, football hooliganism, reckless street fighting, and racist invectives and assaults came to be associated overtly with a brutal nationalist politics of the young; yet, recoded as fashion, much of this repellent political stance gained a different and far broader currency. In other words, the "unspeakable" messages contrived by Beackon and his ilk in urban Britain found expression in defiant styles of self-presentation, taste, and appearance. Instilled as fashion, these astringent messages moved— uncensored—onto the bodies and into the imaginations of a generation.[21]

From as early as Mayhew's explorations of the East End we know that alienation, anomie, sex, violence, and bigotry can be powerfully mediated as fashion. At the close of the twentieth century we also know that these kinds of local stylistic messages can move easily across various global retail and electronic circuits. Though they remain largely latent and relatively harmless as unorthodox or offensive expressions of "taste," the prospect that these elusive messages can be read and deciphered politically is disturbing. We know that there are various paths that the accoutrements of the skinhead fashion have already traced out—as a cryptopolitics with disquieting consequences, as acts of football hooliganism, and as brutal racially motivated thuggery. Style, as an aestheticized basis of solidarity, represents an important pathway by which integralism assumes not just its populist-expressionist form but a fully developed fascist demeanor.[22] Jean-Marie Le Pen has shown with great virtuosity, just how a subtly wrought personal style can be decoded as a wide-ranging authoritarian politics. Indeed, this style is at the heart of Le Pen's charismatic strategy to bridge populism, expressionism, and pluralism. What is transpiring in the East End is perhaps more radical and only plausible as class-based perspectivism is usurped.

Marilyn Strathern notes that as those social distinctions and moral perspectives that mediated understanding of class-based industrial society

are usurped or eclipsed, they are superseded by the hallmark of individualization: "choice" and "styles of life" (1992:145).

> Exercise of choice is shown in the style that the individual affects, not just in
> dress or food but in almost anything that a person does. We might epitomize
> the contrast with ideas in circulation at the turn of the eighteenth and nine-
> teenth centuries by saying that if "then" individual behaviour revealed the nat-
> ural basis of morality, "now" moral behavior is a question of individual style.
> This involves a further cancellation: style and taste are exercised in public, but
> for their own sake, without polite society as an arbiter. (1992:162)

By this nullification, she asserts, "society thereby becomes unimagin-
able," as moral behavior becomes contingent solely on the capacity for
choice. "But what the choice should be between, the norms and canons of
behavior, no longer need lie in institutions outside the individual. The
person is his or her own reference point, a position that requires no nego-
tiation or bargaining with others, least of all with a collective will"
(1992:161–62). This echoes Adorno's characterization of those subject to
this kind of hollowing "freedom of choice," who "experience themselves
solely as objects of opaque processes and, torn between sudden shock and
sudden forgetfulness, are no longer capable of a sense of temporal continuity" as the last traces of their social integration deteriorates. Buford is
equally incisive: "This bored, empty, decadent generation consists of
nothing more than what it appears to be. It is a lad culture without mystery, so deadened that is uses violence to wake itself up. It pricks itself so
that it has feeling, burns its flesh so that is has smell" (1992:262). These
are the dispossessed figures that the leadership of the BNP believe are
being created in ever increasing numbers in urban districts across Britain
and it is these figures whom they seek to enlist in their dubious political
scheme. In the next chapter we will see how the conditions of rootlessness, which create the "new poor" and the "intellectual nomads," also
engender, according to the BNP leadership, conditions that necessitate
authoritarianism. For them the tyranny of style and the style of tyranny
can be fused within a fascist political imaginary.

# Chapter Nine

## AUTHORITARIANISM

THE EXCHANGES with John Tyndall and Michael Newland broached an unsettling message, one that impugns the power of democratic ideals and practices. Tyndall has been a key figure in the groups that have comprised extreme elements of the British nationalist right since the 1960s.[1] He founded in 1982 and officially heads the BNP. In the general election of May 1997 he stood for parliament in East London in the Poplar and Canning Town constituency receiving 2,849 votes (7.3 percent). Newland was press officer for the BNP through the election of 1997 and immediately after Nick Griffin's election to the chairmanship of the BNP in September 1999, he was appointed the party's national treasurer. Newland is one of the party's most articulate partisans. These two characters argue that the corrosive nature of fast-capitalism not only eradicates the array of preexisting social compacts and cultural covenants upon which the nation-state rested; they believe it also precludes the formulation of new democratically instituted social consenses. In other words, in a world where estrangement and exile unfold in one's homeland, social consensus is precarious at best. Nondemocratic means become politically acceptable, if not absolutely essential, to secure social order in their view. They resolve that societal integration must, under these conditions, entail overt authoritarianism. Yet the character of Newland's and Tyndall's arguments and, hence, the courses they plot to an authoritarian order are quite different: one prosaic, the other sublime.

Newland's account continues with the issues raised in the preceding chapter; it portrays how the eclipsing of British industrial society subverts the integrity of certain types of social entitlement. Indeed, Newland struggles to explain his personal predicament in terms of a conventional class-based rendering of society, which, to his chagrin, no longer provides him with a legitimate basis for articulating his claims or, for that matter, for seeking social remediation. Deprived of a moral idiom within which to explain his fate, he embraces the language of the isolated victim. To account for his injury he contrives for himself a pious middle-class victimology in which multiculturalism is the culprit. He goes on, however, to propose a course for recuperation, one that demands a new social order in which totalitarian measures provide the dubious means to restore the collective will of the British people. This leads into the analysis devised by Tyndall, which I initially thought represented a thoroughly unconvincing presentation of an integralist politics. I found his apparent disregard for social and historical contingencies perplexing. Tyndall's mystical invocation of "the will to dominate" and his preoccupation with the leadership principle, his *Führerprinzip*, I found fatuous. He seemed committed to a self-perpetuating radicalism, a radicalism that is pursued even when its aims are impractical, unattainable, or barely fathomable. I changed my evaluation, however, as I began to understand Tyndall's position in terms of its historical roots in the German romantic tradition and its contemporary relevance in relationship to the changed discursive status of society. I began to see how his "apotheosis of the will," which I had initially dismissed as shameless puffery, opened volatile prospects that the BNP leader grasped intimately. In other words, only as I began to admit how Tyndall's salacious rhetoric operated as, if not a penetrating, certainly a cunning reading of the ambiguities of the historical moment, was its potential for dissonant political action betrayed.

The chapter concludes with an assessment of the successful challenge to Mr. Tyndall's leadership by a younger, would-be "modernizer" of the party, Nick Griffin, backed by Mr. Newland in September 1999. Griffin is presented as a forty-year-old former chairman of the British National Front, "who has four children, no criminal record, and a law degree from Cambridge University."[2] He and Newland mounted their challenge through the new communicative and representational technology of the internet. Like Le Pen and his associates, they pursued an integralist politics that is inlaid in the fabric of their adherents' cultural experience and virtually indistinguishable from strategic elements of their styles of life. They combine old virtualism engineered by Sorel and Gramsci with the new virtualism of the internet.

## BLOOD ON THE WALL

Michael Newland draws on issues raised by Edmonds and Beackon to insinuate an overriding question: have the social and cultural covenants that integrated industrial Britain for more than a century been abrogated? He postulates a radical realignment of power among those classes, parties, constituencies, industries, interest groups, and public and private institutions responsible for the construction of Britain as a nation-state. Newland, like his colleagues, has taken it upon himself to interpret this epochal change endowing it with political meaning. He summons an interpretative stance underwritten by middle-class anxieties and grievances. Seymour Lipset developed a classic analysis of fascism as an "extremism of the center," based on what he believed to be the distinctive appeal that Nazism had for the German "middle class."[3] Subsequent research has suggested a far more complex situation. In particular, the role of working-class voters seems to have been more important than previously thought.[4] Nevertheless, there is little doubt about Lipset's general claim that fascism has a peculiar affinity for the middle classes as Michael Newland asserts forcefully.

I met Newland at his home in North London in July 1994. He lives in an attached house on a quiet street not far from the Kentish Town tube station. He is of medium height with white hair and an amiable bearing. Entering his house was treacherous: floorboards were missing in the hallway, studs and patches of insulation were exposed on the walls, there was no working toilet. What appeared to be faded paint or stain was spattered around the entryway. The house seemed to be in some arrested state of renovation. Mr. Newland ushered me into his office. Two or three Union Jacks were displayed. A large fax machine, papers, and texts were strewn on the desk. The shelves were lined with familiar academic books, counterparts to a recent degree course in political science.

Not long before our meeting Newland had been the target of a brutal assault. Early one morning three masked men "in jackboots, wielding ax handles," kicked down the door of his home and beat him. Intervention by neighbors halted the attack and, Newland believes, saved his life. He sustained serious head injuries requiring a stay in hospital. What I mistook for spattered stain or paint around the doorway was dried blood marking the site of the attack. The incident, for which no one was arrested or took credit, darkened his narrative and allowed Newland to indulge in a grim victimology. He attributed the attack to the "Zionist" personnel of the antifascist journal, *Searchlight*, in retaliation for a published letter he wrote to the editor of the *Independent*. The staff of *Searchlight* and members of other antifascist groups believe that the attack was in fact perpetrated by members of Combat 18, a disaffected band of former BNP supporters who seek more radical forms of political action than the electoral approach advocated by John Tyndall. In the *Searchlight* account: "Combat 18's war against the BNP left the BNP's press officer, Michael Newland, hospitalized with broken bones a week before the elections. Newland was attacked in broad daylight at his home in Kentish Town, North London, by three men posing as council workers. He was badly beaten, tied up and gagged."[5] Most shocking for Newland was the idea that political violence could penetrate, albeit briefly, the immunities assumed to shield middle-class personhood.

## Scrap Heap

Newland broods over expectations unrealized. He uses the metaphor of the "scrap heap" to summon images of a life discarded, his life. Like Beackon and Edmonds, he seeks refuge in a reactionary tale of Britain.

The way he extends and elaborates his story, however, allows it to do something quite different than merely provide a sentimental foil for the present. He recasts his regret and disappointment as social claims of a distinctly middle-class order and provenance. Newland is the victim. Middle-class privileges and exemptions have been denied him. He sees himself refused a role as a fully integrated social being by what he regards as the illegitimate practices of multiculturalism masked as age discrimination:

> In Britain, people over thirty-five are barred from nearly all employment. That's why I'm unemployed. We're barred from even applying. We can't go to agencies because they won't take on anybody who is over thirty-five. It's virtually impossible to get a job. And, of course, the people over thirty-five are most of the white population. It doesn't affect the black population so much because they are young. It's been going on for years and the government refuses to do anything about it. It's an absolute scandal. It has forced me on the scrap heap for the rest of my life. The policy is to not employ older people and has been extremely effective in pushing white people out of this society, including myself, I might say. This is one of the main reasons I was drawn into the BNP. There is no doubt there's a concerted effort to get white people out and it's being done in all kinds of ways. It's proving very effective.

The sense of place, which imparted authenticity to appraisals of identity in the portrayals of his working-class colleagues, is attenuated in Newland's disquisition. He is adrift in a middle-class world where "role," particularly as conferred by vocation, is more important in establishing the conditions of belonging. What is central to his politics is the recuperation of a middle-class personhood. The way he seeks to achieve this is to plot a "new" social order—a *Volksgemeinschaft*—that is congruent with his delineation of "British interests," racial solidarity, and authoritarian rule.

Newland is preoccupied with the political economy of Britain's decline from imperial greatness to industrial "backwater," where "prosperity" is in doubt and the reproduction of the middle class in jeopardy. He believes that the integration of the British middle class has been contingent not on the entitlements of the welfare state but on the promise of ongoing economic growth managed by an interventionist state. Under these conditions social justice for the white middle class is assessed in terms of a material standard of living, its moral economy calibrated in relation to a "respectable" style of life. Threats to prosperity fundamentally imperil this social order.

For Newland particular beliefs and values are central for this economic recuperation and the rehabilitation of the white middle class. Authoritarianism is required to reclaim the British nation in the face of failed democratic consensus. He cobbles together a British national socialism that extends beyond Edmond's exclusionary welfarism. For the most part he recycles conventional British ideas that have circulated in mainstream political discourse since the end of the First World War. The ease with which he can fashion a dismal politics from mundane sources is itself arresting; it relies on recourse neither to alien ideologies nor to particularly radical insights. Yet what results is unmistakable:

> *Holmes*: To reestablish such a coherent, stable, and homogeneous society requires extreme action?
>
> *Newland*: Yes, absolutely. That's why we say, quite frankly, we need a far greater degree of authoritarianism in a nationalist government now than we would have needed thirty years ago. The situation has been allowed to deteriorate so far that we can no longer rely on the population to exert the kind of social controls they would have done at one time [in the past]. They will rediscover their confidence after a while; it's just that there will be an interim period in which we will need a far stronger government.
>
> There is no perfect form of government and all governments should be regarded with deep suspicion by the people. Individuals are frail. They get into government, start lining their own pockets, become used to power, cease listening—these are familiar difficulties. There are forms of government needed at particular times. The situation is a kaleidoscope: that which is suitable at one time may not be particularly suitable at another. At the moment we need a fairly authoritarian, nationalist government. Then, after a few years, people will become discontented with that degree of authoritarianism and eventually will discard it. It won't be needed anymore.

Within this very intimate artifice, Newland interleaves fear of expressing his nationalist convictions, dismay about the decline of "trust and friendliness," disgust with media portrayals of "dissolute whites," and contempt for weak-minded clergy. He appraises the "threat" posed by immigrants, the injustice of "official multiculturalism," and the political "sham" of antiracist agendas. A disenfranchised class position quickens his estrangement; personal experience is etched across his cultural critique. What is most illicit about his account is how a middle-class sense of victimhood prepares the groundwork for authoritarianism. When taken as a whole Newland's program, despite its prosaic ingredients, is marked by those demiurges culpable for some of the most searing horrors of a blighted twentieth century.

## Victimhood

Michael Newland believes he has discovered the inherent contradictions at the heart of a multicultural and multiracial Britain. From his critique of multiculturalism he distills not the "factual racism" advocated by Edmonds but an involuted victimhood that supports the racist nationalism of a threatened middle class. He extrapolates from his disenfranchised class position a general crisis of democratic authority, which threatens the integration of Britain. Within his story a series of tyrannies materializes, opening the way for totalitarian measures.

Newland analyzes, as do his colleagues, the global forces that have transformed Britain and the world during the last half of the twentieth century. And, like Edmonds and Beackon, he endows his own claustrophobic depiction of experience with analytical sovereignty. He is concerned with the "stuff of existence," the trust and the friendliness that once rendered the fabric of life in Britain coherent and familiar:

> Simple things like the friendliness and trust [have been lost]. [Before this multicultural Britain] people didn't feel threatened walking down the street as they do now. That's what we [the BNP] want to restore. It's those simple little things of everyday life that are so important. They are the stuff of our existence. The big events are things which only happen occasionally. It is this substance, these minutes of everyday life, which have been progressively destroyed by the political and social changes imposed on us. *Imposed on us* by successive governments completely against the will of the people in this country.

His account takes a *völkisch* turn as he links the symbolic power of the nation with the day-to-day experiences of belonging.[6] Multiculturalism, promoted through political duplicity and ineptitude, violates this congruence, fueling his sense of rupture and inflaming his nationalism. Specifically, an "arrogant" commitment to *assimilation* on the part of British leaders in the 1950s, he believes, defiled national unity and undermined the national will. He insists that assimilation failed. The outcome of this failure is clear. When large numbers of immigrants are allowed to enter Britain with legal protections permitting them to retain their distinctive cultural identities, they inescapably encroach on the cultural identity of "white" Britons. Moreover, when various social preferences are conferred on minorities, particularly in employment, "whites" are inevitably displaced. Thus, the native-born Newland is forced on to the "scrap heap," denied a productive role. He insists that a pernicious multiculturalism is creating societies that people do not want. For him it is tantamount to a betrayal of the moral integrity of the nation.

Newland feels he is subjected to scurrilous defamations. He watches as "poison spews off" the television set every night as portrayals of "dissolute whites" proliferate. White men are wrong, everything about them is wrong, they should just "give up the ghost," "stand aside," and let other people take over. Like Gerd Baumann's informants quoted earlier, he claims that "The white man is afraid!" Newland believes the ethnic character of his community and nation has been ravaged by state sponsored multiculturalism imposed against the will of his countrymen. The respectable, fair-minded, and decent characterology of middle-class Anglo-Saxons must be defended. People who lose their toughness will quickly be displaced by others with greater tough-mindedness. He expresses grudging respect for Muslims who won't stand for any nonsense: "Society needs militancy."

The escalating politics of multiculturalism is also, in Newland's angst ridden view, an expression of the profound failure of parliamentary democracy. He insists that major elements of both the Conservative Party and New Labour promote immigration for crass political ends. The Conservatives want the world to be an "international business park" with the mass movement of population furnishing a constant supply of "cheap labor." They have no interest in the well-being of British society or culture. New Labour embraces immigrants as a vital political asset. Their antiracist rhetoric is merely a cynical cover for shrewd exploitation of immigrants as a burgeoning constituency. The core, middle England, is caught defenseless against these forces. Voters are silenced with no means to thwart democratically this calamitous change. Their will is denied as so-called democratic institutions nullify the creation of a "true" national consensus. The loathsome outcome of the electoral politics of multiculturalism is certain: the eradication of the British nation.

These politics, Newland contends, intrude on an even more intimate level. The British people were once proud of free speech; now they are afraid. He asserts what Baumann's "white English" informants intimate: "Now people avert their eyes and accept restrictions on what they can and cannot say." Politically incorrect views, nationalist views, can cost you your job. To campaign as a nationalist risks arrest and attack, as he knows too well. Others share his views but are too concerned about their position to voice them. It's left to a very few to be "courageous."

Newland asserts that practices of multiculturalism are not merely wrong or unworkable; they are illegitimate and treasonous. They violate the cherished principles upon which the British nation was integrated. Portraying multiculturalism as an instrument of "tyranny" permits Mr. Newland to plot extreme countermeasures. Forced repatriation of non-European immigrants is the most odious of these measures.

## Backwater

The account changes tone as Newland alloys his racialized victimology and his critique of multiculturalism to a political economy. He embraces a national socialist program based on a comprehensive assessment of the destructive capacity of fast-capitalism. Yet Newland's national socialism has an insipid character. By merely taking outdated elements of Labour

Party policy, drawn from the postwar period (1945–75), he fashions a militant agenda for the present, predicated on an interventionist state. Middle-class urgencies surface again, this time as preoccupations over "prosperity." The basic premises of Newland's political economy can be traced back to the work of Oswald Mosley during the 1920s and early 1930s. Mosley was elected as a Labour member of Parliament in 1918 on a platform of "socialistic imperialism."[7]

Newland is emphatic, Britain has moved out of the sphere of prosperity. This message is deeply unsettling for a middle class whose integration within industrial Britain was contingent on an abiding material well-being, if not affluence. Economic insecurity is the symbolic locus of middle-class anxieties. Prosperity, assured by government action, underwrote the reproduction of the white middle class. In a postindustrial Britain the middle class finds itself exposed to the same uncertainties that have historically defined the lot of the working class. For Newland a depopulated and deindustrialized Liverpool stands as the harbinger of things to come. Liverpool has collapsed. When that happens to the whole country, Britain will become a backwater; not only of the world economy, but the European economy. He foresees permanent mass unemployment with service jobs replacing the well-paid industrial jobs. The Fordist industry of the postwar period, the factory-based industry backed up by Keynsian demand management and welfarism, has all been dismantled. He asks, "Where is the industrial base of the future when your industry moves to the Far East? Where is this prosperity to come from?"

The Labour Party, Newland believes, was quite right to raise these questions during the 1970s in its "alternative economic strategy."[8] That approach is consistent with the interventionist priorities he and the BNP want to take.

Newland contends the whole point about economies is that they are not just driven by rational criteria but by beliefs. Economic outcomes are not just about the management of technology and resources; they are about what people believe about themselves and their nation. Doctrines—formulated around national imperatives—must guide state management of the economy. You must have "outside agency to control investment." Capital investment is, in Newland's mind, the "heart of the matter." Lack of investment demonstrates the utter failure of government policy to serve the interests of the British people.

What radicalizes Newland's economic analysis is its linkage to the consummate question posed by nationalism—the disposition of sovereignty. The drift of government policy toward internationalist economic priorities during the 1980s and 1990s is, in Newland's eyes, a sellout. Transference of decision-making powers to the European Union stripped the instruments of economic control from British regulatory agency.

Decontrolled markets, the legacy of Thatcherism, opened British industry to the destructive power of international finance and the full force of fast-capitalism, while government's capacity for economic supervision dwindled. Political control and accountability atrophied. He asks rhetorically, "Where are the instruments which the government will use to relieve unemployment?" Newland sees the decline of national sovereignty as inextricable from his own sense of lost agency. This intriguing maneuver parallels Le Pen's intimate artifice, his distinctive basis of political authority. It is the way that abstract issues, like those surrounding sovereignty and economic decline, are fused directly to the personal experience of adherents, to their lifeworld, circumventing the mediating authority of a public sphere, which is the quintessence of integralist political practice and the basis of its radicalism.

Newland insists people do not realize that power and sovereignty have been lost. The British government no longer has the means it had thirty years ago to intercede in matters of economy. The world has changed. But because open debate has been arrested by those who control the media, nobody knows and nobody really understands the degree to which independence has been relinquished. By warranting that economic reforms are not merely a matter of unsound policies but outrageous compromises of sovereignty, Newland finds "legitimate" grounds to plot extreme, antidemocratic remedies.

## Volksgemeinschaft

Newland sees his British personhood injured by usurpations of multiculturalism, and his middle-class status threatened as the integrative project of the nation-state is challenged by transnational forces. The treatment he prescribes is draconian: recuperation of his British middle-class identity demands construction of a totalitarian order.

After following the circuitous journey through a decaying Britain Newland leads us to the solution. His infamous proposition for national renewal is couched in reasonable terms and moderate language. To reiterate Britain needs a far greater degree of authoritarianism, a government committed to interventionist practices. The situation has been allowed to deteriorate so far that we can no longer rely on the people to exert the kind of social controls they would have done at one time. He temporizes. "They will re-discover their confidence after a while, it's just that there will be an interim period in which we will need a far stronger government." He is a relativist. "All governments should be regarded with deep suspicion by the people." He understands human nature. Individuals are frail. They get into government, start lining their own pockets, and cease listening. Newland is a pragmatist. There are different forms of government needed at different times. "At the moment Britain needs a fairly authoritarian, nationalist government. Then, after a few years, people will become discontented with that degree of authoritarianism and eventually will discard it, since it won't be needed anymore." He is surely deluded.

## ROT

Newland arranged for my interview with John Tyndall. The meeting took place at Tyndall's home in Brighton on a clear summer day in August 1994. His house is on a quiet lane a few hundred feet from the sea. An enormous hydrangea was in bloom in the front yard. Tyndall greeted me at the door, commented on my punctuality and showed me in to a spacious parlor filled with late afternoon sun. He described its decor as Victorian. A child ran up the stairs.

Again, Tyndall has been a central figure in the groups that have comprised extreme elements of the British nationalist right over the past four decades, and he organized in 1982 and officially heads the BNP. Tyndall embellishes many of the themes introduced by his colleagues, but he goes on to derive a very different analytical dimension. He sees himself, like Le Pen, as a diagnostician of decadence and degeneration. He would have the listener engage his positions as "philosophy." Tyndall, like Newland, advocates a nationalism that transcends "place," operating within a highly subjective framework of meaning contoured by an "epistemology" and phantasm of racial distinction. His fascism emerges in an odd alignment with the deeply ingrained street politics of his working-class colleagues.[9] He dispenses with social and historical contingencies. The external social world operates as an epiphenomenon in his scheme, wherein racialized nationalism functions as the authentic moral force and the basis of transcendent action. Although his politics is fundamentally about societal renewal, his vision is *not* underwritten by an empirically grounded political economy. Similarly, the details of history are of little consequence, despite the fact that an overarching historical transformation impels his apocalyptic prognosis and sets the course to the new authoritarian order.

What is important about Tyndall's formulation of an authoritarian British nationalism is that it draws from a *European* integralism. Tyndall appropriates his integralism from the Counter-Enlightenment resonances of the romantic tradition, providing a distinctive course to a national socialist synthesis. The link that Tyndall acknowledges emphatically is to Oswald Spengler, but it goes deeper. Tyndall insists on imposing a sublime conceptualization of society that aligns domains of the social directly with "mind and will." The "apotheosis of the will" is, of course, at the heart of German romanticism and its delineation of society, culture, and biological needs. Isaiah Berlin identifies the axioms of this occult rendering of collectivity:

> [T]o be fully human, that is, fully creative, one must belong somewhere, to some group or some historical stream which cannot be defined save in genetic terms of tradition, a milieu and a culture, themselves generated by natural forces—the *Klima* (i.e. the external world) and physical structure and biological needs which, in interplay with every individual's mind and will, create the dynamic, collective process called society. (Berlin 1976:198)

Berlin goes on to discern within this Counter-Enlightenment demarcation of society the peculiar aesthetic nature of the *Führerprinzip*, the leadership principle, and its potential to generate a fascist political imaginary and field of action:

> It took a more sinister form in the worship of the leader, the creator of a new social order as a work of art, who moulds men as the composer moulds sounds and the painter colours—men too feeble to rise by their own force of will. An exceptional being, the hero and genius to whom [Thomas] Carlyle and [Johann] Fichte paid homage, can lift others to a level beyond any which they could have reached by their own efforts, even if this can be achieved only at the cost of the torment or death of multitudes. (Berlin 1997:321)

What I found initially ludicrous about Tyndall's account was his framing of the leadership principle as the catalyst for social integration and political transcendence. As, however, I viewed his formulation in terms of one of the central theses of this study—that fast-capitalism subverts preexisting conceptions of society both as an empirical and moral tableau—his framework gained a perverse clarity. Put simply, as the operation of British industrial society is increasingly rendered opaque by virtue of a dissonant fast-capitalism, inflammatory forms of political discourse and action become possible, forms that are contemptuous of externally imposed democratic accountabilities. From a Strathernian vantage point, as a rich perspectivism is lost and the discrimination of legitimate class-based social claims undercut, political agendas that are increasingly disenthralled from established patterns of moral scrutiny can gain expression (1992:159).

As we saw earlier, Le Pen is master of this technique creating an integralist political imaginary, unyielding to critical evaluation, within which "racism" and "fascism" are increasingly difficult to define, confront, or oppose. Le Pen's integralism, also based on the authority of "inner truths," creates an alternative basis of legitimacy in the face of an eviscerated public sphere. Tyndall's integralism appears to go further than Le

Pen's in an even more dubious and unsavory direction. He, like Newland, believes that the disintegration of the public sphere is sufficiently advanced that democratic participationism can no longer be sustained and that authoritarianism is the only means of achieving social order. The crucible of his radicalism is the assiduous application of racial hygiene and the apotheosis of the will, which, he is convinced, are capable of transcending preexisting social and historical constraints. Tyndall's fascism is of a classic order: decay abounds and rebirth looms.

He lays out here his own progression from socialism to national socialism to fascism. Though his account is pompous to the point of parody, he demarks a central challenge for an integralist imaginary: the insinuation of the "majority instinct" as a basis of political legitimacy when conventional forms of social consensus are ineffectual and democratic accountabilities are enfeebled. Indeed, he is convinced that historical crises threaten, fomented by the adulteration of democratic institutions and of democratic practices by insipid human frailties. Spengler provides Tyndall with the counterforce to decline and decay: the iron will to dominate.

To transform mind and will into political action requires a peculiar cognitive maneuver, what Berlin calls "political anthropomorphism," by which state, nation, progress, and history are transformed into supersensible agents, "with whose unbounded will I must identify my own finite desires if I am to understand myself and my significance, and be what, at my best, I could and should be. I can only understand this by action" (1997:226–27). This means that "the sacred vocation of man is to transform himself and his world by his indomitable will"(1997:227).[10] Roger Griffin provides an acute portrait of self-styled leaders like Tyndall, determined to fashion themselves as the agents of regeneration, of palingenesis:

> The fascist felt he (and it generally was a "he") had been fatefully born at a watershed between national decline and national regeneration, a feeling that _chosen one to lead_ alchemically converted all pessimism and cultural despair into a manic sense of purpose and optimism. He knew himself to be one of the "chosen" of an otherwise lost generation. His task was to prepare the ground for the new breed of man, _homo fascistus_, who would instinctively form part of the revitalized national community without having first to purge himself of the selfish reflexes inculcated by a civilization sapped by egotism and materialism. (Griffin 1995:3–4; 1993:26–55; 1995:4–12)

Tyndall's integralist politics emerge, as suggested earlier, as deceptively simple personal stories in which his political vision is "anthropomorphized" within an inflected biographical tale. He has, at the close of the century, retraced the basic impulses at the heart of the fascist synthesis.[11]

*Metamorphosis*

Tyndall recounted his own metamorphosis during his reflective exile in northern Germany as a member of the British Army of the Rhine in the 1950s. During this exile he embarked on a quest for inner verities that galvanized his cloying political imaginary. He was a loner, alienated from the other soldiers, not interested in their meaningless distractions. He devoted himself to reflections on his country and its future. Encamped in Germany he discovered a national awareness that had lurked in his subconscious:

> I had a lot of time to think because we didn't have our time well organized and were left to our own devices. I was something of a loner and didn't join in with things my fellow soldiers liked to do in their spare time. I did do a lot of sport but, apart from that, I was a loner. I didn't go whoring and do the things they liked to do. I kept to myself, read a lot of books, went on country walks and meditated. It was during this time that I developed a national consciousness which had always been under the surface, in my subconscious.
>
> If you haven't been beyond the borders of your own country your horizons are limited and you don't think of your country in relation to the rest of the world. When you're sent abroad for the first time, you start to get a look at the rest of the world and you realize that [conditions] in your own country are different from those in the rest of the world. It does, or should, stimulate more of a national consciousness. It did in me anyway. To wear one's country's uniform, I suppose, is an additional thing. You feel the need to be a good ambassador, to behave well, to acquit yourself with dignity and so on; not to let the side down, as it were. All these things, together with the fact that I had abundant time [made me think] about the future of the country I was born to live in. What exactly was my country? It was all of this which steered me to an involvement with politics.

Unlike his colleague whose nationalism was galvanized on the turbulent streets of London, Tyndall discovers an essential Britain at the core of his being. It is a Britain removed from the contemporary moment, though profoundly threatened; an eternal Britain, which he set out to rescue. This brooding steered him toward an involvement with politics and upon his return from Germany he began his political exploration. He scrutinized the major parties but found them unsatisfactory:

> I suppose, if anything, at that time I was closer to Labour than the others because I regarded myself as a kind of socialist. Not a socialist in any way understood by the left wing, but a socialist in the sense that I believed in the community rather than the individual. And so I felt for a time that if there was any party to which I belonged, it might possibly be the Labour Party.

But, as I studied the Labour Party more and more, I couldn't accept the fact that they were not prepared to stand up for the interests of this country. They were against everything I perceived to be in the British national interest. It was this which deterred me from ever becoming more involved with them. I was looking for a combination of something that had a certain socialist dimension, while at the same time, was nationalistic and patriotic; but there didn't seem to be anything around. Then I saw a news flash on television about a small group calling themselves the League of Empire Loyalists. I resolved to look up these people when I moved back to London. Eventually I found them and, although they weren't exactly what I was looking for, I was desperate to be involved in something. Through them, I found out about A. K. Chesterton and I took some literature home to read; most of it was written by Chesterton. I thought this man to be the closest to what it was I was looking for. He had the right approaches, the right ideas. So I joined this little group mainly because I was impressed with him [Chesterton] and felt a kinship with his views.

Arthur Kenneth Chesterton (1899–1973) gave Tyndall's timeless Britain an expansive mythology and distinctive pedigree.[12] Chesterton provided a mythic substance to kindle a politics of national renewal. Chesterton was a prolific journalist, one of the most idealistic and capable polemicists in the British Union of Fascists, who served as Oswald Mosley's press secretary and biographer.[13] In the post–World War II era, Chesterton continued to elaborate on the political program he initially espoused during the interwar period, based on a deeply conspiratorial anti-Semitism blended with authoritarianism and cultural nationalism.[14] "Chesterton was engaged in a constant literary search to provide proof both of the innate superiority of British culture over all rivals, and as a pointer to an ordered, hierarchical society based upon discipline, duty and strict conformity to the needs of the nation and its Empire above those of the individual citizen" (Baker 1985:28).

Chesterton's *völkisch* project sought "truth" in English literature and, through his "pressure group," the League of Empire Loyalists, founded in 1953, opposed the "retreat from Empire" by a succession of postwar British governments. Chesterton found the street corner politics of working-class fascism distasteful and increasingly sought to rehabilitate himself and his politics within a middlebrow, Tory respectability. He brought together various right-wing groups to found the National Front in 1967 and served as its first chairman from 1967 to 1971 (Baker 1985:29). John Tyndall became Chesterton's protégé and successor:

But still, it [the League of Empire Loyalists] was not *really* what I was looking for because it was not a political party. It never aspired to become a political party. It was not even an embryo of a political party. It was a pressure group, and that was the main thing I disagreed about with Chesterton. It was a pressure group to try to influence established political opinion and I saw no future in that [approach]. So, eventually I split with Chesterton, which I regretted, because I liked and admired the man, but we had this strategic difference.

So then I got involved with another group, and yet another group, and there were bewildering comings and goings among various groups over a period of, what, ten or eleven years. None of them were very impressive, none were very effective, but through them I met people. That was the important thing for me; I met people who shared similar ideas.

In 1967 some of these groups, the main ones at the time, merged together to form the National Front. I was in fairly early on that merger and not long after it took place I became more involved. I was in the National Front from 1967 to 1980 and I became its leader in 1972. I remained leader with one small gap of just over a year up to 1980 when there was another split.

If you study the so-called right in Europe you know about this tendency to fragment. It is found everywhere. It is human nature. Anyway, I greatly regretted the split in 1980 but it couldn't be avoided. After this there was a struggle for supremacy between the NF and our faction, which became the BNP. By 1990 our faction clearly emerged as the more successful one, the stronger one. This is where we are now.

Tyndall advances the cultural telos of fascism by embracing its defiantly antirational spirit. However misguided and objectionable the ideas of Edmonds, Beackon, and Newland, they derive from an intimate excursion through a blighted Britain. Analytically, this measure of engagement with an approximation of an empirical world makes their accounts minimally intelligible. Tyndall's depiction is aloof to—even contemptuous of—externalities. He plots a nationalism guided by an interior quest, by "instinct." This retreat to elusive inner truths represents simultaneously one of the most disabling potentials of this kind of politics as well as a source of its sinister power. In order to assess how power is derived from this kind of "political anthropomorphism" requires taking the antirational and profoundly opportunistic character of fascism seriously. The catalyst for this kind of strategic opportunism is a crisis in liberal democratic authority and the occlusion of the public sphere. Crisis creates, at least in the imagination of these partisans, the specific prerequisites for Counter-Enlightenment forms of political agency predicated on the apotheosis of mind and will.

## Domination

The symptoms Tyndall asserts, are unmistakable; all over the Western world ruling powers are incapable of maintaining law and order, incapable of maintaining any kind of moral, political, or legal authority. The economic system is doomed. The world situation will explode, just when cannot be known. Soon. There is a complete spiritual void; thinking people have nothing to believe in anymore. Few people take communism seriously, and the next step for reasonable people will be to desert capitalism. All these things will combine inexorably to bring about the complete demise of the international, liberal, multiracial, multicultural world order. His formulation of nationalism will supersede it as an integrative force. He is emphatic: there will be demands for strong popular leaders, whether democratic or not.[15]

Tyndall, drawing on this metaphysics of domination, sees the chief threat to the Western world in a deep spiritual rot, which has been going on for generations. There is an erosion of a sense of nationhood, an erosion of will, a capitulation to false values. The pursuit of material well-being, the pursuit of comfort and security as the chief goals of society is, for him, preposterous:

> *Holmes*: What is the nature of this "rot"?
>
> *Tyndall*: In a word, liberalism. It's not just liberal political solutions, which are mostly wrong—I suppose there is the occasional case when they might be right; [rather] it is the liberal world view, the whole liberal world view and the whole liberal philosophy and values. With this I am at war—always have been.
>
> *Holmes*: In other words, the power of international capitalism and world markets?
>
> *Tyndall*: Yes. That and the *idea* of the individual. You have two aspects of liberalism: you can say that modern liberalism is collectivist, while traditional liberalism is individualist. I lean more toward the collectivist point of view. I am at war with the *idea* of the individual as an entirely independent unit; one who is allowed to suit himself, do as he likes and acts completely selfishly. I have always leaned more toward the community idea, but the community idea based on *ethnicity*, rather than on common political ideology or a common geographical area. The whole idea of "community" makes no sense to me unless it is an ethnic one. I repudiate the liberal philosophy of a gradual upward progress throughout history. I take a cyclical view of history with periods of resurgence and decline and we are now [close to the bottom].
>
> The whole idea of the pursuit of material well-being, the pursuit of material riches, and the pursuit of comfort and security as the chief goals of society do not fit with my philosophy.

Like Edmonds and Newland, Tyndall leans toward the collectivist point of view. What gives form to his idea of ethnic community is a crude hygiene, based on what he calls "racial interests."

Tyndall is a racist according to his own definition: "a person who believes in the innate inequality of races." A racist believes that races have different capabilities. His racism is unyielding: "Europeans must keep their racial integrity. Differences between races are blatant. It is a mystery to him [the racist] how intelligent people cannot accept this premise, unless their intellect is somehow overruled." His racism is fundamentally different from the factual racism of Edmonds and Beackon. Tyndall's racism arises as an instrumental force by which bigotry is employed to mobilize political support and shape a profane consensus. A racism that can operate in the absence of unbridled enmity, its diabolic character rests on a cynical deployment of hatred and malevolence for purely political ends. He casts his instrumental racism as an expression of realism, fortitude, and transcendence.[16] Indeed, Tyndall sought in my conversation with him to portray his racial phantasm as "humane," if not benevolent.

Tyndall maintained that the only existence "the black man" can have in the "white areas of the world" is as a "subsidized and a kept group," living on welfare and "given employment on the basis of affirmative action rather than on the basis of merit." That is "unhealthy for a race." It is far healthier, as he sees it, for blacks "to revert to an indigenous area where they belong, their natural habitat, which would seem to be Africa." There, "they have a future." "Yes, all fares paid, and a resettlement grant." He would grant this to them, not as an obligation, but as a concession "to remove any accusation of cruelty." He has faith in Western peoples to carry out this forced resettlement "with little pain." "Western races have a humane, decent, kind streak which certainly isn't the case in many other races." If the black races of Africa felt they needed to do to white Britons what Tyndall feels Britain needs to do to them, they would carry out "an ethnic cleansing in a callous and brutal manner." He wouldn't take away black people's houses and say, "Right, you're on the street, we are giving you nothing." "But the world is a brutal place and when your *own* people's future is at stake you have to be prepared to take whatever measures are necessary." He has a young daughter, and he "will do anything which her welfare and her future demands."

## Absurdities

Renewal of authority in the spirit of Spengler is the overriding imperative for Tyndall. To restore Western civilization demands a kind of authority that people will not recognize as democratic. This term "democracy" must be reexamined since in Tyndall's view it fails to reflect the "majority instinct." A singularity—the iron will to dominate—provides him with the structure of motive that can satisfy this majority instinct, and the will to dominate plots Tyndall's dubious course to a new authoritarian order:

> My prescription is the restoration of authority. To put it in Spengler's words, the resurgence of authority. If it will happen at all, if it is possible to restore

Western civilization to any kind of equilibrium, it is going to require something which probably most people would *not* recognize as democracy. It is going to require a kind of leadership which would be called *un*democratic according to modern definition. I would not necessarily designate it as undemocratic because I would say, Who is the greater democrat? The powerful ruler who has no parliament, no committees, and no voting over this or that? One who steers his country in a way that is amenable to the sentiments of the broad population, the silent majority? Or a prime minister or president who works within a nominally democratic framework but who makes decisions contrary to what the people want? How can a person call himself a democrat when, in so many areas, he goes against the majority instinct? This whole term, "democracy," must be reexamined.

*Tyndall likes to invoke Oswald Mosley*: "better a real crisis, than a slow spiritual descent to the grave." This latter is the danger for his nation. The ethnic danger is merely a symptom, since "the nonwhite population is something which can be removed." The real threat is the mentality that has produced the problem, for even without the "nonwhite presence," they would still have this puerile mentality. Losing direction as a nation is what produced the race problem. There is, however, a certainty of victory for his spectral analysis. It lies not in what is to be done but in what "the system" inevitably is going to do. "The system is collapsing; it is not viable." "The system cannot survive and that will create the conditions for victory." Tyndall remains steadfast to fascism's duplicitous rhetoric, decrying precisely those corrupt and dissolute conditions that make the fascist synthesis possible.

Tyndall identifies a series of flaws in the nature and practice of parliamentary democracy that underlie the emerging crisis. Indeed, central to his fascism is the conviction that democracy, like capitalism, harbors profoundly self-destructive dynamics that make crises inevitable. Specifically, he rails against the potential of liberal democracy to attract and promote leaders who will not or cannot represent the "true" interests of the nation. Parliamentary democracy itself "dissipates the will of the people" and "promotes decay." Although Britain is a multicultural society today, there was absolutely no public debate, it was decided by a small minority of powerful people. Now, he insists, "there is a wider conspiracy among certain circles to impose multiculturalism and multiracialism on the whole of the Western world." It is an international agenda. But the majority of those who were responsible for bringing this transformation about in Britain were not, he thinks, conscious conspirators; rather they were "little people," "myopic politicians caught up in the maelstrom of democratic politics." It was all quite simple: "immigrants provide cheap labor," they came in a trickle, people were caught unaware. Members of

Parliament, notably Enoch Powell and, before him, Sir Cyril Osborne, warned that immigration was "getting out of hand" and "it could have explosive consequences." Successive governments recognized these dangers but declined to do anything about it out of political expediency.[17] You have, in Tyndall's vituperative appraisal, "powerless, impotent, small-time politicians who cannot think of the long-range consequences of what is happening." Their only concern is with everyday popularity, opinion polls, votes at election time, and what the media will say. Typical little politicians, "so weak and so cowardly that they won't take any strong action that might get them into trouble." Democratic politics are, in his fascist critique, inevitably compromised by cascading human frailties. But his critique is more subtle; in a Habermasian vein, Tyndall insists that the pursuit of a transient "public opinion" should not be mistaken for the creation of an enduring "social consensus," and he seeks a politics that can exploit this contradiction.

These "newcomers"—nonwhite immigrants—are able to hold voting power.[18] There is in his view an absurdity about this: "these people are off the plane one day and can vote the next," and, to make matters worse, all the major parties are desperate to get their vote. The mentality that led to decolonization, the retreat from the empire, was the same mentality that said, "let more immigrants come in here." It constitutes for him an obscene weakening of the national will to survive. He is unequivocal: "every government must make decisions on the basis of its racial interests." But the power of liberalism in the mass media is formidable; if the government takes action to stop immigration, it will be branded as "racist," which is "the great crime in the catechism of today." "No one wants that tag." This is why, he believes, nothing is done. But, he is adamant, "immigrants" are supremely important because they embody the failure of democratic politics to represent and express "the will of the people"; their presence is "living proof" of the encroaching multiracial and multicultural world order that will destroy his Britain. Thus, the "immigrant" is integral to three fundamental pillars of contemporary British fascism: its rejection of fast-capitalism (which draws South Asians to the East End), its contempt for liberal democracy (which renders "newcomers" a powerful electoral force), and its racism (which renders racial differences irreconcilable).

## No Wimps

His people are very passionate about their ideas, their objectives, their struggle. In that respect they are "militant." There is no doubt in Tyndall's mind that all the violence that has occurred has been instigated by his opponents. The press dishonestly links the BNP with racial attacks, which, he insists, is absolutely untrue. "There is no connection." However, his people are "not wimps"; if provoked they will fight back and "blacken a few eyes." If it is considered extreme or militant to defend yourself, he "pleads guilty." But he never countenanced attacks on the meetings of opponents, never said, "they must be silenced," and never challenged their right to freedom. Tyndall's faith in "free speech" is, however, rather ironic. He is only too happy for his opponents to have "free speech" so they can "condemn themselves out of their own mouths."

Tyndall ponders the meaning of "political respectability." He thinks that the average white East Ender must see the BNP as respectable enough or he wouldn't vote for its candidates. The reason that people elsewhere haven't voted for its candidates is that they don't believe the BNP can win—they haven't crossed that "credibility threshold." If the BNP could be seen as "a real contender," then things would change and it would glean votes from across Britain. Still, he admits, large numbers of people do not see BNP as "respectable." "But what determines respectability?" The political climate is conditioned by the mass media, and "if the mass media decrees that a movement won't be respectable, it isn't respectable."

The "Second World War Syndrome" is involved, he believes. The media links his people with the Nazis, with Hitler, with concentration camps, with mass extermination. But, to the average young person today, the rights and wrongs of World War II are becoming "irrelevant." To link the BNP with Hitler doesn't have the same "emotive force" it once held. That works to his advantage. He is also convinced that the mass media is becoming suspect. Tyndall is fixated on the power of the media, yet he thinks that few people believe what they read anymore. Like Le Pen, he sees the media discredit itself "in the eyes of thinking people" by its lies. Both believe the persuasive clout of the media can be thwarted, if not defeated, by appeals to the day-to-day experience of their audience. Tyndall is convinced that the average white person in Britain distrusts the way the media deals with the racial question because it conflicts with his or her own experience.

This sense of growing popular mistrust of elites and the institutions they represent is evidence for Mr. Tyndall of "immanentization"—that is, the belief that profound historical forces are coalescing that will open the way for insurgent possibilities (Griffin 1993:31). The deterioration of deference throughout society, the false portrayals of the world propagated by the media, the ineptitude and moral dissipation of weak, dithering politicians paralyzed by their own petty self-interests, and the general corruption of those racial imperatives that defined Britain as a white collectivity are merely superficial testimony to a comprehensive subversion of authority across virtually every institutional setting; they stand as confirmation of an acute crisis enveloping the entire Western world. At this climactic turning point all elites are disgraced, and liberal democratic ideals, the hallmark of the old order, are discredited. Tydnall decries the feebleness and ineptitude that created this impending catastrophe, while embracing the crisis as the essential prerequisite for his revolutionary intervention. In the face of escalating chaos, as all forms of liberal-democratic authority are challenged, people will recognize and seek instinctually a forceful restoration of order and an unambiguous rendering of collectivity. This is the spectral moment when "the mind and the will" of the leader are embraced by the populace and then superimposed as the totalizing basis of authority. The "majority instinct," Tyndall is absolutely certain, will legitimize this natural succession to authoritarianism. The instinctual potential is inflamed by the emotional power of racism. This is his path of transcendence by which an integral public is constituted out of inner truths in the wake of a degraded public sphere.

## Leaching

What I found galling about Tyndall's world view is that it is crosscut by thoroughly insipid analysis and outrageously hateful sensibilities. It requires a degree of restraint not to dismiss it as shameless stupidity. Although Tyndall's fascism is of a classic order—a form of populist ultranationalism predicated on the imminence of renewal and rebirth—it seemed to me initially that his synthesis could no longer sustain a revolutionary program. I was inclined to view it as yet another variant of British fascism that creates for its adherents an intellectual refuge wherein alienation is self-imposed and unremitting. Rather than pursuing an active engagement with the world, it seemed clear that Tyndall preferred, despite his assertions to the contrary, intrigue and conspiracy. The kind of aloofness and disdain he expresses toward the contingencies of history and society enmeshed him and his followers in an involuted political imaginary, generating a program that seemed fundamentally obscurantist, insulated from external critique, and under the sway of racism and paranoia. As he concedes, this is a famous path to political irrelevance that has long distinguished radical nationalists in Britain. There was, however, by the general election campaign of 1997 a peculiar accretion of British political discourse that had relevance for Tyndall's baleful vision and that gave his political imaginary a new significance, though it also opened a direct challenge to his style of leadership.

The rebirth of the Labour Party as "New Labour," the outcome of a long process of "modernization" during the 1980s and the 1990s under the leadership of Neil Kinnock, John Smith, and Tony Blair, restored radical possibilities to Tyndall's fascism. The striking ideological metamorphosis of the Labour Party, based on the virtues of the market and the iniquities of welfarism, opened new political ground, which he and his colleagues now seek to infiltrate. Centrally, New Labour scrapped the party's traditional commitment to a socialist political economy; in France where the struggle to eviscerate socialism was led by Le Pen and his associates, in Britain this surgery was accomplished from within the Labour Party. The leaders of the BNP see their claim to social welfarism—albeit one deeply compromised by bigotry and racism—unchallenged by mainstream political forces, while Blair's project of devolution ratifies their nationalist aspirations. By creating the Scottish Parliament and the Welsh and Northern Ireland Assemblies, nationalist sentiments were legitimized within the United Kingdom. Though the aim of this devolutionary maneuver was to forestall more radical separatist initiatives, particularly in Scotland, on the one hand, and orient Britain to full Europeanization on the other, it also meant an English-British nationalism could not simply be dismissed as illegitimate. The BNP leadership is certain that its integralist agenda, with its blending of nationalism and socialism, can provide the sole strategic position from which to oppose fast-capitalism, multiculturalism, and Europeanization.

## WEB OF SIGNIFICANCE

What Tyndall may have not fully grasped, as did those who challenged his leadership in late 1999, is that a new medium and a new political space had emerged that were supremely adapted for their integralist pursuit of intimate artifice. This new medium brutally exposed the outdated style and content of Tyndall's message communicated via his antiquated fascist broadsheet, *Spearhead*. His colleagues, however, did recognize these new possibilities and they drew it to the center of their practice. Michael Newland and Nick Griffin began to exploit the peculiar fit between their integralist message and the communicative and representational technologies of the internet. They found that the internet provided them with a new domain of action that transcends place, where a highly subjective populism can align social action directly with mind and will, where a crude stylistic expressionism joined with the phantasm of racial distinction can operate as instruments of solidarity, and where inflammatory discourses of persecution and victimhood can be expressed free of external scrutiny or accountability. They pursued the challenge of Tyndall's leadership via their control of the BNP's website.

Again, Griffin is portrayed as the young "modernizer," backed by Newland in his endeavor to transform the BNP. In one of his early performances on the BNP website, during the local election campaign of 1997, he demonstrated precisely how his tactics and stylistic approach differed from those of John Tyndall. Immediately following a truly dreary election manifesto prepared by Tydnall, Griffin delved into how "a media-organized scam to entrap members of the BNP in illegal paramilitary activity has failed." The preface to his report reveals not just his flair for conspiratorial repartee, but his commitment to the Sorelian and Gramscian project of wedding a radical political agenda directly to those mundane experiences that encompass the cultural struggles of his followers:

> A media-organized scam to entrap members of the BNP in illegal paramilitary activity has failed. In order to put the whole matter on public record, and to provide a warning to nationalists all over the English-speaking world of the kind of lengths our enemies are now prepared to go to in order to smear and divide us, there follows a necessarily long blow-by-blow account. Take it as a short detective story or spy novelette if you will, but take on board the warning as well. Beware of provocateurs. Stay legal at all times. Fight the rotten liberal system with well-argued publications, education, music, counter-power initiatives, community politics, electioneering, Internet arguments, and every other moral means at your disposal. But understand that extremist posing, confrontation with the Reds or the police, and violent disorder, are exactly what our opponents want to see. Use your heads! (http://www.bnp.net/, May 1997, entitled "How the Cook Report Attempted to Entrap the BNP").

It is not just that Griffin's on-line story is more riveting than the stilted manifesto, though it is certainly a more exciting and intriguing tale.[19] What Mr. Griffin grasps is the already well-known power of the internet to convey a particular type of political story, a story that implicates his audience in the action and in the conspiracy. It aims to break down the space between the participant and observer, allowing Griffin to contrive an alternative (or adjunctive) participatory regime to thuggery, an activism designed to operate on and within the imagination primarily of young alienated males (Buford 1992:149–58). But it is this old project of virtualism—of hegemony—in which cultural obsessions or inchoate fashion are invested with explicit political meaning that binds this activism directly to a new generation of radicals. Again, this goes to the heart of the integralist project whereby cultural production is appropriated for political ends. The internet is the new medium of their intimate artifice.

Finally, there is more than an apparent kinship between Griffin's ideas and practices and those of Le Pen and associates. Those pushing the modernization of the BNP have during the late 1990s sought to emulate what they saw as the French FN's strategy for gaining "respectability" and electoral success. Direct personal links were forged between the BNP modernizers and FN activists. The most significant policy changes to date influenced by this cross-channel exchange came in February 1999 when the BNP leadership decided "to drop its insistence on compulsory repatriation for all nonwhite Commonwealth people, in favour of a policy of voluntary repatriation" (King and Raymond 1999:28–29).

Michael Newland stood as the BNP candidate in the London mayoral elections of May 2000. He received 33,569 first preference votes and a further 45,337 second preference votes. In East London he gleaned a total of 9,920 first and second preference votes cast for mayor (*http:// www.bnp.net/*, May 2000).

# PART THREE

## ATAVISM

## Chapter Ten

## RADICAL SYMMETRY

IN THIS chapter I examine two speeches, one delivered by Jean-Marie Le Pen in Strasbourg at the end of March 1997 and the other delivered by Tony Blair, shortly after he became prime minister, at the Aylesbury housing estate in London in early June 1997.[1] These addresses present two projects of national integration, two social insurgencies, the basic elements of which are, for the most part, radically opposed, yet which at times broach areas of disconcerting congruence.

The peroration, excerpted here, demonstrates how Le Pen, drawing on the incendiary elements of populism, expressionism, and pluralism, generates a stunning political critique of the French power elite on the one hand, and a comprehensive framework for social action on the other. This critique and the social action it envisions open the way toward a Vichy inspired "national revolution." The immediacy that Le Pen achieves in the presentation renders his exegesis a resounding politics of the present—not some nostalgic vestige, but a highly charged politics of contemporary France and Europe. Yet the speech may well have represented the apogee of Le Pen's political ascendancy. Even as he delivered it, circumstances were taking shape that pitted his charismatic leadership of the FN against the local-level routinization and the modernization of the movement by Bruno Mégret. The schism derived from fundamentally different strategies about how the party's electoral success that accrued in 1998 should be exploited. Mégret sought direct power by pursuing coalition arrangements with the major right-wing parties, the RPR and the UDF, to take control of municipal and regional bodies. Over and above the challenge to authority that Mégret's strategic alternative represented, Le Pen has steadfastly resisted any dilution of his agenda that coalition agreements would entail. More fundamentally, Le Pen's vision is emphatically and implacably against the mainstream right. Indeed, the power of his populist rhetoric draws its strength at least as much, if not more, from his revulsion of the right as of the left. As we will see, his excoriating attack on the political establishment leaves scant room for coalition based compromise.

Blair's address represents a vigorous confrontation with the traditions of socialism upon which the Labour Party was founded. Rather than disparaging the powerful, as Le Pen does, his analysis focuses on the delinquencies of the powerless, "the underclass." In the speech he seeks to define New Labour's position on the welfare state and thereby his party's new project of British nationhood. He opens with an acknowledgment that the "underclass" is a product of a misdirected welfarism. He proposes a policy of "welfare to work" to cure the ills of what he awkwardly renames "the workless class," to reintegrate its members into a "one nation Britain."[2] In the process he performs the essential translation of the commercial ethic of fast-capitalism into a political and social agenda of "radical liberalism." It is a liberalism that disrupts traditional solidarities of British society, substituting an aggressive "individualization" as the key axiom of social life.[3] A British nationhood unified across classes is achieved in Blair's model by delegitimizing moral claims based on class distinctions and class dispensations. The project of social justice as it came to be institutionalized within the welfare state is disavowed.

Blair, unlike Le Pen, must attack his own party's history and tradition. Much as the leadership of the BNP suspected, he seeks a virtual elimination of socialism from the Labour Party's doctrine. This internal critique of the very underpinnings of the party has been shrewdly cloaked rhetorically as the project of modernization and the work of the Labour Party's modernizers (Blair 1999).

Like Le Pen, Blair ventures to operate on the soul and psyche of his people to animate their "will to win." By forcefully articulating his agenda of individual duty and responsibility, Blair clears a political space where the traditional project of British socialism no longer has a conspicuous mainstream claimant and, perhaps more important, where the operation of society itself becomes obscure, and the possibility of meaningful social analysis and social criticism becomes increasingly remote. His agenda creates the prospect of a social imaginary in which the relationship between the individual and collectivity is radically recast. But Blairism is by no means a crude extension of Thatcherism. By embracing devolution and Europeanization, Blairism creates new domains within which integralism can operate, where new forms of social and cultural engagement are possible.

## EASTER 1997

During Holy Week of 1997 the Front national held its tenth conference in Strasbourg. Le Pen delivered an extended address to participants at the close of the meeting. His oration constitutes a fully formed statement of European integralism that readily intermingles nationalism and socialism. Again, the speech was delivered at the end of a tumultuous week of street protests. Le Pen claims in the address to be deeply insulted and aggrieved by the violence that swirled around the meeting. This was a disingenuous pose.

Using Strasbourg as a setting for the conference was a strategic provocation. To begin with, the Socialist mayor of the city, Catherine Trautmann—who is also a senior member of the European Parliament—is a longtime adversary of Le Pen. He knew that she would in all likelihood be deeply insulted by the FN conference. Indeed, she removed a statue of Joan of Arc from its public display in the center of the city as a counterinsult. He knew that she and the Socialists would be compelled to sponsor various antiracist and antifascist demonstrations in response. He also knew there was a strong possibility the protests would turn riotous. But this was precisely the drama—with the potential for mayhem—that he sought. Not only does Le Pen use adroitly the violence deployed against him as counterpoint to his basic argumentation; he recognizes it as an integral force that binds his public to him and to his party. It clarifies for his followers their embattled position and their heroic stance. Nor is he ill-disposed to media attention that a confrontation between him and "the red mayoress," as he calls her, would hold. But staging his drama in Strasbourg also provided precisely the European context that further endows his integralist message with an expanded purview, beyond the borders of France, to immure all of Europe. It is classic Le Pen subterfuge.

Having heard a number of Le Pen's addresses, I have noticed that they can have a flat, if not hackneyed, quality when the delivery is merely a reiteration of FN agendas or policies. When Le Pen can orchestrate an emotional instability and bring an ersatz passion to the presentation, however, he becomes a very different figure. The circumstances of the following speech provided the ingredients for just this kind of staging. Le Pen emerges as an enthralling speaker, who can focus passions, for and against himself, with great virtuosity. He deploys techniques that seem to break down the space between him and the listener, endowing his message with unnerving intimacy. And when the speech turns to those whom Le Pen identifies as his political enemies, it takes on a startling bellicosity.

One of the most distinguishing characteristics of Herderian expressionism and populism is that they resist abstraction. Insofar as expressionism rests on the conviction that human voices are artistic forms that convey the essence of human moral and spiritual predicaments, they defy reductive analytical dissection. From this unyielding premise, the creative power of language is inseparable from the content and substance of communication. This is very much the case in the speech that follows, and to capture the force of its expressionism and populism, I have reproduced extended excerpts from it.[4] The speech, although it retains the most refined features of Le Pen's illicit discourse, marks a more significant political breakthrough. In its highly inflected and emotionally charged rhetoric is a fully formed integralist politics of Europe. At the end of the speech I recapitulate the basic elements of the social imaginary; the theory of society, that inspires and informs his exegesis.

## Donkeys Bray

Le Pen opens the speech with a gracious expression of gratitude to his delegates for sharing their Easter time with him in Strasbourg, working on the preparation of the political platform for the then impending elections of 1998. He contrasts the comportment of his supporters with the demonstrators who oppose them. Throughout the speech he deploys the full force of what Blot described earlier as Le Pen's contrastive epistemology and baroque style, which seeks to destabilize the perspective of the listener and insinuate a new basis of "truth":

> What a contrast and what a lesson. On the one hand, the pseudodemocracy of the street, the demonstrators, the banners and the loudmouths, [the rule] of violence and hatred and the havoc which, whether it wants it or not, invariably goes with it. . . . On the other hand, the seriousness, the calm, the labor, the skills, the abilities, the characters, but also the humor and the poetry, and in the evening, the joy and cheerfulness [of the FN delegates]. Everybody has been able to notice that the National Front is made of cool strength. It is the hope of France. A big thank you to all who come from so far away, for setting an example of equanimity, dignity and earnestness, despite the turmoil and the media attempts at misinformation. The donkeys bray and the caravan goes its way.

He quickly launches into a partisan attack that affirms his overarching political critique premised on an account of pervasive corruption:

> Corruption, powerlessness are, indeed, the commanding words of our politicians' universe. Sharing this indignity, it is not surprising that they unite to defend their privileges and emoluments against those who call for the people to judge their excesses and their criminal weaknesses. Political competition like economic competition should stimulate the service of the people. Alas! In the first instance as in the second, the risks it supposes for the competitors can be dismissed in common agreement by connivance and complicity.

The attack goes beyond mere partisanship to an indictment of virtually the entire political establishment who in collusion with big business threaten the integrity of the republic:

> Still they should admit that the foundation of our institutions is the will of the people such as is defined in our constitution and laws. But, for one part, the

democratic spirit has been quelled by technocratic insolence and the oligarchic profit of a few. The people are admitted only when they vote in their favor; they are despised, scorned when they give their confidence to their adversaries. In fact, the French Republic is a theater scenery, an institutional eyewash. They proclaim great principles, they refer to the human rights, they declare their love for democracy and the republic, to the point that their great ancestors of the French Revolution would redden in shame.

His populist invective portrays the democratic institutions of France as sinister illusions meant to dupe the citizenry. But the indictment goes much further, reaching to the deepest assumptions of the Counter-Enlightenment. Le Pen is framing an attack on the classic notion of an ideal man and of an ideal society, which are for him intrinsically incoherent and meaningless (Berlin 1976). The perfectibility of human beings through the application of universal principles founded on reason is in his view not just absurd but, as in the case of contemporary France, responsible for sustaining a political class entirely devoid of moral substance:

> In France, appearances are democratic. We have a parliament, a civil service, laws and rules, a judiciary, an army, a police, a social security structure . . . and even citizens who are subject to taxation and which we take into consideration for one month [during the election campaign], each five or seven years at best, provided they vote correctly, that is to say for the system. But our Assembly has no initiative to draft laws, nor freedom to discuss nor to vote them. It is a registration chamber which has to make believe. In fact, it is like the political class, the government, the administration and the Economy with a capital E, that is to say big business largely dominated by a sprawling bureaucracy.[5] Under their leadership and under their responsibility, the State—which made our Nation and its greatness—is degrading and ruining it. To compare, civil servants represent in France 25 percent of employment, 16 percent in Germany.

Le Pen sees the heroic purpose of the FN to challenge this monstrous sham, to break through the veil of appearances to reveal another reality:

> This dinosaur, which devours 60 percent of the national wealth, was brought out of its torpor when the National Front trod upon its tail, and since then, it tries to straighten up again its crest of spines, to shake up its scales and to hurl, with its toothless mouth, some onomatopoeic flatulence. But it has strength only to eat and to curse. The French people have just one right: to pay. To pay for the deficits of the state, of the social security, of the national and the nationalized firms . . . to pay for unemployment, for immigration, for the National Education. But, the more they pay, the worse things get.

He proceeds to marshal his all too familiar rhetorical device to link the ills of France to immigration. By so doing he exposes the intimate fears and resentments of various segments of the French public, their anxieties about an encroaching lawlessness: their growing sense of powerlessness:

> Income taxes are more and more numerous, heavier and heavier, more and more stifling, more and more unfair too, for the great firm in deficit will pay its taxes fraudulently, like the crook, the slave trader and the peddler; or like the majority of immigrants, unemployed, on social benefits or family assistance . . . sheltered in lawless areas which have become legal or above all illegal fiscal paradises. Imagine what would become of the bailiff who came to seize the unpaid-for television set or came to process the eviction of the refractory tenant, or the employee who came to cut off the water or the gas unpaid for, in neighborhoods where the police and even the firemen no longer enter and for a very good reason!

From his indictment of contemporary democratic practices he proposes another view of the state, based on plebiscitary "democracy":

> Some accuse us of antiparliamentarianism because we say that we don't queue in front of a cinema where no film is shown. It is wrong. We say that according to our constitution there is only one political legitimacy: that of a people rightly and loyally informed, appointing freely and through honest modes of ballot, those the people judge reliable. The referendum's field must be widened and the people must be enabled to pronounce themselves on the great questions of our time and thus avoid the sly intellectual dictatorship of those who control the media and the [public opinion] surveys.

He plots an alternative means to harness the will of the people, to circumvent the debased institutions of liberal democracy. To defeat the sly intellectual dictatorship of the establishment, Le Pen seeks to deploy the plebiscite, the referendum. The plebiscite is not an instrument for reasoned appraisal of public issues; rather it is a vehicle to establish expressionism and populism at the center of public discourse. Its strategic aim is to liberate the power of the irrational, the unconscious, and the intuitive.

## Sacred Realm

Le Pen hits the full force of his exegesis when he turns to the state of the nation. He renders the nation not merely a political but a sacred realm. The nation is under siege; the establishment, the political class, those appointed to protect and defend France, have abrogated their responsibilities. They are silent while the sacred patrimony is plundered:

> Do the Nation and its servant the State still exist anywhere else than in history books and in the hearts of patriots? What are its territorial boundaries, its independent and controlled space since we have, in accordance with interna-

tionalist ideology and the Maastricht Treaty, erased the borders and thus the customs? Who is a citizen? What are his or her rights and duties? Is the foreigner at home in France? But who must pay then?

He draws on the occult resonances of blood and earth:

> Is there still for the French people a common destiny, a will to live together, within a proud but not necessarily haughty identity? Is the land—not only the one which our landscape and our crops grow on—still present in our minds and in our hearts, the one, sacred place, where our ancestors and our fathers are buried, and the one for which, for two millennia, those who have given their life and blood to defend it have died, the one at last which we bequeath to our children after we pronounce our "nunc dimittis"?

Le Pen insists that the language of nation has been abandoned, depriving the state and its citizens of collective purpose. All that remains are "sinister utopias" demanding yet further regimes of vacuous "modernization" and traitorous "internationalization." The French citizens are being transformed into mere consumers, mere voyeurs:

> The political class no longer answers these questions, silent in shame or fear. Before it came to power, these questions were so much taken for granted that they were not asked. Nowadays, they are blurred, indirectly approached by the mental AIDS of the ruling class, by the pressure of foreign influences and interests. Never like today has France been threatened in its existence and its essence. And for the people to be defended and protected, these questions must be answered. People do not need a national defense if there is no nation, no homeland—if they are just a herd of consumers or television viewers, or voyeurs, and are not aware and responsible actors: if they are not citizens. There is no national defense without nation and nationals, and no nationals without national preference. There is no national defense without homeland and without love of the homeland.
>
> So it is not enough, as we are told, to modernize and to adapt ourselves. An army needs to know what we want, where we are going, with what means and how? The government is destroying it all because it no longer conceives the army as French, at the service of France, but as a part of an international police force at the service of an international government: sinister utopia, horrible betrayal.
>
> Everything is accomplished in the silence of "the great cemeteries under the Moon." We heard no minister, or representative, or general or admiral's door slamming. The order seems to be: "Gentlemen, France is dying, do not disturb its agony."

Le Pen's use of metaphor is grandiose, his attack relentless. But what is distinctive about his rhetoric, even when it verges on the ludicrous, is the way it achieves that pseudo-intimacy noted earlier, that connects him with the listener. He speaks with an intelligence that seems thoroughly attuned to the experience of the listener; his language is highly refined but emphatically antielitist. By this means he creates an errant basis of legitimacy.

## We Talk

Le Pen will speak out proudly as a patriot for his sacred patrimony with its glorious past. It is a past that fills him with respect, humility, honesty, and gratitude. Haughty empires fall, but the nation endures. He emphasizes its human scale, which allows the nation to serve the wants and needs of the people. From these mysterious reciprocities, from this love, he summons the defiant will to resist those forces within and without which threaten France:

> Well! *We* talk, *we* know what has to be done and we say it. We have a will. The will to defend the Homeland, the Nation, the State, because they are the worthiest property of the French people of today and tomorrow.
>
> Against the Euro-internationalists, we defend the Nation. We defend it, not only because we love France as its sons—this would be respectful—not only because we admire its glorious past, but out of gratefulness and honesty. We know very well that we can never—even if we were the greatest scientist, the greatest poet, the greatest musician of all times—give back to her what we owe her, but also because we know (and this is true for all the nations of the world and it explains in fact why the nationalists of Europe and tomorrow, those of the world, are beside us in the struggle) that the nation today, while haughty empires are falling apart, is the most effective human-scale political framework to ensure the security, the freedom, the dignity, the identity, the prosperity of the citizens, of our people.

But he makes it unmistakable who and what constitute the real enemies of the nation and what constitute the contemporary terms of struggle:

> So obviously enough, internationalism—the doctrine of an international government, which claims to be justified by an internationalization known as unavoidable and profitable for the economy—is today the sworn enemy of nations and patriots. They [patriots] are indeed the only ones to oppose the Big Brother's on-the-move dictatorship.
>
> But, as far as the economy is concerned, the destruction of borders gives our production and jobs away to the unfair competition of countries which have no social taxes. For twenty years we have been forewarning that this policy, implemented at home by the right as well as by the left, would result in ever growing unemployment and a continuous fall of wages, thus leading the way to revolutionary destabilization. On the other hand, exportationism ends up in the giv-

ing up of our home market and in the loss of self-sufficiency, the guarantee of our freedom.

This is one of the most fundamental integralist claims: it is not the abstract principles of the republic but the mysterious endowments of the nation that are the true guarantors of human freedom. Hence, only the patriot can defeat "Big Brother's on-the-move dictatorship."

## Venom

Le Pen's critique turns venomous when he addresses his enemies and the enemies of his party. He points to rampant corruption, hypocrisy, and ineptitude on the part of the political establishment. He scorns "sly intellectuals," "the privileged ones," and their elite discourse. Again, he is scathing in his attack on the media, as an appendage of the political establishment, that misrepresents "reality" and debases the "truth." The "red mayoress" and what Le Pen sees as fraudulent protests against him and his party, however, ignite the full force of his rhetorical fury:

> The left, the right, the media, the trade unions, the masonic sects, that is to say all the privileged ones, all the prebendaries of the system mobilize in their hysteria in order to try and contain the National Front's compelling rise. Compelling because our successes are only partially due to a movement which has no television, or radio, or mass press, no representatives [in parliament], 4 mayors out of 36,000; rather, our successes are due only to courageous and dedicated militants who are committed to fight for a true and a good cause. Our electoral advancements are mainly due to the public's awareness that they are being robbed, duped, betrayed by those in charge and by those who are paid to defend them. . . .
> I am happy that there are here numerous foreign politicians and hundreds of French and foreign journalists who will be able to testify to what they saw here. Those who are going to discover the real face of the National Front are undoubtedly numerous and this face has nothing to do with the gross and deceitful caricature usually drawn of it. Regardless of the facts, it is stated on the one hand that the National Front has no political program or that the latter is no good, that it is against the republic, against democracy, that it is antiparliamentarian, racist, xenophobic, anti-Semitic, that it is insignificant and powerless for some, frightening and dangerous for others. Its assailants charge it with hatred and violence while they are precisely those people who attack FN meetings with an iron bar in their hands. The establishment is panicking.

He goes on to link each of his opponents to wider historical dramas, restaging his struggles on an epic scale:

> Strasbourg is in a state of siege, not because of the National Front Conference as [mayor] Trautmann would have it, but because of her friends. We have held

ten conferences in France in twenty-five years, there never were more than a few policemen in the street. If today there are more than two thousand, it is because of the threat to public order represented by the demonstrators who have come in subsidized buses and trains to intimidate, to threaten, and, for some, to attack our conference.

With disdainful hypocrisy, the red mayoress thinks she has discharged her responsibility when she calls for peace, like the arsonist shouts "fire" after he spreads gasoline. To the left, they are short of breath and imagination. They endlessly watch their former government ministers, their representatives, their senators, their mayors, compromised in criminal affairs.

He associates his opponents with cadres of parasitic supporters who enact counterfeit democratic protests:

The antifascist front neck and neck with the communists whose hands yet, like those of Lady Macbeth, remain indelibly stained with the blood of the 200 millions of communism's martyrs, neck and neck with the sitting-room anarchists, social betrayers and old-Stalinists, friends of Maastricht, arm in arm with the prebendaries of the national companies, the fake trade unionists, and the café intellectuals. They take action with the complicity of hired editorial writers, professional petitioners and marchers, compelled to be there [at the anti-FN demonstrations], for fear of being evicted from the trade-union local or community machinery, where they are thriving.

They forget that the democracy they crow about is not the law of the street, of the demonstrations, of the loudmouths or the fist. Democracy is the law of the vote. One man, one vote. And if you were ten thousand or twenty thousand to have come from all over France [for demonstrations in Strasbourg], you would still only be a twentieth or a tenth of the voters I have gathered in my name in [the election in] two departments of Alsace.

And two months of a campaign of steady lies, provocations, insults, the call of more than a hundred parties of the left and trade unions from across Europe, the support of the mayoress, that of [Daniel] Cohn-Bendit's Trotskyite comrades, was necessary to rouse a few thousand demonstrators.

I understand that the left suffers from stomach pains when they see the workers, the employees, the unemployed voting for the National Front. They are collecting the price of betrayal. The right, they are hugging the walls. The marches are none of their business. They do not need this; they have the television, which they refuse to the National Front. Less than three hundred Alsacians came to listen to a delegation of their little runts.

He turns to a belligerent comparative history, daring, if not threatening, journalists in the audience to abandon their derisive comparisons equating his movement with fascism and Nazism:

In the few weeks, in fact since [the election in] Vitrolles and the undoubted and undoubtedly democratic victory of our friend Mégret, the craziest accusations, the most scandalous qualifying terms have been ascribed to us. From extreme right, a parliamentary geographic location to which we object, we have moved to extremist right, to neofascist, then to fascist and at last *reductio ad hitlerium*, to Nazi. Look closely, ladies and gentlemen of the press, and, if you dare, write that what you saw here is a reedition of the Nuremberg Conference—you would make the whole world laugh.

Those who write this are ignoramuses or liars. Fascism and Nazism were two totalitarian movements of socialist, equalitarian, revolutionary thought with like origins. . . . [Their leaders] were inspired by French revolutionary extremists who advocated terror as a means of government. Those who are making this judgment upon us, their friends, their allies, are responsible for the gulag. On this matter, I would like to denounce here the lie of the antiracist activists who are doing a real job as agitators, subsidized by considerable amounts of money coming from the taxpayers' pockets.

Le Pen focuses his exegesis back to the mayor and her insulting removal of the statue of Saint Joan. Her tactic symbolizes for him precisely the violation of a true French history that can confer sanity and coherence on human affairs. Rather, he thinks, she and the political establishment prefer distortions of history that draw simplistic truths in black and white:

A nation only has a future if it keeps a fair and sane vision from its past, with the right part of light and shadow. If we shame the people or if they are ashamed of their past, they have no future. If political parties, in the 1930s and in the dark years, may be ashamed of their cowardice and mistakes, this has nothing to do with our movement whose leaders were not born at that time. . . . The National Front is a national patriot movement which Ms. Trautmann thought she was insulting when she brought down the statue of Joan of Arc, but *they* [members of the FN] scrupulously respect the rules of democracy and of the republic. Not only in words but also in deeds.

Ms. Trautmann, never have our militants attacked your meetings or your conferences as your bullies are. Never did we appeal to hatred, as a representative of the majority, surely a little drunk, did on television. Never in fact did we scapegoat immigrants or others. We have always said that the only ones responsible were the French politicians, incapable and corrupt.

We are neither racist, nor anti-Semitic, as this conference shows. In fact, we have militants of all races and all colors. But we do not accept attacks or insults from anyone, neither by whites nor Catholics, nor by Jews nor blacks, nor by thugs, nor penpushers. We are not xenophobic but Francophile, which should be quite allowed in France and which is not always allowed since there are politicians or magistrates hired to deny us the right to exist. The deluge of insane talk poured over us does not impress us nor does it intimidate us; on the contrary it strengthens us and roots us in our resolution.

## Treason

Contemporary political scandals take on a fateful significance in what Le Pen sees as the moral struggle for recuperation. Corruption is not merely evidence for him and his colleagues of personal malfeasance; rather it stands as proof of ongoing traitorous betrayals of the nation by mainstream political parties. Scandals are cast as acts of sedition. Each new expression of political corruption by those opposed to the NF is thus subject to a spurious historical appraisal whereby contemporary political "affairs" serve to erode the calumny of Vichy. Le Pen lays out a bill of particulars that amounts to a charge of treason against the broad swath of the French establishment:

- the death of the republican state: France is no longer more than a virtual republic and a democracy of appearances. The establishment is cut off from the people to the point that they disdainfully construe as "populism" and as "demagogy" that which yet makes the essence of democracy: the government must answer the citizens' needs and expectations. . . .

  The sovereign institutions are in a state of crisis and the confusion of the powers is spreading: judges pretend that they make the law . . . the police play the role of social-workers . . . the republican schools no longer play their role of integration and civic education, the army is becoming a mercenary troop at the service of the new international order.

  In the hands of the establishment . . . the state rises against the nation and against the French people born of French parents: the recognized aim of the establishment is indeed to dissolve the nation-state, that is to say France.
- the setting up of the Maastricht order which is going to withdraw from the state the first attributes of sovereignty (the currency, the control of the borders, and budgetary control). . . .
- by the opening up of the borders in the name of Anglo-Saxon liberal dogmas.
- by the submission to the law coming from abroad, the law of foreigners: already . . . more than 40 percent of the laws are made in Brussels.
- by the capitulation before . . . immigration. . . .
- by the submission to the human rights ideology without the citizen, conveyed by the . . . media and the supposedly moral authorities, which, in fact, is a weapon of war against the people and the nation. . . .
- by the setting up of a totalitarian order which, every day a little more, threatens freedoms: the freedom to research, the freedom to spread one's thought . . . the freedom of the press . . . and more and more the freedom to meet . . . and the freedom to join the political movement or the trade union of one's choice. . . .
- the establishment spreads violence and hatred when they vilify the French people who join the national movement when they make them second-class citizens.

- the establishment betrays France when they introduce foreign preference and when they refrain from pushing back immigration.
- the establishment betrays national independence when they dissolve our country in European federalism, when they reintegrate our military forces in NATO, when they submit to American domination and when they reduce our defenses. . . .
- the establishment falsifies History when they want to persuade us that our country has always been a land of immigration and when they pretend that France is guilty for the horrors of the Second World War.
- the establishment betrays the Republic and democracy by disregarding the citizens' equality before the law, by creating special rights for foreigners and by trying to introduce quotas. The establishment threatens the Republic when they remain deaf to the people's demands for more security, less immigration, less taxes.
- the establishment spreads concern and despair by letting unemployment and poverty grow.
- the establishment lets a climate of civil unrest progressively set in by exposing a growing part of the electorate to the condemnation of the media.

   The establishment accuses the national movement of exploiting the French people's distress, even of provoking it, whereas we are only expressing and answering it. On this point, the establishment does precisely the opposite of the national movement: they are deaf to French preoccupations and do not answer them. We are fighting for a great change, for a genuine liberal, fiscal, social, familial, moral, popular, cultural, democratic, republican, national alternative.

These attacks go beyond mere partisanship to a militant integralism that is uncompromising and inherently unconstrained by the restrictions of mainstream political participationism. It is this remarkable latitude for populist critique—poised against the left and the right—that generates a distinctive rhetorical power, one that limits its expression within a parliamentary framework of coalition and cooperation.

## Alternative

Le Pen espouses a political program that is and must be removed from what he sees as the corrupt practices of the political establishment. He sets out a systematic integralist alternative that has clarity and immediacy:

   The social alternative is the will to carry out, for the benefit of the whole people and their welfare, the fundamental political reforms without which there will not be any straightening up of the economic situation, and thus no remedy for the social disaster. It is not a question of assisting the French people and of seeing that they evolve from diploma-awarding training to RMI [minimum welfare payment] while awaiting retirement pension or preretirement pension, but it is a question of ensuring employment within our borders. . . . The social alternative also means the raising of low wages . . . it means the defense of workers' social security by the most appropriate combination of health and pension benefits.

Our alternative is familial because it envisions a great family policy by the reevaluation of family allowances, the creation of parental or maternal salary. Families in charge of children are, indeed, the most affected by impoverishment.

Our alternative is familial because it offers to restore to the family its key role in the education and the teaching of the child. Our alternative is familial because it is based on the respect of life. Our alternative is familial because without a dynamic change of our demographic trend, France is doomed.

He reasserts the classic integralist formula. Social, economic, and political recuperation is only possible through a prior restoration of the moral and spiritual integrity of the nation. The instrument for this recuperation is a democratic populism that can ignite the will of the people and engender a liberatory insurgency:

Our alternative is moral. It aims at replacing a corrupted political class. A political class corrupted by scandals, corrupted by business. But also corrupt by the loss of the spiritual dimension of life, the loss of the meaning of their mission and of their role. A political class forgetful of their being here to serve the people and the nation, not the lobbies and the foreign interests, which no longer respect the spirit of democratic institutions.

Our alternative is popular, some even say populist, and we are not ashamed. Quite the contrary, we are proud of it. We are proud to defend a program that answers to the people's expectations: surer, more deeply rooted, more French cities. Yes, our alternative is popular because it proposes to reduce immigration and this is what the French people want. Yes, our alternative is popular because it proposes to punish criminals and to reestablish the death penalty for murderers and this is what the French people want. Yes, our alternative is popular because it proposes to put some order in France and this is what the French people want.

Democracy is the governing of the people, by the people, and for the people. It is not the people's government by the lobbies and for the prebends! The democratic alternative is the reestablishment of the parliament's powers. . . . The democratic alternative is to make the people the ultimate arbitrators of the great choices. The democratic alternative is not to make of the French vote an act without consequences; it is to make of the French vote the hub of decision making on French matters.

The law of democracy is that of the ballot boxes, that of the universal suffrage. One man, one vote: this slogan was good for [Nelson] Mandela and cannot be denied to Le Pen. The will of the people expresses itself not in the opinion polls, or in the street demonstrations, but in free and fair elections. European policy, immigration policy, the death penalty, taxation policy, it is for the people to decide by means of the referendum and a referendum of popular initiative.

Populism becomes the means to reengage the French people with the cultural genius and grandeur of the nation:

> A people's culture is related to its history, its past of events, lives, adventures, discoveries, struggles, artistic, literary, poetic creations. They give it an originality, an identity of its own, a synthesis of spirit and matter, of genius, talent, and labor.
>
> The state's role is to preserve and to enhance the cultural patrimony, to ensure its promotion in France and in the world, as well as to ensure the passing on of cultural and artistic knowledge and the promotion of our language, to contribute to Humanity's treasure by sustaining its national specificity. The state must not impose the fashions of its time, leaving this initiative to the artists and the patrons whose efforts it can fiscally support.

The Republic is recast as the vehicle for the protection of a distinct French nation and its people:

> Our alternative is republican because we want to give the republic back to the French people, the One and Indivisible Republic. But today the Republic is taken over by corrupt people—corrupt people who forget to serve France but do not forget to help themselves, corrupt people who are dishonest in the way they run public matters and political matters. Those who pretend to embody the republican tradition betray it. The Republic is the institutional expression of the nation's sovereignty—not submission to a new world order—a device of the American empire, not the submission to international organizations. The Republic is guarantor of the national security, it is the same law for all, all over the territory, not the law of communities, not the laws of the bands. The Republic is the equality of right, not the "positive discriminations" or ethnic taxation—in the American way. Yes we say that there must be equal rights for all French people. Yes we say that the meaning of republican equality, threatened by the return of privileges, must be rediscovered by:
> - the suppression of positive discrimination measures and of foreign preference (which are contrary to the 1789 Declaration).
> - the effective respect of the secularism principle (whereas today the debate on secularism conceals the preference for religious minorities).
> - the reestablishment of the rule of law all over the territory (reduction of the "sanctuarised" suburbs) and on all those who inhabit them (for example, the

suppression of the social agencies' actual tolerance concerning polygamous practice of foreigners). . . .

Liberty, equality, and fraternity are refracted through this integralist lens as principles of exclusion, differentially conferred on those who are deemed French and those who are deemed foreign.

## Synthesis

He concludes with an ardent synthesis that captures the form and content of his theory of society, its metaphysical underpinnings, its moral affirmations, its pragmatic aims:

> At last, of course and above all, the national alternative is the nation's choice and the giving up of internationalism and federalism. The national alternative is the recovery of national independence.
>
> The national alternative implies the reconstruction of a modern and credible national defense, on the basis of a budget of about 5 percent of the GDP. The national alternative is the choice of the nation's independence by breaking the chains of international organizations: the UN, NATO, the European Union. It is also the denunciation of the Maastricht and Schengen treaties, the reestablishment of borders, the negotiation of agreements to create a Europe of nations and the maintenance of the national currency.
>
> The national alternative is the reestablishment of the supremacy of the French law over foreign laws, treaties, European laws and directives. The national alternative is the establishment of the national preference principle, it is the reform of the nationality code and the repeal of double nationality, the introduction of the one-year—instead of ten-year—resident card, the organization of family groupings by country of origin [in ethnic ghettos].
>
> What the national alternative means is a France that recovers the pride of its past and of its heritage and that rejects attempts to create a sense of guilt and shame. So, yes, dear friends, dear companions, dear comrades, within the frame of the laws of the republic . . . our mission is not only an electoral mission, a political mission; it is a historical mission: for France and for the French people, first of all, but also for the peoples of Europe and for the peoples of the world who want to keep their identity.
>
> Our mission is to act so that France recovers its full sovereignty at the dawn of the twenty-first century: political, economic, monetary, cultural, diplomatic, military sovereignty by freeing ourselves from the chains of international organizations. Our mission is to mobilize the energies of the peoples struggling to defend their identity against the international order. Yes, we must give to France its traditional role of leader of the nations again, of an awakening of the people, and to assert loudly and strongly the right of the people to govern themselves.

In these times of great danger for the very existence of France and the French people, the necessity remains to call once more, relentlessly, for the patriots' unity.

Their love of the Homeland is the cement of their unity and the continuity of France.

**With us, neither right, nor left: France!**

Again, what is stunning is how Le Pen, drawing on what seems an outdated social imaginary, achieves such immediacy in his presentation. It is an immediacy that renders his exegesis a resounding politics of the present, a highly charged politics of contemporary France and Europe. The great power of this politics is its intimacy, its way of foregrounding experience, its way of operating as if it were indistinguishable from a style of life and a practice of belonging. These proclivities allow elite and subaltern sensibilities to intermingle in a volatile amalgamation that can span the traditional domains of left and right.

## Society

The dissonant theory of society that informs Le Pen's vision operates on three levels. The national socialist synthesis generates a logic or rationale for political practice as well as a strategy for opposing "Big-brother's on-the-move dictatorship." It is predicated on the sanctity of human collective endeavors, endeavors that must remain uncompromised and unsullied by crass materialism, technocratic pretense, and cosmopolitan cant. Collective history, values, and sentiments of the nation are treated as sovereign, determining the norms of society and the policies of the state. Populism, expressionism, and pluralism underpin the operation of Le Pen's national socialism. They establish the rules of human association, the character of human affinity and difference, the preeminence of human creative self-expression, and the enduring conditions of belonging (as well as the circumstances of alienation and estrangement). They provide access to the forces of the irrational, the unconscious, and the intuitive. They are, in turn, sustained at a yet deeper level by the mysterious registers of mechanical solidarity. At this deepest reach of society, legitimate forms of relationality are ultimately rooted in sacred symbols, in sentiments of blood and earth.

## THE WILL TO WIN

What follows is a deceptively simple speech, certainly as compared with Le Pen's panegyric. It is a speech that operates in a number of different registers. Blair opens with compassion and moderation. He recounts how the poorest people in Britain have been forgotten for the eighteen years of Conservative government. He proposes a new moral economy that can integrate the nation and create a new vision of national purpose. His analysis takes the point of view of the majority, privileging neither the interests of the wealthy nor the poor. Middle-class Britain, what he calls "comfortable Britain," is at the center of his social doctrine. Members of this middle class have been subject to new forms of insecurity as a consequence of the recessions and industrial restructuring of the 1970s and 1980s. This creates a common experience of economic vulnerability that, he believes, can link the interests of middle-class Britain to those of the underclass. He seeks to define the new era by a new ethic for "civic society" based on the purportedly simple idea that "we are all in this together."

Blair's account moves from this moderate register, to an engagement with insurgent sensibilities taking shape at the "radical center" of Britain. He sees a new mechanism aligning society and community spurred by the increasingly individualistic nature of modern economic, social, and cultural life. With a rather bold stroke he seeks to superimpose this emerging individualistic calculus onto the consciousness of the underclass, thereby drawing its members into his optimistic rendering of a "one nation Britain." This transfiguration is framed in liberatory rhetoric: empowerment, not punishment. It challenges the members of the underclass to jettison the legacy of "fatalism" and the "dead weight of low expectations" imparted by welfarism and to embrace an ethic of responsibility and "the will to win" that can spur his new Britain. Newman's observations in Chapter 6 suggest that the prerequisites for this conversion of underclass values is already in place. Newman decries precisely these individualistic and antisocial sensibilities that have surfaced among members of the underclass; they are, ironically, the predispositions that Blair seeks to foster and to harness as a new basis of integration.

Blair envisions a new bargain among all members of society, but particularly with the young. What is needed is a morality grounded in the core of British values, the sense of fairness and balance between rights and duties. The basis of this decent society is an ethic of mutual responsibility or duty. It is something for something. A society where we play by the rules. You only take out if you put in. That's the bargain. As Samuel Beer notes caustically, "Blair states the defining purpose of that [decent] society in a vivid oxymoron, 'compassion with a hard edge.' What he means is sharply expressed in his warning to young people not to lapse into dependency but to work to improve their skills, to avoid crime, sloth and disorderly conduct" (1998:25). These are the ethical foundations drawn from Thatcherism, which Blair has chosen to impel his social insurgency. He articulates his vision with great clarity:

> I have chosen this housing estate to deliver my first speech as Prime Minister for a very simple reason. For 18 years, the poorest people in our country have been forgotten by government. They have been left out of growing prosperity, told that they were not needed, ignored by the Government except for the purpose of blaming them. I want that to change. There will be no forgotten people in the Britain I want to build.
>
> We need to act in a new way because fatalism, and not just poverty, is the problem we face, the dead weight of low expectations, the crushing belief that things cannot get better. I want to give people back the will to win again. This will to win is what drives a country, the belief that expectations can be fulfilled and ambitions realized.
>
> But that cannot be done without a radical shift in our values and attitudes. When the electorate gave the Conservatives their marching orders after 18 years of government, they did so for more than reasons of political fatigue and "time for a change." They did so also because they thought that the values underpinning the Conservative government were wrong.
>
> The 1960s were the decade of "anything goes." The 1980s were a time of "who cares?" The next decade will be defined by a simple idea: "we are all in this together." It will be about how to recreate the bonds of civic society and community in a way compatible with the far more individualistic nature of modern economic, social and cultural life. . . .
>
> Today there is a possibility of an alliance between the haves and havenots. Comfortable Britain now knows not just its own form of insecurity and difficulty following the recession and industrial restructuring. It also knows the price it pays for economic and social breakdown in the poorest parts of Britain.
>
> There is a case not just in moral terms but in enlightened self-interest to act, to tackle what we all know exists—an underclass of people cut off from society's mainstream, without any sense of shared purpose.
>
> Just as there are no no-go areas for New Labour so there will be no no-hope areas in New Labour's Britain. To be a citizen of Britain is not just to hold its passport, it is to share its aspirations, to be part of the British family.
>
> But this new alliance of interests to build on "one nation Britain" can only be done on the basis of a new bargain between us all as members of society.
>
> We should reject the rootless morality whose symptom is a false choice between bleeding hearts and couldn't care less, when what we need is one grounded in the core of British values, the sense of fairness and a balance between rights and duties.
>
> The basis of modern civic society is an ethic of mutual responsibility or duty.

It is something for something. A society where we play by the rules. You only take out if you put in. That's the bargain. . . .

Blair, like Le Pen, espouses a species of populism that seeks to circumvent pivotal social distinctions in order to engage the entire British nation. He too seeks to act upon values, to engage the will of the British people, to overcome fatalism, and to create new possibilities for action. The proximate challenge is to reintegrate the dispossessed of Britain. Where his populism differs from Le Pen's is in its appeal to self-interest and its faith in the individual's willingness to participate in a civic bargain aimed at aligning social rights with civic duties:

> We must begin by being clear about the legacy we have inherited. Some people are doing well, but too many are left behind and falling down. It is a legacy that previous generations of Conservatives would have felt ashamed of. After several years of economic growth, five million people of working age live in homes where nobody works. Over a million have never worked since leaving school.
>
> For a generation of young men, little has come to replace the third of all manufacturing jobs that have been lost. For part of a generation of young women early pregnancies and the absence of a reliable father almost guarantee a life of poverty, and today Britain has a higher proportion of single parent families than anywhere else in Europe.
>
> These are the raw statistics. You can add to them the 150,000 people who are now deemed to be homeless; what may be as many as 100,000 children not attending school in England and Wales; the fact that nearly a half of all crimes take place in only a tenth of the neighborhoods in a country that has the worst crime record in the western world; the dozens of ailing schools that threaten another generation with unemployment and failure; housing estates cut off by failing bus services and where only a third of homes have a phone.
>
> Behind the statistics lie households where three generations have never had a job. There are estates where the biggest employer is the drugs industry, where all that is left of the high hopes of the post-war planners is derelict concrete. Behind the statistics are people who have lost hope, trapped in fatalism.
>
> If we are to act effectively it is vital that we understand how we got here. The industrial revolution of the 19th century created a new working class. Millions of people became key players in the economy—but lacked the basic rights to vote, rights of association at work, rights to security in old age. Then it fell to the Labour Party—and similar parties around the world—to bring that new class into the mainstream of society, through new rights and a comprehensive welfare state.
>
> Now at the close of the 20th century, the decline of old industries and the shift to an economy based on knowledge and skills has given rise to a new class: a workless class. In many countries—not just Britain—a large minority is play-

ing no role in the formal economy, dependent on benefits and the black economy. In 1979, only one in twelve non-pensioner households had no-one bringing in a wage; today one in five are in that position.

Without skills and opportunities people become detached not just from work, but also from citizenship in its wider sense. With each generation aspirations are falling. So that whereas a generation ago even the poorest believed that they had a chance to make it to the top, now children are being brought up on benefits and without hope.

Earlier this century leaders faced the challenge of creating a welfare state that could provide security for the new working class. Today the greatest challenge for any democratic government is to refashion our institutions to bring this new workless class back into society and into useful work, and to bring back the will to win.

The previous government failed that challenge because it believed that a divided Britain was sustainable. That we could afford to forget about a workless minority. That it might even be the price to be paid for competitiveness. But they were proven wrong. . . .

Blair provides a dismal picture of encroaching poverty in Britain at the close of the twentieth century. To reclaim the Labour Party's traditional commitment to societal transformation in the face of a new constellation of human struggles, he must jettison precisely those historical commitments to welfarism that were at the core of the party's covenant with the working class. Depending on one's perspective, Blair's analysis can be read as either courageous or disloyal insofar as it identifies at least part of the degradation and dependence of the underclass as the outcome of misdirected welfarism, of a welfare system that imparts values that are at best inappropriate, at worst simply wrong.

## Early Actions

The changes we seek will take many years and will involve many difficult choices. There are no quick fixes. But since the election we have made a quick start in dealing with this legacy. There have been no excuses, and no prevarications. And in every area, we have given substance to the claim that we will govern for the majority, on the basis that everyone has the opportunity and everyone the responsibility to contribute. . . .

In the absence of a clear philosophy of rights and duties the welfare system can discourage hard work and honesty. The benefits system penalizes the husband or wife of an unemployed person who takes up a job. It makes couples better off when they live apart. It locks people into dependence on benefits like housing benefit and income support when it should be helping them to get clear of benefits. It offers little incentive to work part-time, or for irregular earnings.

30 percent of people live in a household dependent on a means tested benefit, which discourages work and encourages people to hide any money that is earned.

The task of reshaping welfare to reward hard work is daunting. But we must be absolutely clear that our challenge is to help all those who want to work but are not working with the jobs, the training and the support that they need. That is why I am asking social security ministers to look at all the key benefits and apply a simple test—do they give people a chance to work or do they trap them on benefits for the most productive years of their lives. . . .

What we are talking about is empowerment not punishment, so that as many children as possible can grow up in working households with expectations of a job themselves.

What unites these policies is the idea that work is the best form of welfare—the best way of funding people's needs, and the best way of giving them a stake in society. They will help the under 25s who are the first generations since the war to expect their standard of living to be worse than their parents'.

What Blair proposes is to make the values of the welfare state congruent with what he sees as the emerging values of a wider political economy. Though he focuses on the circumstances of the underclass, he clearly has the entire nation in mind, his "one nation Britain." Again, he sees the fundamental challenge "to recreate the bonds of civic society and community," to make them compatible with the increasingly "individualistic nature of modern economic, social and cultural life." This is a radical agenda that seeks national integration not under the modernist banner of "solidarity" but under the communitarian aegis of "responsibility."

## The Ethic of Responsibility

To reverse the slide toward a divided nation, we also need to tap a wider ethic of responsibility. The making of one nation is not just a job of government. It is the task of everyone, a responsibility that applies as much at the top of society as at the bottom. . . .

In the 1960s people thought government was always the solution. In the 1980s people said government was the problem. In the 1990s, we know that we cannot solve the problems of the workless class without government, but the government itself must change if it is part of the solution not the problem.

We must never forget that a strong, competitive, flexible economy is the prerequisite for creating jobs and opportunities. But equally we must never forget that it is not enough. The economy can grow even while leaving behind a workless class whose members become so detached that they are no longer full citizens. . . .

Here in Britain our task is to reconnect that workless class—to bring jobs, skills, opportunities and ambition to all those people who have been left behind by the Conservative years, and to restore the will to win where it has been lost.

That will to win is what drives every country. There already is a new sense of hope and optimism in the country. People believe that there are new options, new possibilities. And I want everyone to be part of them.

This is a new government with a new sense of purpose. A government that believes in giving everyone the chance to succeed and get on in life. It is a government that has a will to win. To those who have lost hope over the last 18 years, I offer them a fresh start. The best thing any government can offer is hope and this is what I bring today.

## Deviation

Despite the more measured and less extravagant tone of his address, Tony Blair's proposal is no less radical than Jean-Marie Le Pen's. He too seeks to operate on society, to refurbish its moral substance. He reviews the traditional commitments of British socialism and finds them deeply compromised. "Today the leader of the Labour Party is telling us that the founding of the Labour Party was a great mistake and that he looks forward to reversing that fatal deviation" (Beer 1998:23). Indeed, Blair argues, the welfare state has become "the problem." He accounts its cost and burdens for government.[6] Its moral "costs" are perhaps the most devastating: fatalism, low expectations, the crushing belief that things cannot get better. It locks people into dependence on benefits like housing benefit and income support when it should be helping them to get clear of welfare. In the absence of a clear philosophy of rights and duties the welfare system can, he believes, discourage hard work and honesty. The welfare state creates a divided Britain and validates the workless practices of the underclass. Indeed, he suggests that welfarism threatens the very integrity of the British nation. Today the greatest challenge for any democratic government is, in his view, to refashion institutions to bring this new workless class back into society and into useful work, to redeem its members from worthlessness and inspire in them the will to win.

Work, Blair tells us, is the best form of welfare—the best way of funding people's needs, and the best way of giving them a stake in society. Enterprise offers salvation for the underclass. It creates new bonds of community compatible with the individualistic nature of modern economic, social, and cultural life. It is no longer an evil, no longer the instrument of exploitation, no longer the mechanism of injustice, but the dynamic medium for the creation of a new individualism. The capitalist regime need not be understood against the backdrop of the old satanic mills or of epic historical struggles pitting rich against poor. The system is to be appraised, in Blair's judgment, by a very narrow calculus. Duty and responsibility are the central axes of this new political economy.

These values emerge relatively unmediated by a social imaginary; rather they gain coherence only when fused to the agency of the autonomous individual within a competitive market economy. This is the political economy of empowerment, rather than punishment.

## Astringent Bargain

With each reference to the "workless" class in Blair's speech I find myself substituting "worthless" class. This misreading seems hardly an accident. Indeed, what the speech declares with striking clarity is that the fate of the working class no longer provides the central defining preoccupation of the Labour Party. The apprehensions of Beackon expressed in chapter 8 are essentially correct: New Labour has no use for the working class. The historical value of the industrial proletariat is exhausted, its romance spent. This renunciation of socialism is an audacious move by New Labour. And, though it has been gradually taking shape over the past two decades, its utterance as government policy, particularly by a Labour prime minister, is stunning. What is left are hapless figures like Derek Beackon, the workless man, who feels utterly betrayed, or the precarious members of the middle class like Newland. They become yet more absorbed in their involuted victimology.

The bargain that the prime minister extends to what he estimates as perhaps five million members of the workless class of Britain is elegant. It provides a clear formula for its reintegration into the land of hope and glory. For those who will not or cannot embrace the principles of a one nation Britain, however, the bargain is far more austere. What it promises, or threatens implicitly, is an altered status of a very different sort. It offers the underclass or workless class the status of the "new poor," as described by Zygmunt Bauman, who are fated to slip beyond the reach of political surveillance and intervention. Bauman articulates the unacknowledged premise of the one nation Britain. To restate Bauman's assertion: "The new poor are fully and truly useless and redundant, and thus become burdensome 'others' who have outstayed their welcome" (1997a). They constitute a new postindustrial "public," a paradoxical public that will, by virtue of Blair's political economy, no longer be of public concern. By obscuring or debasing the moral distinctions that adhere to the conditions of the poor, Blair can govern from the standpoint of the majority by dismissing as illusory differences of class, on the basis that everyone has the opportunity and everyone the responsibility to contribute. There is no doubt that his proposal to redraw the borders of national integration around the abstract principles of market exchange and the unfolding contingencies of individualization will create a New Britain.

What the retreat from socialism achieves inadvertently is the subversion of a comprehensive understanding of society. It was a British rendering of society upon which not only socialist politics was based, but also the medium through which a much broader sense of cultural coherence was conferred on social relations. "Society" served as the discursive space within which the terms of debate on social justice were calibrated. Above all, it provided an architecture—particularly as it came to be materialized within the welfare state—for national integration. E. P. Thompson has eloquently depicted how this rendering of society, embracing old solidarities that pre-date the industrial revolution, rooted the Labour Party and its project of a socialism within a distinctive British historical experience forged through generations of class-based struggle. New Labour has not only jettisoned but repudiated this cultural figuration of society along with the moral authority of class-based dispensations. For many in Britain the lifting of this outdated social imaginary is exhilarating, the discrediting of its simplistic and cloying moral interventions long overdue.

As argued in chapter 6, Margaret Thatcher's appeal to sections of the middle and working classes was based on the insinuation of a wide-ranging ambivalence about authority. Thatcher recognized that the Labour Party's agenda of social reformism and progressivism, intended to protect the interests of the working class, ratified its subaltern position. She relentlessly equated welfarism with dependency and subordination. Her ardent advocacy of individual enterprise and contempt for the entitlements of socialism subverted precisely those social values of deference to authority that have kept people in their place. Thatcher, in her authoritarian fashion, had found a way to become the champion of a compelling type of "agency." Tony Blair learned this lesson well. The election of the New Labour government further ratified this profound shift in public sensibilities; its victory was experienced across Britain with a genuine sense of release, if not liberation.

Perhaps the leaders of the BNP gleaned the implications of the Labour Party's new message before the rest of us. For them it is not merely the modernization of the party but the betrayal of the old social compact that orchestrated class collaboration and integrated an industrial Britain. Nonetheless, they see something hopeful in New Labour's program. What they recognized in Blair's political vision is the creation of a social imaginary where the BNP's reciprocal obsessions with national integration and social alienation appear reconcilable. They discern, as Emile Durkheim did a century ago, the inflammatory potential of anomie: "Social man necessarily presupposes a society which he expresses and serves. If this dissolves, if we no longer feel it in existence and action about and above us, whatever is social in us is deprived of all objective foundation. All that remains is an artificial combination of illusory images, a phantasmagoria vanishing at the least reflection; that is, nothing which can be a goal for our action" (1951:213). The odd characters that inhabit the prior two chapters of this text share with Durkheim an appreciation of the objective foundations of social reality, its significance for political actions, and its implications for personhood. The leaders of the BNP also know that those people, whose grasp of the social grounding of existence has ruptured, possess sensibilities that can inflame a stupefying politics. Their predilection for a brutal capriciousness propelled by "instincts" defines the margins of the political bargain proposed by Blair. On this marginal landscape where the BNP ranges a searing configuration of integralism can take form. It is here that alienation and anomie can sustain, paradoxically, solidarity and a fierce politics.

# Chapter Eleven

## ECLIPSE

THE TEXT concludes with an assessment of two ways that history can be revised and deployed politically in response to advanced European integration: the implication of one is ominous, the other more hopeful. Both rely on the eradication of pivotal historical distinctions upon which the moral discourse of society has rested during the twentieth century. The two figures I use to illustrate these revisionist interventions are the former MEP, Franz Schönhuber, and the Nobel Peace Prize laureate, John Hume, MEP. Their divergent positions summarize many of the central preoccupations of the text. The account by Schönhuber has an added significance, insofar as it helps explain a peculiar incident in the closing months of the decade that threatened to put an end to the political career of his comrade Jean-Marie Le Pen, an appropriate punctuation for this text.

### Details

With the exceptions of overt racism and overt anti-Semitism, the form of "historical revisionism" known as "Holocaust denial" represents the most controversial variant of the integralist insurgency; one that would seem to thoroughly discredit any effort at putting a moderate face on this type of politics. Le Pen, of course, has insinuated himself at the heart of this virulent controversy with his now infamous assertions that gas chambers are a mere "detail of history." For this offense he was tried and convicted in a French court in the late 1980s.[1] Like many of his other outrageous performances, his offense seemed initially almost inadvertent, perhaps even a misstatement or misquote. Gollnisch tried to put a salutary interpretation on this earlier infraction of his confederate:

> It was [during an interview in September 1987] when they pressed him to say exactly what he thought about the thesis of a paper written about the history of concentration camps during the Second World War. He [Le Pen] said, "I am not an historian, I am interested in how things are now." Then they asked if he believed in the Holocaust. [He said], "I recognize that millions of people died." [The interviewer then asked], "But would you like to say how they died?" [Le Pen responded], "Well it's a matter of detail." Now that word, "detail" can have two meanings in French: something which is part of a whole or something which is insignificant and of no interest. It is very clear, when you hear the

whole tape [of the interview], he said the way people were killed was of little matter compared to the fact that they were killed. But the media went on to use this [response] against him [Le Pen] as a political weapon.[2]

In 1997 Le Pen repeated "the detail of history" statement on at least two separate occasions, once in a *New Yorker* interview and again at a news conference in Munich. Le Pen was in Germany promoting a new book by his friend and former colleague, Franz Schönhuber, entitled, *Le Pen the Rebel*. True to the title, Le Pen used the occasion to clarify his earlier inflammatory declaration: "I will say it again, the gas chambers were a detail in the history of the Second World War. If you take a thousand-page book written on this war you will see that fifty million people died, the concentration camps fill two pages and the gas chambers take up 10 to 12 lines. That is what you might call a detail." The statement opened him to a series of new, more aggressive legal prosecutions. Nine civil rights groups filed a complaint based on the Munich incident in the same French court that found Le Pen guilty in 1987. They won a judgment requiring Le Pen to pay a substantial fine to publish the text of the French court's disparaging decision in a dozen French newspapers (Whitney 1997). More significantly, in late 1998 at the behest of a state prosecutor in Munich, the European Parliament by a vote of 420 to 20 stripped Le Pen of his parliamentary immunity, which exposed him to criminal charges under German law; Articles 130 and 220 of the German Criminal Code make it an offense to approve of, deny or present as inoffensive any act committed under the Nazi regime.[3] In June 1999 the German court found him guilty and subjected him to an unspecified fine.

Le Pen's willful reiteration of the obnoxious claim suggests that, far from a faux pas, the assertion holds a central place in his integralist vision. Yet, it is hard to fathom the purpose of this apparently self-destructive ploy, which may well contribute to terminating his career and fatally splitting his political movement.[4] The fact that Le Pen chose to make his derisive pronouncement in a German city with Franz Schön-huber at his side suggests, I think, a curious intentionality. Indeed, Le Pen, in making his tendentious comment, was deferring to Schönhuber's proj-ect, the project of an integralist history.

Schönhuber, as one of the founders and former president of Die Re-publikaner, a small German nationalist party, made a career of shaping an integralist politics out of "war stories" (Leggewie 1990). Schönhuber published a best-selling series of accounts of his war and post–World War II experiences. The crucial feature of his populist history of the war and its aftermath is that Schönhuber "lived it from within" as an eighteen-year-old volunteer in the *Leibstandarte* SS Adolf Hitler.[5] What resulted, as he described it for me in an interview at the European Parliament, was a defiant history—a "horrifying totality"—in which Germans were, like the Jews, "victims."[6] He insisted that prevailing modes of historical narration do not conform to the real experience of National Socialism. Although his message seems to be morbidly preoccupied with the past, his politics are emphatically about the present, about a unified Germany within a unifying Europe. His project is oriented to finding a means by which Germany can "escape" what he calls "its Babylonian captivity," "the reigning image of Germans as criminals."

Schönhuber's narrative relies on flagrantly discrepant memories of Nazi rule: he recalls twelve years of awesome power and achievement, yet he knows it as a period of unspeakable terror and destruction. For him, "to revive National Socialism now would be idiotic." What remains refractory, however, is some incomprehensible truth about those twelve years. The density of time, the complexity of circumstance, the scale of struggle, the breadth of misery extend beyond reach, and certainly beyond crude objective appraisal. In the extremes of exhilaration and despondency lurks an incandescent material, the substance of German identity. This is the inner landscape upon which his highly refined integral history rests. He rages against those who judge without experience. He avows that good and evil cannot be calculated on some abstract moral index. It is a past, he insists, that must be read from within, a past that yields certainties that are incommensurable with other histories based on mere external observation. The German establishment believed—under the sway of American pragmatism—that it need only "give people a good life and the German people will forget their problems and forget their past."[7] He utterly rejects this cynical view. He crusades for a German history for Germans, that accounts for their struggles, their courage, their honor even in the face of the most discredited cause of the twentieth century.

Schönhuber's stories ratify a portrayal of German experience that relies on the full force of the Counter-Enlightenment and its saturnine eschatology. That tradition allows him to embrace the staggering contradictions of the twentieth century while adamantly repudiating an "Americanized" history, a reductively rendered "victors'" account "imposed" on Germans. German children, he asserts, are prevented from knowing their real history because "the world will not tolerate a free-thinking Germany." This is precisely what Le Pen was intimating by his assertions: Germans should not be dominated by the external facts—mere "details of history"—that have constrained them as a nation since the Second World War.

Schönhuber, in league with Le Pen, ventures to usurp factual, empirically oriented history with the inner truths and emotional enthrallments of an exculpatory, integral history. They understand that the historical facts of the Second World War have established the moral parameters of mainstream political discourse in Europe. To render the sublimities of their politics truly viable, they must discredit *that* history, its moral constraints and its ethical restrictions. It is by no means the mere details of history that they seek to challenge; it is the facts of history. In place of these facts they endeavor to instill their liberatory narratives, narratives that can sustain a construal of collectivity that draws on the full force of populism, expressionism, and pluralism. It is, in their view, the only means by which "true" freedom can be restored to Europeans and the intellectual legacy of the Counter-Enlightenment reclaimed.

## Europeanization

John Hume, MEP, too embraces a radical approach to history, one that interweaves Catholic social doctrine and French social modernism. Using familiar elements drawn from the European project, Mr. Hume is able to conjure an emancipatory revision of Irish history that revealed those new political and institutional possibilities that ultimately led to the Good Friday Accord of 1998. He had in fact recognized the potential of this Europeanized approach to the history of Ireland as early as the 1970s, and he tenaciously fought for its recognition over the course of three very difficult decades of Irish history. What he proposed was a classic application of the idea of Europe as formulated by the founders of the EU, a formulation that seeks to transcend integralisms of both Republicans and Unionists by tracing a path of deliverance out from their fraught inner landscapes. In the spirit of Schuman and Monnet, he sought to insinuate the European idea in order to disable precisely those distinctions upon which Irish sectarianism rests.

Since 1979 Hume has been leader of the Social Democratic and Labour Party [SDLP] in Northern Ireland. The central agenda of the party is nonviolent Catholic nationalism, civil rights activism, and urban socialism. Hume entered politics through the Catholic civil rights movement in Derry in the late 1960s. He was elected to the Stormont Parliament in 1969, to the European Parliament in 1979, and to the British House of Commons in 1983, holding the latter two positions concurrently. In spring of 1997 Hume gained a powerful ally, an ally who was well versed in social Catholicism and the metaphysics of European integration, the Right Honorable Tony Blair, PM. Blair's framework for the devolution of Scotland, Wales, and Northern Ireland dovetailed with Hume's historical answer for the Irish question. In the fall of 1998, he and David Trimble, leader of the Ulster Unionist Party, were awarded the Nobel Peace Prize for their campaign for sectarian reconciliation. Hume framed his revisionism as follows:

> You must understand that the Irish problem is European in its origin. In the protestant tradition it is European. In the Catholic, nationalist tradition it is

also European. For example the Battle of the Boyne was [part of] a European war. The Danes were there, the Dutch were there, the Germans were there, the French were there on both sides, the Irish on both sides and the Scots. They [the Europeans] have long since settled [their disputes]. The Irish still hang on.

After the French Revolution, the French invaded Ireland to assist the Irish republicans. England responded by passing the Act of Union between England and Ireland. In a sense, the British-Irish problem resulted because the English regarded Ireland as a back door for her European enemies. That is the center of the conflict over sovereignty and independence. Now the European Community has changed the fundamental nature of the quarrel. Both Ireland and Britain now have pooled their sovereignty and inter-depend at European levels.

But there is a legacy of the past. That legacy is a deeply divided people, with divided loyalty. I would hope that we could find a European approach to resolving these differences. If someone had said 50 years ago that you would have a united Europe, when the slaughter [of World War II] was at its height, when millions were dying, you would have said he was a nut case. But it has happened. The great achievement of the European Community has been—this is underestimated by those who only look at economies and markets—the enormous saving of human life. Europe discovered that the answer to difference is not rivalry or conflict or war. It discovered that the real key to stability is the acceptance of difference. The essence of stability and unity is the acceptance of diversity. The United States recognized this as its founding principle. . . . It has the message in its foundational documents. People driven from Europe because of intolerance decided they weren't going to let it happen again—"*E Pluribus Unum.*" Europe only discovered this [lesson] after the Second World War.

Hume went beyond the mere idea of Europe to a direct embrace of its institutional formulaic, its science, political economy, and metaphysics of solidarity, which he translated into a simple Irish vernacular as the acknowledgment of "common ground." He began this process, which culminated in the signing of the Good Friday Accord on April 10, 1998, as a member of the power-sharing executive under the Sunningdale Agreement in 1973 and with his participation in drafting the Anglo-Irish accord of 1986, which gave Dublin a limited say in the affairs of Northern Ireland. He gave me a copy of an SDLP discussion paper dated April 1981 in which the institutional structure of the EC is directly superimposed on Northern Ireland and the Republic and an escape from history is plotted:

> *Hume*: What they [the founders of the EC] agreed to do was to leave the past behind. As you know, people in Ireland still call up the past to justify the present and, of course, paralyze the future. They continually whip up the old emotions. The next thing they did was establish a set of institutions that respected difference and permitted them to work toward a common ground. The

common ground initially being coal and steel and subsequently the wider economic community. By working toward a common ground over the last generation, by spilling sweat and not blood, the barriers broke down, and they evolved into a united Europe.

I am asking that the same formula be applied to Ireland. I am saying to the Irish government and the British government to declare the past over. Declare that you are going to build institutions in Ireland, North and South, that respect differences but which allow work toward a common ground—the common ground again being economic. That common ground is very strong at the moment, because the interests of Ireland, North and South, are closer than the interests of any part of Ireland and Britain. . . . There is a need for the Irish to find institutional arrangements to create a common ground. They can then grow together at their own speed into a united Ireland. That is the strategy I am pursuing. It may be successful, it may not. It is inspired by the European example.

*Holmes*: Wasn't this precisely the aim of the Anglo-Irish accord?

*Hume*: Yes, the Anglo-Irish agreement was modeled, if you look at the institutional arrangements, [on the European Union]. There is the Anglo-Irish conference modeled on the Council of Ministers [of the EU]. Its secretariat is the equivalent of the commission [of the EU]. There is a parliamentary tier exactly modeled on this institution [the European Parliament].

*Holmes*: You have taken advantage of the political [as opposed to the economic] possibilities of the European idea as it relates to nationalism?

*Hume*: The nationalism that created the world wars was about territory instead of about people. If you go back to the last half of the nineteenth century and the first half of the twentieth century, you see that conflict was about the right to territory, not the rights of people. What Europe has discovered is that its humanity transcends nationality. My argument about Ireland is that it is a unified piece of earth. It's the people that are divided. You cannot unite people by force. You cannot say that because a majority of the people on that territory want it to have a particular governmental form, it has to have that form. Democracy is not merely majority rule [in the late twentieth century]; democracy is majority rule with the consent of the entire community, particularly when there is a divided community.

Hume's vision of a European formula for the peaceful integration of North and South is central to the institutional provisions and language of the three "Strands" of the Good Friday Agreement. In the spirit, if not letter, of Jean Monnet's model, Strand One of the agreement creates an Executive Committee and Assembly, Strand Two establishes a North/South Ministerial Council, and Strand Three specifies a British-Irish Intergovernmental Conference: the three strands seek to weave crosscutting institutional relationships that circumvent or transcend preexisting

power relationships for the purposes of, in Hume's language, construct-
ing new institutional ties that create a literal "common ground" for the
Irish people, irrespective of borders.[8]

## INSTABILITIES

These two efforts by Schönhuber and Hume to revise history and thereby
reformulate contemporary social possibilities represent the opposed positions that demark the borders of the political economy surveyed in this
study. Yet, as I have suggested throughout the text, these positions are at
the close of the century inherently unstable.

Hume creates for his politics of reconciliation an optimistic, Euro-Irish
populism crafted for the purposes of superseding an entrenched history of
sectarianism. It is a shrewd and courageous intervention. By summoning
a European purview, he recasts sectarian histories not as the parochial
victimologies common to integralist strategies, but as elements of a
broader political and cultural tableau implicating other peoples and other
histories of Europe. This recalls the pluralist vision intimated a decade
earlier during my encounters with the leaders of the Movimento Friuli.
What the Irish must do, according to this formula, is obvious. They must
redefine themselves not in terms of a spent nationalism or divisive sectarianism, but in terms of what Hume still believes is a viable modernist
project of Europe. Thirty years of bloodletting has made this an appealing
alternative for the majority of the people of Ireland as the referendum on
the accord in 1998 demonstrates. Hume is not prone to self-doubt. Yet
the formula he proposes provokes questions, the central questions that
dominated the first part of this text. Can the science, political economy,
and metaphysics of solidarity that has underpinned the European project
withstand the kind of corrosive transformations that advanced European
integration itself brings to Ireland, Britain, and rest of the EU? Can the
modernist project of society still provide a compelling moral framework
and institutional practice to mediate fundamental human differences in
the face of a fast-capitalism that flattens social distinctions, obscures perspective, and renders consensus at best elusive?[9] In the face of these questions, the pluralist problematic looms as the central cultural challenge of
European integration, its essential possibility and its abiding limitation.

Those integralists like Le Pen, who seek to exploit this cultural problematic, recognize acutely the failures of the EU's modernist agenda, its
interim nature, its apparent lack of a moral center (Anderson 1996). They
see the modernist project of the EU as an anathema to their claims of
cultural distinction. They retain an ardent faith in the sovereignty of collective practices rooted in populism, expressionism, and pluralism. The

distinctions they summon not only provide a basis for action; they also provide a discriminatory rationale for an ethics of inclusion and exclusion. Above all, they retain a faith in collectivity tied to a discrete cultural milieu. Like Le Pen, Schönhuber insists on the deeply flawed character of the EU, but he also recognizes the instability and transience of his own political and historical aspirations.

Schönhuber betrayed a pessimistic assessment of his own fate and that of Le Pen and their respective German and French cohort. He invoked a temporality, one that suggested an eclipsing of their struggle. They were succumbing on "biological grounds," as he put it; they were old and dying off. He did not, in the spirit of the old soldier, fear death, but what he found acutely disquieting was the prospect of his political vision being debased by a new generation of Europeans, alienated from their own history and estranged from their own society. Without his integral history, a Germany of the young is being created that is increasingly divorced from its Germanness, its cultural genius. What he dreads is not so much a demise of integralist politics, but the proliferation of forms of integralism that are increasingly unstable, deprived of their *Führerprinzip*, and thus devoid of any mediating ideas save a fierce preoccupation with racism, anti-Semitism, and violence. These criminalized forms of integralism he knew were already taking hold among the young in rough neighborhoods of Germany. He recognized in their thuggish fascination with violence and bigotry the predispositions that recalled for him the SA men, the storm troopers, from his Nazi youth. Hence, what disturbs Schönhuber is the issue of succession, how his and Le Pen's heirs, the modernizers and the thugs, will use or misuse their collective histories, their creative legacies.

Le Pen and Schönhuber no doubt approve of the emergence of Jörg Haider as a notably skilled heir to their legacy; he has refined core elements of Le Pen's integralist insurgency as well as key aspects of Schönhuber's revisionism. Haider describes himself as a "modernizer," with, as he asserts, a very similar reformist program to that of Tony Blair, a claim the British Prime Minister has rejected vehemently. As a result of his party's electoral success in late 1999, the Austrian Freedom Party entered a coalition government in February 2000 with the appointment of six of Haider's leadership cadre to senior positions including Susanne Riess-Passer, vice chancellor; Karl-Heinz Grasser, finance minister; Herbert Scheibner, defense minister; Michael Krueger, justice minister; Elisabeth Sickl, social affairs minister; and Michael Schmid, minister of infrastructure. While these are powerful ministerial positions within Austria, these portfolios also confer membership in the Council of Ministers implanting Haider's associates at the heart of the EU's decision-making structure. Haider, however, resigned his leadership of the Freedom Party within a few weeks of taking power, presumably as a tactical move to appease an unprecedented offensive on the part of leaders of the EU to discredit him and his party as paragons of intolerance and antidemocratic values. Like Le Pen, Haider is more than capable of turning these denunciations to his advantage by simply portraying the EU's action as an arrogant usurpation of the will of the Austrian people.

What Haider's rise demonstrates is not merely that integralism is gaining a dynamic European cast while assuming an increasingly conventional veneer, but rather that a well-defined path has been cleared along which integralists of various persuasions can enter the political mainstream and pursue their distinctive orientation to power.

## PROXIMITY

What makes integralism an intriguing and troublesome subject for analysis is that it embraces cultural aspirations that are not generally understood as the basis of legitimate political contestation or worthy of serious anthropological depiction. This is ironic, given the affinities of these integralist ideas with the theoretical concepts that have defined the development of cultural anthropology (Wolf 1999:26-30). I initially portrayed this kind of political formation as an "illicit discourse." At the end of the study the illicit character of this politics seems, if anything, even more vexing as its committed partisans seek to redefine the relationship between individuals and collectivities. As I have suggested throughout the text, it is the unsettling potential of this politics to join, fuse, merge, and synthesize what might appear to be incompatible elements that is at the heart of its distinctive power and its perplexing ethical character.

From my earliest encounters with the practitioners of this insurgency, I was struck by how thoroughly they tested my own position and the integrity of my own observations. What I found unnerving was that as one entered or engaged this kind of political framework, it was very difficult to sustain an oppositional stance. I watched as those who attempted to oppose publicly integralists like Le Pen were themselves forced into a treacherous position of narrowly defining them as bigots or fascists and thereby foreclosing analysis and truncating political response. What is particularly disconcerting, as the speech in the preceding chapter suggests, is how effectively integralists can turn this kind of attack back against their critics, liberating the full force of their insurgent message. I have tried to circumvent this hazard by examining integralist agendas, not as reactionary aberrations, but as compendia of ideas and practices in their own right drawn from a formidable European intellectual tradition with which anthropology itself has an unsettling kinship. And as I have tried to show throughout the text, only by acknowledging the proximity of integralist ideals to more conventional political and cultural aspirations can we assess their intricate nature and their abiding danger.

This stance, derived from the work of Isaiah Berlin, imparted a specific interpretive strategy by which I allowed my informants' accounts to emerge on their own terms as, if not always coherent, certainly compelling symbolic compositions. I tried to keep my analysis as close as possible to their words, while encouraging them to provide the conceptual grounding for their at times salacious interpretive positions. My enduring interest in these political figures was not in their charismatic repartee or their lurid charms, but in their willingness to talk about how they understood the transformations unfolding around them and how they rendered these transformations politically meaningful. At the center of this metamorphosis is the status of European society as a moral framework, analytical construct, and empirical fact. I found these figures capable of endowing these epic changes with not just a powerful narration, but also a critical language, a language that drew on "inner truths" for its authority. What was most trying about the project was just this act of deference to the language and concepts of their fugitive politics; what was compelling was the recognition that this kind of politics can mediate fundamental transformations of European society.

I have also suggested that integralism can emerge as a far broader and more covert phenomenon. It can align cultural awareness and consciousness in a way that constitutes a pre- or postpolitics, wherein populism, expressionism, and pluralism operate as quiescent practices of collective belonging or virulent idioms of estrangement and alienation. Indeed, for the ethnographer, this manifestation of integralism may well be the most consequential, insofar as it provides a means to gain access to protean formations of experience and to inchoate struggles. It can allow ethnographic access to domains where acute and deeply felt human dilemmas are encrypted as prosaic narratives of past and present, as styles of life, as taste, as fashion; where abhorrent racial and ethnic distinctions are valorized; where personal injury and insult coalesces as cloying victimologies; where open political contestation is superseded by an intimate artifice defying conventional forms of abstraction, analysis, or public scrutiny. It is this emerging or reemerging field of European experience that I have begun to survey in this text. Integralism emerges out of this analysis both as a response to profound political transformations and, under special circumstances, as a politics in its own right. My overriding purpose in developing and using integralism as an analytical construct is to understand the refiguration of human collectivities, the shifting nature of society, and the stark dilemmas these changes can pose for the individual.

There is, however, one further issue incited by integralism: how do we engage it ethically and morally? Again, it is the peculiar proximity of integralism, by which our own values, and our own analytical conceits, are refracted back at us, that makes integralism so deeply unsettling. Unsettling too, is Berlin's emphatic assertion that populism, expressionism, and pluralism—the central components of integralism—imbue not just romanticism and fascism but also much of what constitutes the highest ideals of the humanistic tradition (1976; 1979; 1997). We are thus challenged ethically to probe not merely what constitutes acceptable or legitimate forms of expression and action, but rather to account simultaneously for reason and unreason, for the rational and the irrational, for the imperatives of the Enlightenment and the Counter-Enlightenment. For the ethnographer working in Europe, this means going beyond reflexivity to subtle and sustained forms of moral inquiry, inquiry that focuses on the deeply ambiguous nature of human belief and action. This is by no means a novel proposition. The first anthropologists to work in Europe in the twentieth century pursued precisely this analytical challenge in their classic studies of the social organization of small-scale European communities (Campbell 1964; Pitt-Rivers 1961). In delineating the concept of integralism I sought to reclaim this anthropological tradition in a way that allows engagement empirically and ethically with a very different constellation of historical circumstances and within very differently constituted ethnographic settings.

# NOTES

CHAPTER ONE
INNER LANDSCAPES

1. Berlin defines the Counter-Enlightenment tradition in the following rather dense passage: "Aggressive nationalism, self-identification with the interests of class, the culture or the race, or the forces of progress—with the wave of a future-directed dynamism of history, something that at once explains and justifies acts which might be abhorred or despised if committed from calculation of selfish advantage or some other mundane motive—this family of political and moral conceptions is so many expressions of a doctrine of self-realization based on defiant rejection of the central theses of the Enlightenment, according to which what is true, or right, or good, or beautiful, can be shown to be valid for all men by the correct application of objective methods of discovery and interpretation, open to anyone to use and verify. In its full romantic guise, this attitude is an open declaration of war upon the very heart of the rational and experimental which Descartes and Galileo had inaugurated" (Berlin 1979:18–19).

2. I have described the time, place, and general circumstances of these conversations in the text. All were conducted in English except the encounters with Jean-Marie Le Pen, which were in French and the encounters with Roberto Jacovissi and Marco De Agostini, which were in Italian. Though I met with most of these individuals on a number of occasions, it was generally the first encounters that proved most provocative and provided the material used in this text. These were usually scheduled appointments while the subsequent encounters were more chance encounters, for example in the offices, restaurants, hallways, or meeting rooms of the European Parliament. In most cases I was able to tape record some or all of the conversations, but I also relied heavily on handwritten notes jotted down during and immediately after these meetings.

3. Jane Cowan (1997) refers to these as "idioms of belonging."

4. The theme of the Counter-Enlightenment runs through Berlin's entire distinguished oeuvre and serves as one of the central unifying themes of his scholarship. See Wolf's concise summary of the Counter-Enlightenment tradition (1999:26–30).

5. "[Fascism] is not so much irrational as anti-rational, seeing the most distinctive human faculty not in the reason celebrated in the Enlightenment, humanist, and positivist tradition, but in the capacity to be inspired to heroic action and self-sacrifice through the power of belief, myth, symbols and *idée-forces* such as the nation, the leader, identity, or the regeneration of history" (Griffin 1995:6).

6. I use Christopher Herbert's (1991) account of the development of the culture concept in the nineteenth-century European ethnographic imagination in the second part of this text.

7. Harvey (1989) has stressed the importance of speed as "time-space compression" in the rise of modernism and as a distinguishing feature of the postmodern condition. See also Strathern 1992:143.

8. Balibar sees the usurpation of philosophies and agendas championing universality by the fact of a true globalization, a real interconnection of humankind. He also acknowledges how the sheer velocity of a technologically advanced and fully globalized capitalism liberates transformative processes that outpace philosophical design and sociological observation (1995:50).

9. Moravcsik (1998) has traced with great thoroughness the intricate process of decision making from the Messina Conference to the Maastricht Treaty, which instituted fast-capitalism within the EU.

10. This designation, of course, also sidesteps the notoriously difficult question of how to define "fascism" itself (see Griffin 1993).

11. Another compelling way to view the fascist predispositions of integralists like Jean-Marie Le Pen is offered by Roger Eatwell: "During the 1980s an academic boom industry developed in France, and elsewhere, dealing with the question of whether the FN could reasonably be termed 'fascist' or 'neofascist.' Most French academics tended to reject the tag, in part a reflection of a long-running tendency to play down the importance of fascism in France: instead they preferred 'Poujadist,' 'Bonapartist,' and especially 'National Populist.' What these arguments glossed over was that, in a sense, the FN was all of these things. It was deliberately vague about its core: Le Pen specifically denied that it had an ideology, portraying it more as the defense of common sense, a good populist theme. Recent developments within the FN, however, tend to indicate that there always was a core and its name is fascism. This is not to argue that Le Pen, or leading members of the FN, like [Bruno] Mégret, are closet Nazis—though the party clearly has this side at the local level. The point is related to a more fundamental ideology, to an attempt to create a new holistic community, to achieve a radical change in the nature of socioeconomic organization" (Eatwell 1996:325).

12. "[A]ntimaterialism was not just a negation of liberalism, whether in the form found in the 'social contract' school of thought or in the one represented by English utilitarianism, which from the beginning implied the democratization of political life and the reform of society. To an equal degree, toward 1900 antimaterialism also represented a rejection of the main postulates of Marxist economics and an attack on the rationalistic foundations of Marx's thought. It was the revolutionary syndicalists, those dissidents and nonconformists of the Left, who by means of their criticism of Marxist determinism created the first element of the Fascist synthesis in the first decade of our century" (Sternhell 1994:8).

13. See Adamson (1989:411–35; 1993) and Griffin 1992. Herf 1986 portrays the character of this intellectual tradition in Germany.

CHAPTER TWO
FLOWERING OF CULTURES

1. Smith (1999) provides a rich appraisal of precisely these elements of Raymond Williams's work and their relevance for anthropological inquiry.

2. See Jacovissi's (1980) nationalist manifesto.

3. By the early 1990s this political agenda was largely assumed by the Lega nord led by Umberto Bossi (Cole 1997; Schneider 1998). The ethnographic texts

by Cole (1997) and Carter (1997) examine the prospects of a multicultural and multiracial Italy.

4. This vision has come to be referred to as the "Europe of regions." See Nelde, Strubell, and Williams 1996.

5. The pivotal meeting took place on the steps of the cathedral between Herder and a young Goethe. The soaring Gothic style captured for Herder the "architectural style that best embodied the organic truths" he sought. "And his [Herder's] influence may well have swayed the young Goethe, himself delicately poised between classicism and Romanticism, toward the latter. During Goethe's long life he would veer back many times in the other direction. But for the moment he became an apostle, even plunging into the collection of local folklore and ballads around Alsace in a burst of Herderian zeal" (Schama 1995:237).

6. Subsidiarity has served as a template of the federalism forged between the German Federation and the Lander under the Basic Law. Though the term is not used explicitly in the text of the Basic Law, subsidiarity can be traced through a series of its provisions, notably Articles 30 and 72 of the Grundgesetz (Emiliou 1992:388–90). The fundamental assumption imparted by these articles is that "all government competence is presumed to lie with the Lander" (389). The express purpose of these provisions was "to limit centralization to the absolute minimum" (389). The effectiveness of this restraint on centralization is open to question given the tendency since 1949 to strengthen federal legislative powers in Germany. Nonetheless, the constitutional reality (*Verfassungswirklichkeit*) that has emerged from five decades of German postwar history is one of a deep commitment to "co-operative federalism," which Emiliou defines as "The political principles that . . . emphasize the primacy of bargaining and negotiated co-ordination among several power centers; they stress the virtues of dispersed power centers as a means of safeguarding individual and local liberties" (390n33). From my own experience at the Parliament, I found this notion of cooperative federalism deeply ingrained in the political values and ethics of virtually all German politicians I encountered, regardless of political party. Moreover, they equated these values and ethics explicitly with a subtle rendering of the concept of subsidiarity. I found it somewhat ironic that the German Social Democrats whom I encountered seemed, if anything, more enamored with the concept than their Christian Democratic compatriots. The successful political application of the principle of subsidiarity in the case of German federalism has endowed the concept with a broad-based legitimacy among those seeking a federal Europe.

7. All six of the foreign ministers who subsequently signed the European Coal and Steel Community (ESCS) Treaty were Christian Democrats (Judt 1996:40; see Berstein, Mayeur, and Milza 1993).

8. There is no doubt that national interests have been, and continue to be, prominent in Community/Union politics since its founding. One need only look at the circumstances surrounding the formulation of the Schuman Plan (Monnet 1978). Indeed, a powerful theoretical view of the EU holds that it is merely a new medium with new rules for the pursuit of national aspirations. See Milward 1992; Moravcsik 1998.

9. "The Treaty Establishing the European Economic Community" (signed in Rome on March 25, 1957) and the "Single European Act" (signed in

Luxembourg on February 17, 1986, and The Hague on February 28, 1986) are the two major treaties that serve as the constitutional documents upon which Community law and institutional operations are based. The "Treaty of European Union" (signed in Maastricht on December 11, 1991) made fundamental constitutional reforms that extend European integration toward monetary union and the formation of a federal polity.

10. The treaty came into legal force on November 1, 1993; however, the implementation of its provisions will continue into the first years of the twenty-first century.

11. In many respects this task was made easier by the publication by Marc Abélès of *La vie quotidienne au Parlement européen* (1992). His ethnographic study covers precisely those domains of the Parliament's internal organization and activity that allowed me to pursue alternative issues.

12. See Monnet's discussion of his method of convergent action (1978:232–48; Duchêne 1995). For a highly critical appraisal of Monnet's overall contributions to integration, see Milward's 1992 chapter entitled "The Lives and Teachings of the European Saints."

13. I present a full definition of the term in the next chapter. However, in an expression of the difficulty of satisfactorily defining subsidiarity, the *Times of London* goes so far as to claim that the "principle of subsidiarity is meaningless or even a misleading phrase in English" (*Times*, September 18, 1982, quoted in the *Oxford English Dictionary*, 17:59). Emiliou further notes, "On this there is a general agreement that there is no agreement on the definition of this concept. A narrow approach to the content of the principle of subsidiarity may result in a very limited scope of examination" (1992:383).

14. From the standpoint of the European Commission, "[C]ultural affairs and cultural policy fall within the remit of Directorate-General X, which is responsible for information, communication, culture and audio-visual media" (Weidenfield and Wessels 1998:58).

15. Presumably "peoples" constitute "nations" or "ethnic groups." Article 2 in contrast speaks of "ever closer relations between the *states* belonging to it [Europe]."

16. A more expansive formulation is noted by Shore, who worked in the offices of the European Commission: "Despite the problems inherent in the use of such categories, the notions of 'European culture' and 'European heritage' permeate official Community documents. Much of this follows a familiar pattern in which European culture is defined as a type of 'civilization' whose most important sources include the Judaeo-Christian religion, Greek-Hellenistic ideas of government, philosophy and art, Roman law, Renaissance humanism, the ideals of the Enlightenment and the Scientific Revolution, Social Democracy and the rule of law. This representation of Europe follows a familiar historical route: Greece-Rome-Christianity-Renaissance-Western democracy" (1993a:792). These apparently innocuous demarcations of Europe can nonetheless surface as veiled anxieties with far more troubling connotations, connotations that have a tenacious hold on the EU, as suggested by the thirty-six-year-long effort of Turkey to become a candidate for EU membership.

17. The report was subsequently published as Glyn Ford, *Fascist Europe: The Rise of Racism and Xenophobia* (1992).

18. Insofar as I was examining the delineation of an integralist agenda, I focused on an impassioned oppositional stance to the European project. This opened a very different perspective on the "uniting of Europe" from that defined by the classic work of David Mitrany, Ernst Haas, Leon Lindberg, Joseph Nye, Paul Taylor, Robert Keohane, and Stanley Hoffman. These theorists have examined the internal dynamics, the "invisible" hand, of integration; the intricate "prerequisites" and "spillovers" that punctuate each stage of the process; they have also shaped the debate on the specific outcomes of the transference of governmental competencies and powers from member states to the institutions of the EU in terms of "intergovernmental" versus "supranational" processes. Alternatives to these "functionalist" approaches have emerged around models of "flexible integration" as the possibility looms of perhaps twenty-five to thirty very different polities with contingent EU membership. In this view a "hard core" of European states is surrounded by concentric circles of states, which participate in economic and political integration with different rates of convergence.

CHAPTER THREE
SCIENCE AND METAPHYSICS OF SOLIDARITY

1. The Parliament also has administrative offices in Luxembourg.

2. The foresighted work of Herzfeld laid the ground work for this analysis by elucidating the origins of the European discourse of society (1987) and the symbolic roots of bureaucracy (1993). Zabusky (1995) was the first anthropologist to address Europeanization in terms of an emerging social order. She was also the first to recognize the sacred modern character of this nascent social order from within the European Space Agency.

3. Lipgens pointed out in the mid-1980s "that the European Community . . . as yet hardly possesses a historical consciousness of its own" (1985:ix). Lipgens, along with his colleagues at the European University Institute in Florence, has made an enormous contribution to correcting this deficit.

4. See the excellent political biography by Ross (1995).

5. The classic work on French economic planning is Pierre Massé's *Le plan ou l'anti-hasard* (1991). The preface of this edition is written by Jacques Delors.

6. See Delors 1989; 1991.

7. Delors played an important role within the "reconstruction group" of the Confédération Française des Travailleurs Chrétiens that became Confédération Française et Démocratique du Travail (Ross 1995:17).

8. "Delors is a man of action for whom ideas are terribly important: present and future must be connected by lucid theory and analysis, both then to be confronted with what is morally desirable. . . . At the intellectual center of this was the thought of Emmanuel Mounier and personalism, a progressive form of Catholic anti-individualism" (Ross 1995:17).

9. "'Social' meant more than merely the brute fact of association. A man was not truly social unless he was aware of his dependence on society and actively accepted his debt to others. Social life depended on mutual consent to mutual protection against mutual risk. [According to Rousseau] the social contract was the culmination of a conscious agreement signaling the ascent from the realm of force and necessity to that of freedom. Since the highest stage of sociality was

mutuality, it followed that the mutualist contract would be the road to social peace. Through the socialization of risk guaranteed by, but not created by, the state, the conditions of justice were made possible. Insurance companies had done just that; society should follow their example.

"If this was socialism, then it was of a new type, one starting from collectivism and moving toward individual liberty. Neo-Kantian socialism combined the liberal economists' notion of freedom with the socialists' concept of justice. [Léon] Bourgeois was careful to underline his differences from the socialists on the question of the State. The State was not an end in itself but only a protection. Its main role was to apply sanctions to violators of the common quasi-contract. Risks, not property, would be socialized" (Rabinow 1989:187).

10. After successfully restructuring his family's cognac business, Monnet found employment with an American merchant banking firm, Blair and Co., which led him through a series of international finance projects, including securing loans for Romania and Poland to support their currencies. He also served a brief tenure as vice-president of Bancamerica in San Francisco, followed by a year in Shanghai devoted to founding a Chinese development bank (Monnet 1978: 150–211).

11. See Nathan's account (1991: 67–85). A quotation attributed to John Maynard Keynes credits Monnet's labors with shortening the Second World War by a year (Mayne 1991: 114–28).

12. See Bloch-Lainé and Bouview 1986 and Mioche 1985. (See also Duchêne 1991: 86–113).

13. In his memoirs he recalls how, at the outset of the planning process, he solicited the views of a "few exceptional men," who outlined a somber, though familiar, analysis. "Their diagnosis was crisp: by modern standards, France was appallingly backward" (Monnet 1978:233). He immediately put this pessimistic appraisal to political ends with the slogan "modernization or decadence": "There was a very real danger, indeed, that France might content herself with frugal mediocrity behind a protectionist shield. This, after all, had been a national tradition. But I knew that the mere allusion to such a possibility would be enough to win support from the new, Resistance generation and to carry the day with General de Gaulle" (Monnet 1978:238).

14. He recounts his pledge to De Gaulle: "I don't know exactly what has to be done . . . but I'm sure of one thing. The French economy can't be transformed unless the French people take part in its transformation. And when I say 'the French people,' I don't mean an abstract entity: I mean trade unionists, industrialists, and civil servants. Everyone must be associated in an investment and modernization plan" (Monnet 1978:234–35).

15. Monnet articulates a position that intersects with David Mitrany's rendering of "functionalism." Functionalists argue "that integration is a process that has its own internal dynamic and that if states cooperate in certain limited areas and create new bodies to oversee that cooperation, they will cooperate in other areas through a kind of 'invisible hand' of integration" (McCormick 1996:13). The functionalist or neofunctionalist approaches, which dominated theorizing on integration, can be summarized as follows: "In the minds of the Community's founding fathers the fusion of economic interests, that began with the establishment of

the Communities [ECSC, EAEC, EEC], would automatically generate or at least foster conditions favorable to the more far-reaching political integration" (Borchardt 1989:26). In this view the modernist logic guiding European federalism is the outcome of incremental steps by which governmental competencies, furthering economic integration, are transferred from member states to the Community. The sheer managerial demands of regulating wide-ranging economic matters would in themselves impel—without conflict—the gradual formation of a polity of a federal type. Thus, the Single European Act (1986), which legislated the single market, inevitably led to the Maastricht Treaty (1992) creating political union.

16. Hoffmann has noted that this statist strategy established by the Planning Commission "had been largely responsible for the spectacular transformation of post-1950 France into a major industrial and exporting power (something many foreign experts had deemed impossible)" (1997:45).

17. Ian Paisley, MEP, famous for his anti-Catholic, antipapal, and anti-EU tirades, noted sarcastically that it was, after all, the Treaty of *Rome* upon which the European project was based, thus confirming in his mind that the Vatican was the guiding force behind European federalism.

18. See Maritain 1950; Amato 1975; and Hellman 1981.

19. As early as the spring of 1940 Jacques Maritain had formulated an agenda that was to become the ideological core of the noncommunist resistance movement in France. Maritain left France in January 1940 and worked in the United States for the duration of the war. His writings were influential not merely among Catholic militants, but across the French Resistance. During the war they were published clandestinely and widely quoted in the underground press, including in one of the first resistance pamphlets printed in November 1941 and distributed throughout southern France, in which he proposes a federal Europe to prevent the recurrence of war (Lipgens 1985: 274–75): ". . . a European federation whose members would all agree to the diminution of sovereignty necessary for the purpose of organic institutional cooperation. No doubt there will be many a profound and terrible upheaval before we reach that goal, but we believe [federalism is] the only hope for Europe and Western civilization" (Maritain, quoted in Lipgens 1985:276).

20. The Catholic critique was radical though by no means novel, following by more than a generation the emergence of communist and socialist movements across Europe. Furthermore, the Catholic movement was in fact a strategic effort to thwart rapid growth of the forces of the left, particularly in rural areas across Europe. In the case of Leo XIII his encyclical (in English, *Of New Things*, also known as *The Condition of Working Classes*) was a specific response to the long and extreme conservatism of the pontificate of Pius IX (Newman 1967). See Habermas's analysis of neo-Thomism (1987 1:372–376).

21. For a critical appraisal of Emmanuel Mounier's work in this regard, particularly as editor of *Esprit*, see the chapter entitled, "Spiritualistic Fascism" and the "Conclusion" of Sternhell 1996.

22. The modern application of subsidiarity dates from the famous papal encyclical *Rerum novarum* (1891) in which Leo XIII, drawing on the writings of Thomas Aquinas, sets out the basic tenets of Catholic social doctrine. The first explicit use of the term comes in the encyclical of Pius XI, *Quadregesimo anno*

(1931), which reviews the development of Catholic social teaching in the forty years after *Rerum novarum*, later elaborated upon by John XXIII in *Mater et Magistra* (1961) and *Pacem in terris* (1963). "It is a fundamental principle of social philosophy, fixed and unchangeable, that one should not withdraw from individuals and commit to the community what they can accomplish by their own enterprise and industry. So, too, it is an injustice and at the same time a grave evil and a disturbance of right order, to transfer to the larger and higher collectivity functions which can be performed and provided for by lesser and subordinate bodies. Inasmuch as every social activity should, by its very nature prove a help to members of the body social, it should never destroy or absorb them" (Pius XI *Quadragesimo anno* (1931), quoted in Mulcahy 1967:762). Pius XI's definition of subsidiarity follows immediately upon his assessment of the liberal state, and it is clear that he sees the concept serving as the basis of a wide-ranging Catholic political economy.

23. "[A]s a number of contemporary philosophers and political theorists have recognized, Aquinas shares with his mentor, Aristotle, a belief in the human capacity to identify goals, values and purpose ('teleology') in the structure and functioning of the human person that can provide the basis of a theory of ethics that responds to the argument of the eighteenth-century philosopher, David Hume, that values cannot be derived from the facts of human existence" (Sigmund 1988: xxvi).

24. I borrowed the ideas of the "sacred modern" from Smart 1997.

25. "The concept of inherent structural limits is, in a sense, a key to an understanding of Aquinas's approach. It enables him to develop a theory that maintains a middle position between faith and reason, rationalism and empiricism, individualism and collectivism, and authority and participation. If medieval political thought can be described as involving two principal traditions—a populist tradition 'ascending' from the community and a theocratic monarchist tradition 'descending' from God—Aquinas can be seen as representing both" (Sigmund 1988:xxiii).

26. The central institutional focus of the movement was originally Catholic Action founded by Maritain: "The essential purpose of Catholic Action was to exert a strong Catholic influence on the secular society, shaping the social milieu according to Catholic ideals. However, since the Church made a strong distinction between the role of the clergy and laity in society, limiting the sociopolitical activities of clergy, Catholic Action focused on training lay people to carry out the mission of exerting Catholic influence" (Smith 1991:80). Catholic Action became the basis of the Christian Democratic political movement. See Power 1992; Evans and Ward 1955.

27. The position taken herein is that subsidiarity refers to a range of concepts and formulations that delineate a political economy. See Millon-Delsol's (1992) elegant text, which provides an excellent introduction to these issues, and Zorgbide 1993. For a basic introduction to Catholic political economy, see Rommen 1955. For the application of subsidiarity to the constitutional challenges of European Union, see Emiliou 1992.

28. These deliberations over the disposition of powers are framed in terms of governmental "competencies." Competencies refer to the legally circumscribed

authority over specific domains of governmental action. The relationship between sovereignty and competency is not always clear. A very rough equivalence can be drawn between the sum of governmental competencies and sovereignty. Sovereignty, however, can also be interpreted as the power to allocate or retain competencies by a governing entity.

29. These same encyclicals blended with Marxist concepts became the basis of "liberation theology." See Smith 1991.

30. It can also be traced, as suggested earlier, through the work of Jacques Delors within the Europe Commission (Ross 1995).

31. See Mayne and Pinder with Roberts 1990.

32. Tindemans's first cabinet position required that he plan the transition from a "unitary" to a "federal" state. The creation of a "regionalized Belgium" was an effort to resolve the conflict between Francophone and Flemish-speaking communities (Tindemans 1972). He noted in an interview in 1991 that in developing the plan he made a careful study of the available scholarship on federal systems.

33. By far the most important outcome of this political economy in the post–World War II period was the displacement of laissez-faire philosophy with that of the "social market" (1977).

34. For a full summary of the European Commission's position on subsidiarity, see European Commission 1992.

35. Taylor's (1991: 109–25) intriguing article explores some of the possible outcomes (*International Herald Tribune*, June 6, 1997, p. 6).

36. For many observers European Monetary Union (EMU) is the most important federalist goal of the EU (Taylor 1997:35).

CHAPTER FOUR
CULTURAL PHYSICIAN

1. "The aim of the Cercle Proudhon, wrote [George] Valois, was to provide 'a common platform for nationalists and leftist antidemocrats'" (Sternhell 1996:11). Valois went on to found *Le Faisceau* in 1925. Weber comments on the analytical unease this marriage provokes: "The connection of socialism and nationalism has existed for a long time; it is like one of those common-law unions which practice and habit render commonplace and extremely unremarkable. Less so, if only because theoretical discussion has insisted upon the incompatibility, is the ideological alliance of the two, an alliance . . . that has never lacked supporters in France since the days of Barrès" (1991:262–63).

2. "[Sorel] regarded Marxism as a whole, including Marx's own works and the codification of Marxism by Engels, Kautsky, and Bernstein as a kind of receptacle that could be voided of its original contents and filled with another substance. This principle applied not only to the means but also to the end of revolutionary action" (Sternhell 1994:22).

3. Sternhell notes: "Marxism was a system of ideas still deeply rooted in the philosophy of the eighteenth century. Sorelian revisionism replaced the rationalist, Hegelian foundations of Marxism with Le Bon's new vision of human nature, with the anti-Cartesianism of Bergson, with the Nietzchean cult of revolt, and

with Pareto's recent discoveries [regarding the role of elites] in political sociology. The Sorelian voluntarist, vitalist, and antimaterialist form of socialism used Bergsonism as an instrument against scientism and did not hesitate to attack reason. It was a philosophy of action based on intuition, the cult of energy and *élan vital*" (1994:24).

4. In one of the most remarkable and overlooked texts in European anthropology, Mintz (1982) examines another radical variant of Marxist revisionism, the anarchosyndicalism inspired by Michael Bakunin.

5. There was an earlier presaging of this synthesis: "speaking in 1896 over the grave of a typical nationalist buccaneer, the Marquis de Morès, Maurice Barrès had taken care to explain that Morès was both nationalist and socialist. As for himself, said Barrès, he never feared to insist upon the intimate union of nationalist and socialist ideas. So much so that when two years later he stood for election at Nancy, his program was headed 'Nationalism, Protectionism, and Socialism,' and his supporters were the members of the Republican Socialist Nationalist Committee" (Weber 1991:262).

6. "Proudhon, of course, owed his privileged place in *L'Action française* to what the Maurrassians saw as his antirepublicanism, his anti-Semitism, his loathing of Rousseau, his disdain of the French Revolution, democracy, and parliamentarians, and his championship of the nation, the family, tradition, and the monarchy" (Sternhell 1996:56–7).

7. The two most important theoretical texts on the French right are Réne Rémond's *Le droites en France de 1815 à nos jours* (1982) and Zeev Sternhell's *Ni droite, ni gauche. L'idéologie fasciste en France* (1983). In the 1996 English edition of Sternhell's text there is an important—indeed devastating—critique of the work of Rémond and his followers, principally their critical restraint when it comes to French elites and their involvements with Vichy. The legacy of Vichy remains in the public imagination through prosecutions of crimes against humanity from Klaus Barbie and Paul Touvier, to the trial of Maurice Papon (see Rousso 1991; Judt 1992).

8. "[T]he public sphere means 'a sphere which mediates between society and state, in which the public organizes itself as the bearer of public opinion'" and it is within this context that a "communicatively generated rationality" emerges and new emancipatory possibilities are created. "It eventuated from the struggle against absolutism ... and aimed at transforming arbitrary authority into rational authority subject to the scrutiny of a citizenry organized into a public body under the law" (Eley 1994:298).

9. This possibility forms a central anxiety pervading the work of Habermas (1991).

10. This compares with 15.7 percent of the vote for Jacques Chirac's Rally for the Republic (RPR) and 14.2 percent for Valéry Giscard d'Estaing's Union of French Democracy (UDF).

11. "As president of his own party, Le Pen navigated successfully among the treacherous currents of right-wing extremism, remaining faithful to parliamentary tactics despite its meager results during the first decade (the 1970s)" (Fysh and Wolfreys 1992). Le Pen's fidelity to parliamentary tactics is noteworthy given

the way the electoral system "works against the FN" on the national level: "There is no doubt that the electoral system does not work in the Front's favor. The Communist Party, for example, won some 9 per cent of the first ballot vote at the 1993 Legislative election. It emerged with 23 seats; the National Front, whose first ballot tally was over 12 per cent, emerged with none" (Marcus 1995:6).

12. For a good summary of the electoral history of Le Pen's party, see Simmons 1996, and for a masterful analysis and insightful description of the work of Le Pen and his associates, see Marcus 1995. Both texts provide good summaries of the FN's immigration policies (Marcus 1995:73; Simmons 1996:143–68). For excerpts of interviews with Le Pen in English, see Marcus 1995:6–9 and Gourevitch 1997:110–149.

13. Weber's descriptions of the French romantic nationalists echo the contradictory sensibilities that imbue Le Pen's style of presentation: "It is perhaps in the nature of the modern romantic to visualize himself as a cool-headed positivist. . . . no self-respecting nationalist would be anything but rational. Yet the lyricism pierces through the sober surface, the cloven hoof of passion peeps beneath the vestments of positivism, and, in the end, our national socialist returns to the great nineteenth-century tradition of sentimental, adventurous romance—national and social because a hundred years ago national and social activity was considered romantic. With Chateaubriand's René he calls on long-awaited storms to rise" (Weber 1991:278–79).

14. They were members of the Technical Group of the European Right, which in the early 1990s was small, comprising only fourteen members of the Parliament. It was composed of ten members drawn from the French Front national, two from the German *parteilos*, one from the Deutsche Liga, and one from the Belgian Vlaams Blok. Four members of the Italian Movimento sociale italiano-Destra nationale and one member of the German Die Republikaner sat with the nonattached members (NI) of the Parliament, although they shared extreme right-wing views with the European right. See the conclusions to Marcus 1995.

15. See Le Pen 1989. To grasp the centrality of Le Pen's position on immigration, it is important to cast it against the social history of immigration in France. Again, see Noiriel's excellent study (1996).

16. The figure who has drawn most effectively on Le Pen's integralist model is Jörg Haider leader of the Austrian Freedom Party and governor of Carinthia. In January 2000 he entered negotiations with the leaders of the Austrian People's Party to form a new national government after polling second in the elections of October 1999. He appears to be the true heir to Le Pen's European legacy.

17. This is by no means a new phenomenon. Eatwell finds "antifascism" deployed by the left against Action français (AF) in the 1920s, and he detects, even in the earliest expressions of antifascism, an element of "shadowboxing." "It was, therefore, almost inevitable that the AF would become branded as fascist by left-wing opponents who were quickly finding a practical benefit to antifascism—namely, the power of the cause to rally together the forces of the center-left" (1996:197).

18. Stoler raises a broader theoretical issue in this regard: "Is there something to learn about the nature of racism from discrepancies and commonalities in the

stories we tell about them? Perhaps more troubling: are these anti-racist histories so much a part and product of racial discourse that they are, despite intention, subject to its regimes of truth?" (1997a:184).

19. The myth of rebirth or "palingenesis" is central to Roger Griffin's definition of "fascism." *"Fascism is a genus of political ideology whose mythic core in its various permutations is a palingenetic form of popular ultra-nationalism"* (Griffin 1995:4; emphasis in the original).

20. Alain Touraine was quoted in *Le Monde* (1990) arguing that "The national question is replacing the social question at the center of political life" (Simmons 1996:256). "[Bruno] Mégret argues that the old distinctions between Left and Right are no longer relevant. Previously, he says, the political process was a debate between Marxists and liberals over the social and economic organisation of a country. 'But today,' he claims, there is a new debate 'between nationalism and cosmopolitanism, between identity and internationalism'" (Marcus 1995:130).

21. Obviously, this rhetoric does not persuade all listeners. To many this populist tactic only confirms the racist nature of his intimate politics.

22. The nature and consequences of this development are analyzed in the excellent article by Stolcke (1995).

23. See Kaplan's (1986) biographical sketch and intriguing conversation with Bardèche.

24. Todorov (1993) gives an extended treatment of the development of "race" and "nation" in French thought. Arendt (1951) examines the broad influence of Gobineau's *Essai sur l'inégalité des races humaines* (1853) in France during the early twentieth century. See also Berlin's three articles (1990).

25. "Le Pen's awareness of the mobilizing appeal of the immigration issue has led commentators to compare him with various populist nationalist figures such as Enoch Powell and Pierre Poujade. This fundamental error, seeing the Front National as little more than a single-issue movement, is reflected in the disastrous complacency of many analyses. . . . Since the early 1980s it [the FN] has ruthlessly exploited the immigration issue. . . . Yet in 1974 the theme was absent from the FN's ten point election program [and in the FN's 1977 program] no mention whatsoever is made of immigration" (Wolfreys 1993:420). This is somewhat misleading, given that leadership of the Ordre nouveau (ON), the organization that created the Front national and named Le Pen as its leader, had in the late 1960s "believed it had found an important new electoral issue: opposition to immigration. About eight percent of France's population was foreign, a figure that had remained unchanged throughout the twentieth century. But within these figures, there had been a marked rise during the 1960s of immigrants from North Africa, especially Algeria. . . . The ON line was that having pushed the French out of Algeria, Arabs were now set to take over the rest of France. Immigration, therefore, seemed the ideal topic, combining economic fears, racist sentiment, and pandering to the obsession of an important part of the party's hard core" (Eatwell 1996:316).

26. Stoler notes in the work of Foucault a theoretical premise for this kind of political maneuver. "For if Foucault is right that one of the defining features of racism is its 'polyvalent mobility,' that it may vacillate and be embraced by those

opposed to and beleaguered by the state at one moment and become an integral part of the technologies of state rule at another then the fact that racial discourses contain and coexist with a range of political agendas is not a contradiction but a fundamental historical feature of their *non-linear*, spiraling political genealogies" (1997a:191).

27. "The most interesting and difficult part of any cultural analysis, in complex societies, is that which seeks to grasp the hegemonic in its active and formative but also its transformational processes" (Williams 1977:113).

28. Le Pen is drawing on elements of what Michael Herzfeld (1997) calls "cultural intimacy" and making it a form of overt political practice.

29. Le Pen, quoted in Taguieff 1991a:43.

30. It constitutes a comprehensive rejection of cosmopolitan agendas or what Le Pen increasingly refers to in the mid-1990s as the *"mondialiste"* lobby. "Apparently, cosmopolitanism was too overtly anti-Semitic and therefore too inflexible to serve in the vocabulary battle. This did not mean that the Front was about to abandon anti-Semitism, but the advantage of *mondial* in all its versions was that it lacked historical baggage" (Simmons 1996:222-23).

31. See Taguieff 1989; 1991b.

32. Le Pen 1984, quoted in Vaughan 1991:222.

33. "As evidence of how open the National Front is, Le Pen cited its leadership's domestic arrangements. 'It's amusing,' he said, 'when the Party's administrative team is accused of narrow-minded nationalism, because almost all of its leaders are either sons of immigrants or married to foreigners. It is true,' he insisted; 'for example Bruno Gollnisch, one of our stars, is married to a Japanese woman and as for me, my wife is half-Greek'" (quoted in Marcus 1995:8-9).

34. I have described this as an "illicit discourse" (Holmes 1993:258). Foucault uses a more delimited denotation of the concept. "[I]llicit discourse, that is, discourses of infraction that crudely named sex by way of insult or mockery of the new code of decency; tightening up of the rules of decorum likely did produce, as a countereffect, a valorization and intensification of indecent speech" (1978:18).

35. It is, however, clear that his advisors, who participated in the work of the French New Right, have read these theorists and employed them in the shaping of FN policy, as we will see in the next chapter.

36. Le Pen was deeply involved in the presidential campaign of Jean-Louis Tixier-Vignancourt in 1965. It was a campaign that was centrally concerned with putting a "moderate face" on the extreme right, while employing the mass media as the vehicle for getting this message across to the French electorate (Eatwell 1996: 310-12; Simmons 1996:53-56).

37. Stoler describes the specific dynamics of this discursive field (1997a:194-201).

38. Milza (1987) has noted that the muted nature of bellicosity and militarism in FN ideology is one important element that distinguishes the FN from truly fascist groups. The more bellicose side of Le Pen's attack can be unleashed with calculated effect, as we will see in chapter 10.

39. Bruno Mégret remarked to Philip Gourevitch: "If we compare Le Pen to Hitler, it makes Hitler sympathetic, because for many French people Jean-Marie Le Pen is sympathetic" (Gourevitch 1997:148).

CHAPTER FIVE
AN ESSENTIAL SOCIOLOGY

1. During a subsequent celebration of Fête de Jeannne d'Arc a group of on-lookers pounced on a Moroccan student and threw him into the Seine, where he drowned.

2. At another FN festival, the Fête Bleu Blanc Rouge, later in the year, a party official commented to Jonathan Marcus: "See, we are not monsters with two heads, just ordinary people." Marcus concurred, "He is right; it is the very nor-mality of much of the National Front's world that surprises" (1995:2). Marcus also finds the FN festival reminiscent of Fête de l'Humanité sponsored by the French Communist Party and he notes "the various National Front Circles, asso-ciated journals, children's activities, and so on have created a sort of far right counterculture, almost a mirror image of that created by the Communists, and for very similar reasons. By establishing this web of interlocking organizations, a whole world is created in which the activist can feel at home" (1995:3–4). See Kertzer's (1980) classic study of this kind of cultural struggle between right and left in Italy.

3. Jean-Marie Domenach uses the notion of the *moi idéal* to capture the kind of aura fostered by the operation of Le Pen's sense of grandeur on M. Johnston's imagination: "the form taken by the desire to conform one's wish for grandeur to models that can be heroic, aesthetic or artistic, and to love oneself through these ideal representations" (Domenach, quoted in Hoffmann 1997:46).

4. A "Frontist" structure is one that serves to harness a mass membership and also effectively, if not formally, encourage dual membership both in the FN and in a sect or tendency to which members with an ideological bent owe their first loyalty. This means that both the party program and the declared strategy for achieving power can be interpreted to their own satisfaction by potentially conflicting groups within the Front (Fysh and Wolfreys 1992: 310).

5. The Ordre nouveau grew directly out of the events of 1968: "Anti-immi-grant politics were central to another organization that emerged in the aftermath of 1968, a movement that reflected [a] . . . new strategic direction taken by the extremists at this time. The group, which had its roots in a series of meetings that took place during late 1969, was called New Order (ON). Unlike the ND, which was a small and relatively homogeneous group, the ON was meant to link differ-ent types of nationalists, both fascist and nonfascist. From the former category, it attracted François Duprat, who in the late 1960s had written a sympathetic his-tory of the SS for Bardèche's publishing house, and who was beginning to show a marked interest in Holocaust denial arguments. Among the leading nonfascists was François Brigneau, who had served with the Milice under the Vichy govern-ment, and who was editor of the extreme-right weekly *Minute*.

"New Order wanted to model itself on the Italian Social Movement, which managed to combine within one organization violent activists and those who sought a more respectable electoral strategy. Although the leaders of the ON were eager to develop the latter side, they were well aware that they could not ignore the former: most of the two thousand or so members who joined during 1969 and

1970 came from violent extremist organizations—and in some cases held joint membership with street-fighting units" (Eatwell 1996:315–16).

6. Marcus also points out that Le Pen has always remained steadfast to the founding statement of the FN: "*La Droite sociale, populaire et nationale*" (1995:130).

7. See Taguieff's (1994) critical analysis of the ND. Benoist sets out his vision in two major works (1977; 1979). There was an interesting debate between Benoist and Taguieff published as "Vous avez dit différence?" *Le Nouvel Observateur*, September 25, 1987.

8. "Much like the English Fabian Society at the turn of the century, GRECE adopted the tactic of permeation—that is, of spreading new ideas and a new vocabulary throughout the political elite on the extreme right and, through it, GRECE hoped, the entire French political spectrum" (Simmons 1996:210).

9. The breakthrough is usually dated to the election in 1983 of the late Jean-Pierre Stirbois, then general secretary of the FN, and three colleagues to the municipal council of Dreux, a small city of thirty five thousand outside of Paris. The character of the election was very important in establishing the local level tactics of FN (Simmons 1996:72–77). See the insightful text by the former Socialist mayor of Dreux, François Gaspard (1995). Gaspard examines the underlying sociopolitical changes that provided an opening for the FN (see Marcus 1995:52–72).

10. The *solidaristes* were "advocates of a 'third way' between communism and capitalism, strongly anti-Marxist, anti-Zionist, and anti-American" (Marcus 1995:36). Despite its frontist structure, the FN does not permit organized factions or tendencies. They exist nonetheless, albeit informally. For a brief overview of the shifting factions or ideological groups within the FN, including the *solidaristes*, see Simmons (1996:198–202).

11. As is the general practice in French politics, Gollnisch continues to hold in the late 1990s a series of elected posts concurrently. As noted earlier, the conversations with Gollnisch took place at the offices of the European Parliament in Strasbourg.

12. Again, as Sternhell notes, "The Sorelian voluntarist, vitalist, and anti-materialist form of socialism used Bergsonism as an instrument against scientism and did not hesitate to attack reason. It was a philosophy of action based on intuition, the cult of energy and *élan vital*" (1994:24).

13. Gollnisch was self-consciously shaping, as part of a broader effort orchestrated by Le Pen and his supporters, an ideological counteroffensive to the accusations of covert racism on the part of the FN. Taguieff's text (1988), in many ways set the terms of this debate.

14. "Le Pen himself believes that the place of anti-racism in the Socialist party's outlook is akin to that of anti-clericalism in the ideology of the Third Republic—a campaign to mask the questionable legitimacy of those in power" (Marcus 1995:108).

15. Wieviorka summarizes this kind of critique articulated by Gollnisch: "that anti-racism is an ideology which has come to the aid of the failing socialist, communist or Marxist ideologues, an instrument manipulated by left-wing actors

with no political project; above all, anti-racism has itself been accused of fomenting racism, of precipitating processes leading to the racialization of society, or exacerbating such processes. . . . The end result of the anti-racists' denunciation of racism, according to the most virulent critics, has been to encourage it, just as the end result of promoting a multicultural society has been to racialize social relations through construction of groups who define themselves, or are defined, in terms of race" (1997:140).

16. *Le Nouvel Observateur*, September 7–13, 1989, p. 28, quoted in Johnson 1991:243. "Blot's career is typical of a number of high civil servants who worked in the mainstream right and then decided to throw in their lot with the National Front. He began his administrative career in the ministry of Interior, worked for the Planning Commission, and then from 1978 to 1983 with a high official in Chirac's RPR. From 1984 to 1986 Blot worked for Charles Pasqua, the hard-line minister of the interior in the 1986 Chirac government" (Simmons 1996:215). My conversation with Blot took place in Strasbourg in April 1991.

17. See "Qu'est-ce que le Club de l'horloge?" in Club de l'horloge, 1985.

18. Yvan Blot is one of the founders and former presidents of the Club de l'horloge. "These [right-wing political clubs and think tanks] mirrored the establishment by left intellectuals, civil servants, and politicians in the 1960s of left-wing clubs such as the Club Jean Moulin devoted to modernizing socialist doctrine. The extreme right was motivated by the same factors as the left; disillusionment with the existing political parties, disaffection from political elites, and a desire to break out of the political ghetto in which it had languished since 1945" (Simmons 1996:208).

19. "The dichotomisation of politics into right and left is an integral part of the Revolution's legacy to republican France. The full endorsement of the organising myths, which underpin the regime, is held to be the birthright of the left. In contrast, the ideological credentials of the right remain perennially open to challenge" (Vaughan 1991: 211).

20. "The Club de l'Horloge defines itself above all as anti-Socialist and declares its goal as 'preparing for the period after socialism by contributing to a renewal of the political ideas of the opposition' " ("Qu'est-ce que le Club de l'horloge?", quoted in Simmons 1996:215).

21. His disillusionment with Chirac is chronicled in an interview with *Le Monde*, June 2, 1989.

22. See Blot 1992.

23. Bruno Mégret is emphatic on this point: "[W]e don't believe that the history of France began in 1789. [We believe] that this revolution was a rupture which was damaging to France and that the ideas which flowed from it are not part of our outlook. Above all, the way they are currently put into practice, with what we call the 'ideology of rights of man,' is something that is very negative. Therefore we reject the rupture of 1789" (quoted in Marcus 1995:103). The publication of Martin's 1990 text provided the leadership of the FN with an historical precedent upon which to demonstrate partisan resistance to the destructive force of the Revolution and a symbolic framework—the badge of Les Chouans—to oppose the republic (Marcus 1995:2).

24. As Simmons points out, this kind of epistemology creates enormous potential for the proliferation and manipulation of right-wing conspiracy theories (1996a:225–28).

25. I spoke to Johnston on a number of occasions in 1991 and 1993 in Brussels and Strasbourg. The conversation excerpted below took place in Brussels in March of 1991.

26. "Le Pen has launched a strong campaign against the use of the appellation 'extreme Right' to describe the Front. It is an intellectual subterfuge, he says, an attempt to give the Party a diabolical image" (Marcus 1995:130).

27. The actual Catholic character of the FN is somewhat ambiguous. The party is strongly supported by fundamentalists most notably members of the Chrétienté-Solidarité, but whereas "51 percent of mainstream right voters were either regular or occasional practitioners of the Catholic faith, fully 59 percent of those who voted for the National Front identified themselves as nonpracticing Catholics" (Simmons 1996:83).

28. The percentage of immigrants in the population of France has remained remarkably stable for decades (Noiriel 1996).

29. This is despite Blot's impeccable technocratic credentials. Indeed, Blot even worked on the French Planning Commission founded by Jean Monnet.

30. Bruno Mégret has noted: "The semantic superiority of the left helped its culture and then political influence. Language is a form of subtle code. In choosing a word, one's thoughts are inscribed, sometimes even without wishing it, within a pre-established ideological schema. To speak of 'social classes,' or 'workers,' of the 'proletariat,' is not innocent. To utilize these words is to push forward Marxist doctrine" (1990: 166, quoted in Simmons 1996:215).

CHAPTER SIX
SOCIETY AND ITS VICISSITUDES

1. "Out of the very contradiction between the interest of the individual and that of the community the latter takes on an independent form as the *State*, divorced from the real interests of individuals and community, and at the same time an illusory communal life. . . . It follows from this that the struggles within the State . . . are merely the illusory forms in which the real struggles of the different classes are fought out among one another" (Marx and Engels, quoted in McLellan 1974:146).

2. This is a story generally traced back to the writings of Giambattista Vico (see Berlin 1976). Vico's writing is also the starting point of Herzfeld's (1987) account of the emergence of a critical anthropology of Europe.

3. Another transient resident of Brussels, Charles Baudelaire, analyzed the deep cultural limitations of modernist societal constructions by way of his aesthetic critique (Starkie 1988).

4. Castellina was interviewed at the European Parliament in Brussels in March 1991.

5. The PCI changed its name to Partito democratico della sinistra (PDS) and ultimately its group affiliation in the European Parliament, moving to the Social-

ists. Castellina broke with the PDS, refusing to enter the Socialist Group, and participated in the founding of the Refoundation Communists in Italy. See Kertzer's (1996) pivotal account of the internal struggle that led to the breakup of the PCI and the founding of the PDS. See also the more general account of the transformation of Italian politics as a whole in Caciaglil and Kertzer 1996.

6. Again, this is how an integral politics of the left operates. Again, see Kertzer's classic text (1980).

7. See Lemke and Marks 1992. See also Gaffney 1989.

8. The encounter with Newman took place at the parliament's offices in Brussels in 1991 and 1993.

CHAPTER SEVEN
CALL IT FASCISM

1. This should by no means be construed as a full ethnographic account of the political life of the East End. Although leaders from the major antiracist groups in Tower Hamlets as well as leaders of the major Bengali community organizations were interviewed, their accounts are not included herein. To do justice to the rich political life of these variously constituted community organizations requires a fuller ethnographic treatment. Fortunately, Eade (1989; 1990; 1991) has published a series of fine-grained analyses of these issues. This body of work constitutes an excellent introduction to the history and political anthropology of the Bangladeshi community in Tower Hamlets.

2. Again, the BNP is the successor to the (British) National Front. A number of journals have chronicled in great detail all the events covered in this chapter from an antiracist and antifascist stance. The most important and most thorough is *Searchlight*, which carefully monitors and interprets neofascist activity in Britain and Europe. For an excellent portrayal of the BNP during the 1993–94 period, see Copsey 1996.

3. See the historical analysis by Husbands (1982). See also his definitive text on the National Front (1983).

4. The history of Afro-Caribbeans in London dates to 1555. The most recent wave of immigration dates from the arrival of five hundred immigrants aboard the S.S. *Empire Windrush* in 1948. A small community of Indian seaman was already present around the Docklands in the mid-nineteenth century (Merriman 1993:170). The most important phase of recent immigration to Tower Hamlets commences with "the arrival of around 5,000 migrant workers between 1954 and 1956. Settlers were drawn from one Bangladeshi district in particular, Sylhet" (Eade 1991:85).

5. As of April 1992, Annual Report 1993–94:47.

6. Baumann draws on the local census of 1991 of Southallian "ethnic groups" for the following breakdown: "Indian," 50 percent; "Pakistani," 7 percent; "Other Asian," 3 percent; "White," 30 percent; "Black-Caribbean," 5 percent; "Other categories," 3 percent (Baumann 1996:48).

7. Baumann insists on italicizing "culture" and "community" throughout his text to emphasize "local meaning and usage of the terms" as opposed to their "reified" usage in the dominant discourse (1996:xiii).

8. Baumann notes, however, that: "[In 1963] the right-wing British National Party gained 27 per cent of Southall votes at council elections campaigning on the slogan 'Send them Back!'" (1996:56). It was the exodus of the white residents that ultimately weakened nationalist politics in Southall.

9. In Payne's axiom: "The number of neo-fascist and right radical groups has actually increased, in bewildering and kaleidoscopic variety, following the basic rule of thumb 'The more insignificant, the more of them'" (1995: 498).

10. This is simply a realignment of the premise of Sternhell's remarkable book: "This book is based on two assumptions. The first is that fascism, before it became a political force, was a cultural phenomenon" (1994:3). The argument in this part of the text is that a dismal political movement, the BNP, can be used to gain access to a much broader cultural movement, one that embraces a deeply alienated public.

11. Griffin (1996a) argues systematically that fascism will not directly threaten the British nation or state.

12. "Inevitably each fascism will be made in the image or 'imagining' of a particular national culture, but even within the same movement or party its most influential ideologies will inevitably represent a wide range of ideas and theories, sometimes quite incompatible with each other *except at the level of a shared mythic core of palingenetic ultra-nationalism*. Fascism is thus inherently syncretic, bringing heterogeneous currents of ideas into a loose alliance united only by a common struggle for a new order" (Griffin 1995:8).

13. This alignment opens the way, at least in theory, for syntheses that go beyond George Valois's formulation of "nationalism" plus "socialism" equals "fascism." The implication is that fascism can achieve ideological integration of unlikely elements under conditions where democratic forms of consensus building are thwarted.

14. Max Horkheimer's dictum "whoever is not prepared to talk about capitalism should also remain silent about fascism" has deflected attention, particularly in Marxist analyses, away from fascism's anticapitalist nature (Horkheimer 1995:272–73).

15. Griffin is explicit: "The main risk which fascists pose to society, apart from the concrete acts of hatred and violence they inspire, is that of putting onto the agenda of mainstream politicians misgivings about the desirability or sustainability of a multi-ethnic, multi-faith society, and alarms about the contamination of alleged cultural 'purity' by foreign influence. Once such issues can be openly debated as genuine 'problems' requiring 'solutions,' purportedly liberal states can come all too easily to collude with the forces of racism and ultra-nationalism" (1996a:164).

CHAPTER EIGHT
FACTUAL RACISM

1. Edmonds and Beackon were interviewed separately in July 1994 at the former-BNP headquarters in Welling.

2. The "factual" character of this racism is deeply ironic. It does not imply, as we will see, a fixity of meaning; rather it reveals the fluidity of racial discourses,

their ability to emerge from very different political impulses even among an insular group of political activists. Again, Stoler, drawing on Foucault, further notes "that racial discourses contain both 'erudite' and 'subjugated' knowledge, and thus genealogically build on the concerns of those privileged purveyors of truth, those with 'erudite knowledge' as well as those whose knowledge has been disqualified or denied access to the realm of valorized knowledge" (Stoler 1997a:191–92).

3. In the fall of 1993 an anti-BNP "Unity" march through Welling, estimated by *Searchlight* (1993, no. 221) at more than forty thousand participants, turned riotous when the police tried to block protesters from passing in front of the BNP headquarters.

4. Baumann (1995) argues that the complexities of the urban districts of London must be seen as going well beyond mere distinctions between and among "ethnic" groups or "cultures." "What is interesting about urban 'ethnicity,' and in particular its discursive devices of 'ethnic' and 'community,' is its capacity to hide the very multiplicity of linguistic, regional, national and other cultural cleavages that cut across each other. Any of these cross-cutting cleavages, and several others such as religion and caste, can take on the significance of 'ethnic' or 'community' boundaries, depending on context" (1995:738). Cohen (1993) provides an excellent depiction of the Notting Hill Carnival as a vehicle for transformation and integration within a multicultural district of London.

5. See Husbands 1983 and Sibley 1995.

6. The notion of the organic intellectual comes, of course, from Antonio Gramsci. "Mr. Edmonds is not only one of the better educated, though nevertheless crazy, BNP leaders. . . . His wife is a former Oxford student with a good job in computing at London University. She . . . has been openly critical of the 'Jew-obsessed losers' with whom he has surrounded himself" (*Searchlight*, no. 229:3 [1994]).

7. I have accounts of eight individuals who participated in the confrontations described in this section. I have also drawn heavily on the narrative of these events as reported in *Searchlight*, no. 220 (1993). *Searchlight* has been a valuable resource for this analysis, providing a strong alternative perspective.

8. The homicide of Gurdip Singh Chaggar in 1976 created a very similar community response in Southall, with protest organized by groups of young Asians and Afro-Caribbeans, confrontations with the police, and ultimately the infamous Southall "race riot," provoked by activists from the National Front, on August 23, 1979 (Baumann 1996:58).

9. "The Anti Nazi League (ANL) was launched on 10 November [1977]. . . . The League was launched as a broad initiative, drawing together sponsors from right across the spectrum of radical politics. . . . The League's founding statement drew attention to the electoral threat posed by the NF and their associates. The danger they represented was once again conveyed by reference to the Nazism of Hitler" (Gilroy 1991:131).

10. The events of September 1993 are reminiscent of an earlier election, also punctuated by violence, which first galvanized the Bengali community to political mobilization. "Active involvement in local political institutions and policies was encouraged by the events surrounding the 1978 borough election which involved

opposition to the National Front and the murder of a young Sylheti garment worker, Altab Ali, on the night of the poll" (Eade 1991:86). The murder was followed by a rampage by members of the National Front down Brick Lane (Eade 1991:88). It also recalls a now mythologized confrontation between Oswald Mosley's "Blackshirts" and antifascists, which took place around the corner from Brick Lane on Cable Street, "The Battle of Cable Street" on October 4, 1936. Oswald Mosley arrived for a march through the East End "with a motor-cycle escort and standing up in the open Bentley doing the fascist salute in his new uniform—he walked up and down the columns of blackshirts inspecting them while the crowd, beyond the lines of police, began to charge, and here and there broke through" (Mosley 1991:377–78). The march was delayed while the police (six thousand were present) tried to push their way through Cable Street. A melee ensued between the police and the various antifascist groups defending their barricades on Cable Street. Mosley was ordered by the police to halt. He complied and had his men march away from the fray. Thus, this famous "battle" was, in fact, a confrontation between the police and antifascists, of whom eighty-three were arrested.

11. See "Demands for Action after BNP Boss Walks Free," *Searchlight*, no. 229 (1994):3–5.

12. Buford's (1992) account of his participation at a social gathering of the National Front captures the popular view of the style and the temperament of supporters of the extreme right. See also Alan Clarke's 1983 film *Made in Britain*.

13. See Smith's (1999) discussion of the relationships among the welfare state, civil society, citizenship, and culture in France and Britain.

14. He rejects this as an expression of mere "nostalgia," which he forgoes as a "weak word."

15. The "alien wedge" is a term coined by Enoch Powell.

16. There is a substantial literature on the "official" and "unofficial" immigration and its control. Again, for a general overview, see Hiro 1992:200–203, 250–51, 257–58.

17. This is in reference to Enoch Powell's incendiary speech in Birmingham on April 20, 1968. The speech is filled with carefully crafted phrases and images to engender, if not ignite, white fear. "Under the circumstances, to enact the 1968 Race Relations Bill (then before Parliament) was to 'risk throwing a match on to gun powder.'" Concluding, he saw ahead, like the Roman, "The River Tiber foaming with much blood" (Hiro 1992:246–47). Enormous public support followed in the wake of the speech, as did calls for censure. Ultimately, Edward Heath dismissed Powell from the shadow cabinet (Powell 1969;1978). Nevertheless, Enoch Powell continued to be the most important critic of Britain's immigration and race policies until his death in 1997. John Tyndall acknowledged an earlier formulation of this position by Sir Cyril Osborne, MP, in the 1950s.

18. The leadership of the BNP is not keen to divulge the exact number of its active members. The estimates that seem most plausible during the mid-1990s were in the neighborhood of 250 core members of whom fewer than 100 are serious activists. In 1997 for the first time since its formation in 1982, the BNP stood 50 candidates in a general election. The party leaders tried to sidestep the implications of the election: "The overall average vote is not particularly mean-

ingful" (http://www.bnp.net/, May 5, 1997). The results were, in fact, paltry with only a handful of candidates attracting 5 percent or more of the vote. In the local elections in the spring of 1994, the party stood candidates for 29 council positions across England. In London they received 13,731 votes or 8.39 percent. This compares with the apex of the National Front's popularity twenty years earlier when it fielded 90 candidates and gleaned 114,000 votes averaging close to 10 percent of the poll in several London districts (Gilroy 1991:118). By contrast, Oswald Mosley's British Union of Fascists at its apex in 1934 claimed 50,000 members (Griffin 1995:172).

19. In the local election of May 1994, when he lost the Millwall position, he increased his vote to 2,051. As he notes: "So, I increased my vote by almost 600. We should have won on that but there was a very big turnout." For coverage of the May 1994 local election see *Searchlight*, no. 226 (1994):3–7.

20. "I dreamed I was in Yorkshire, going from Gomersal Hill-Top to Cleckheaton; and about the middle of the lane I thought I saw Satan coming to meet me in the shape of a tall, black man, and the hair of his head like snakes." John Nelson, stonemason of Birstall, quoted in Thompson 1966. Gilroy (1991) uses the same quotation at the outset of his introduction.

21. See the *Searchlight* issue on "White Noise," no. 280 (1998).

22. This is worked out theoretically by Berman (1989).

CHAPTER NINE
AUTHORITARIANISM

1. Durham (1991) and Gable (1991) give an excellent summary of John Tyndall's early role in the labyrinthine development of the extreme right in Britain. For a more theoretical treatment, see Taylor's (1993) analysis.

2. Griffin's police record is, however, not free of entries. In 1998, for example, he came under criminal prosecution for publishing a racist magazine. See note 19.

3. Lipset 1960.

4. See Mühlberger 1991.

5. From an editorial under the heading "Beyond Beackon," *Searchlight*, no. 228 (1994):2. In Mr. Newland's own recollection of the event, "Tales of Tyranny—Two and a Half Years as a 'Nazi' Press Officer," he continues to argue that it was "left-wing Zionists" who perpetrated the attack and not "hooligan right-wing types in an internal feud" (http://www.bnp.net/, July 1998).

6. "In its radical forms . . . *völkisch* thought implied that the nation was endowed with a mysterious essence which could be sapped by such 'decadent' forces as socialism, materialism, cosmopolitanism and internationalism, all of which came to be epitomized for some in the Jews" (Griffin 1993:85–86).

7. His socialism took form under the influence of the Birmingham Labour Party and emerged as a synthesis of the monetary theories and socialist planning of J. M. Keynes, the concept of "underconsumptionism" worked out by J. A. Hobson, and the ideas of "social credit" as formulated by C. H. Douglas. See Thurlow's excellent summary of Mosley's transition from socialism to nationalism (1987:40–45).

8. In our conversation in 1994 Newland summarized his political economy as follows: "Indeed, the Labour Party during the 1970s developed what was called

"the alternative economic strategy," which, to a certain degree, is much in our direction. In fact, it was the first time the Labour Party moved toward a protectionist stance. That had always been the province of the Conservative Party. Until 1870, free trade was seen as very advantageous to the British because of their empire and because we were the first in the industrial revolution. But after 1870, countries like Germany began to develop economically and free trade no longer served our interest. But, somehow, we have never managed to come to grips with the debate and what to do about it. There have been attempts from time to time, like Joseph Chamberlain (1836–1914) in the early 1900s, who tried to define and protect our own sphere of economic influence. Similarly, [Oswald] Mosley tried to do something in the 1920s. But they both failed. The Labour Party never took it on board until 1970, but they did it for other reasons and became unelectable."

9. This misalignment is particularly pronounced in Tyndall's relationship with the former members of the BNP who moved to Combat 18. Again, see "Combat 18 Proscribed as Tyndall Runs Scared," *Searchlight*, no. 224 (1994):5.

10. Adorno found in Spengler's work an analogous substance: "This is the conception of the moving force of history, of 'souldom,' of the enigmatic thoroughly inward, inexplicable quality which sometimes appears in history in a particular type of man, or as Spengler sometimes calls it, 'a race.' But the metaphysics of 'souldom' has consequences more far-reaching. . . . One could call it a latent philosophy of identity" (1967:67).

11. Eatwell summarizes these element as follows: "Among the most important were: between a conservative view of man constrained by nature and the more left-wing view of the possibilities of creating a "new man"; between a commitment to science, especially in terms of understanding human nature, and a more anti-rationalist, vitalist interest in the possibilities of the will (one of the factors which attracted the philosopher Heidegger to Nazism was his belief that the fall into inauthentic modes of existence in modern society was reversible); between the faith and service of Christianity and the heroism of Classical thought, between private property relations more typical of the right and a form of welfarism more typical of the left" (1992:189).

12. See Thurlow 1974 and Baker 1985.

13. After his resignation he joined the British army and fought to defeat Hitler. "Chesterton, never a Nazi, was genuinely horrified by Hitler's policy of genocide and, unable to comprehend the racially-motivated drive to imperialist war by the Nazis (he believed that other peoples could never become Aryanized, each nation being culturally distinct), he was left with little choice but to fight those he had previously considered his closest allies. He was also fearful that his most extreme cultural and conspiratorial writings of the thirties would be associated with Nazi genocide" (Baker 1985:28).

14. See Chesterton 1965.

15. Adorno comments on the dual character of this kind of claustrophobic framework inspired by Spengler: first, its peculiar sympathy with the plight of the iron-willed leader and, second, its inability to conceive any system not premised on a monolithic commitment to domination. "The interest which is decisive for this attitude is domination. All of Spengler's categories are determined by this concept. His sympathies are with the rulers, and when speaking of the immense intelligence and iron will of modern industrial leaders, the philosopher of

historical disillusionment can gush like one of the pacifists he is always mocking. His entire image of history is measured by the ideal of domination. His affinity for this ideal gives him profound insight whenever it is a question of the possibilities of domination and blinds him with hatred as soon as he is confronted by impulses which go beyond all previous history as the history of domination" (Adorno 1967:61).

16. Sternhell has observed a similar instrumental and opportunistic role of anti-Semitism within the "integral nationalism" of L'Action française. Charles Maurras wrote: "Everything seems impossible or terribly difficult without the providential appearance of anti-Semitism. It enables everything to be arranged, smoothed over, and simplified. If one were not through patriotism, one would become one through a simple sense of opportunity" (quoted in Sternhell 1996:46).

17. Again, for a thorough analysis of these issues, see Paul 1997: chaps. 5, 6, and 8.

18. As noted earlier, the history of Afro-Caribbeans in London, these "newcomers," stretches back to 1555 (Merriman 1993).

19. Griffin also provides a raucous account of his own trial in April 1999 on charges of incitement to racial hatred. Putting his legal training to work, he acted in his own defense without a barrister or solicitor. The trail is claimed as a resounding moral victory for the BNP, though Griffin was found guilty by the jury.

CHAPTER TEN
RADICAL SYMMETRY

1. Le Pen's speech was retrieved from the FN Home Page, http://www.front-nat.fr/, October 27, 1997. It is titled, "Xth Conference of the National Front March, 29th , 30th , 31st in Strasbourg: Closing Speech of Jean-Marie Le Pen." The copy of the speech by Blair was supplied by the Labour Party, John Smith House, London, June 25, 1997. It is titled, "Speech by the Prime Minister, The Rt Hon Tony Blair MP, at the Aylesbury Estate, Southwark, On 2 June 1997," and marked "Check against Delivery."

2. There is little doubt that the new prime minister intends this program of welfare reform as a centerpiece of the radical agenda he envisions for his government. " 'Division among radicals almost 100 years ago,' Tony Blair told the Labour Party last year, 'resulted in a 20th century dominated by Conservatives. I want the 21st century to be the century of the radicals' " (Beer 1998:23).

3. Blair has embraced a sophisticated theoretical treatment of the dynamics of "individualization" as rendered by the Theory, Culture, Society Group composed of Ulrich Beck, Anthony Giddens, and Scott Lash. Moreover, Anthony Giddens became a very important senior advisor to the prime minister. Beck gives an optimistic depiction of this phenomenon: "The individualized everyday culture of the West is simply a culture of built-up knowledge and self-confidence: more and higher education, as well as better jobs and opportunities to earn money, in which people no longer just obey. Individuals still communicate in and play along with the old forms and institutions, but they also withdraw from them, with at least part of their existence, their identity, their commitment and their courage. Their withdrawal, however, is not just a withdrawal but at the same time an emigration

to new niches of activity and identity. The latter seem so unclear and inconsistent not least because this inner migration often takes place half-heartedly, with one foot, so to speak while the other foot is still firmly planted in the old order" (1994:20–21).

4. Obviously, translation in and of itself violates to some degree Herder's postulates. Catherine Garibal-Couot provided excellent assistance in the translation of this text retaining, as much as possible, its expressionist and populist efficacy.

5. Le Pen makes a play on words for which he is infamous using the term *énarchie* to imply the anarchy of bureaucrats. An *énarque* is a graduate of the Ecole nationale d'Administration (ENA), the school that trains the administrative elite of France.

6. "First because there was no way of avoiding it the cost of a workless class falls on businesses and people in work. The Tories never guessed that social security spending would double since 1979, that it would rise from 9 percent of GDP to 13 percent, nearly £100 billion, that crime would more than double or that benefits for lone parents would now cost £10 billion each year. Yet these were the predictable consequences of their policies, since while they talked of cutting crime and social security costs, their policies were in fact fueling them—and loading extra cost onto every one from taxpayers to hospitals to insurance companies. . . .

"The second reason the Tories were proven wrong is that the people of Britain found it morally unacceptable that so many should have no stake. They saw it as an offence against decency that work should be allowed to disappear from so many areas of the country, work to be replaced by an economy built on benefits, crime, petty thieving and drugs. For a country famous for its sense of fair play it was a source of national shame that visitors should see beggars on the streets and that Britain should have shot up the international league tables for inequality" (Blair 1997).

CHAPTER ELEVEN
ECLIPSE

1. "On 28.1.88 the 14th Chamber of the Court of Appeal of Versailles confirmed the ruling rendered on 23.9.87 by the Departmental Court of Nanterre which condemned Mr. Le Pen to pay a symbolic one franc indemnity to each of nine associations and three survivors of the deportation who filed complaints against him. . . . In describing the gas chambers as a 'detail' of World War II, the Versailles Court ruled . . . that [the assertion] was consenting to the horrible (event)" (Ford 1992).

2. The dialogue used in this chapter is drawn primarily from conversations with Gollnisch at the European Parliament in Strasbourg in May 1993 and with Schönhuber in Strasbourg in July 1994, and Hume in Strasbourg in April 1991.

3. Le Pen further delved into his dark rendering of historical details and facts through an oblique anti-Semitism. His anti-Semitic maneuver necessitates a mimesis of Jewish victimhood, appropriating its tropes and, thereby, devaluing its singular moral gravity through spurious equivalence. "Asked in Strasbourg if he would obey a summons to go to Munich to testify, Mr. Le Pen answered derisively, 'My condition is that they guarantee I will not immediately be sent to Dachau or Buchenwald,' he said, referring to the concentration camps Hitler built

outside Munich and near Weimar." He punctuated his anti-Semitism with a counterblow at German politicians, the largest national group in the European Parliament, who voted to lift his immunity. He reminds the German Social Democrats, Christian Democrats, and Greens: "Let us not forget that I am the victim. . . . It wasn't I who invented the concentration camps, but the fathers, grandfathers and uncles of my German colleagues here" (Whitney 1998).

4. Within the same week of his loss of parliamentary immunity, Le Pen was also convicted of assaulting a Socialist politician, Annette Peulvast-Bergeal who was campaigning against his daughter in the legislative elections of 1997 in the Paris suburb of Mantes-la-Jolie. In November an appeals court upheld Le Pen's conviction sentencing him to a three-month suspended jail sentence and a one-year loss of civil rights which would have precluded him from leading his party in the 1999 European Parliamentary elections. Le Pen appealed the conviction to the Court de Cassation, which lifted the conviction, allowing Le Pen to stand for reelection. The events of the fall of 1998 precipitated an internal crisis within the Front national and an open challenge to Le Pen's leadership by Bruno Mégret.

5. "He [Schönhuber] was assigned to the division in the Leibstandarte SS Adolf Hitler, served on the southern front, and was awarded the Iron Cross Second Class for bravery at Bastia in Corsica, where in September 1943, after Italy's defection, his unit withstood the attacks of a greatly superior Italian force and made good its escape to Elba" (Craig 1989). See Schönhuber 1981; 1983; 1987.

6. Moeller (1996:1008–48) has analyzed the character of this rhetorical maneuver and the broader political movement of which Franz Schönhuber was a part. Moeller demonstrates: "how in the first postwar decade stories of expellees from eastern Germany and Eastern Europe and German prisoners of war imprisoned in the Soviet Union were crafted into rhetorics of victimization in the arena of public policy and in the writing of 'contemporary history'. . . . Focusing on German suffering . . . made it possible to talk about the end of the Third Reich without assessing responsibility for its origins, to tell an abbreviated story of National Socialism in which all Germans were ultimately victims of a war that Hitler started but everyone lost" (1996:1013). Through this victimology, equating the suffering of Jews and Germans and blurring the lines between victims and perpetrators, an exculpatory history was crafted.

7. Schönhuber recapitulates in a political vernacular many elements of the famous *Historikerstreit*, the historians' debate, of the 1980s. For far more than a mere summary of this debate, see Maier 1988. For a collection of the relevant exchanges in the debate, see Knowlton and Cates 1993. See also Eatwell 1991; Lipstadt 1993.

8. The executive and the democratically elected Northern Ireland Assembly are designed to operate "on an across-community basis" with a voting system ("parallel consent" or "a weighted majority") to insure that "all sections of the community are protected." The council, like its EU counterpart, is composed of ministers of the Northern Ireland Assembly and the Irish government. Its function is "to reach agreement on the adoption of common policies, in areas where there is a mutual cross-border and all-island benefit." The council, supported by a joint secretariat, staffed by members of the Northern Ireland civil service and Irish civil service, is charged with a broad range of shared competencies over agriculture,

education, transport, environment, health, urban and rural development, waterways, tourism, fisheries, social security, and social welfare. The council is responsible for the implementation of EU policies and programs and ensuring that the common interests of the North and South are represented before relevant EU institutions. The Intergovernmental Conference as agreed to in Strand Three, is charged with all nondevolved powers particularly those covering security matters, the areas of rights, justice, prisons, and policing in Northern Ireland. More generally, the conference with its own joint secretariat, is charged with promoting bilateral cooperation at all levels of "mutual interest within the competence of both Governments"; of holding regular and frequent meetings concerning nondevolved Northern Ireland matters, at which time the Irish government can express views and table proposals; and of reviewing the implementation of the Good Friday Agreement as a whole (Northern Ireland Peace Accord 1998).

9. The difficulties encountered implementing the Good Friday Accord reflect this potential.

# BIBLIOGRAPHY

TREATIES AND AGREEMENTS

Northern Ireland Peace Accord. April 11, 1998.
Single European Act, Luxembourg and The Hague. February 17 and 28, 1986.
Treaties establishing the European Economic Community (EEC) and the European Atomic Energy Community (Euratom), Rome. March 25, 1957.
Treaty of Amsterdam, Amsterdam. October 2, 1997.
Treaty on European Union, Maastricht. February 7, 1992.


OTHER SOURCES

Abélès, Marc. 1992. *La vie quotidienne au Parlement européen*. Paris: Hachette.
———. 1995. "Pour une anthropologie des institutions." *L'Homme* 135:65–85.
———. 1996. *En attente d'Europe: Débat avec Jean-Louis Bourlanges*. Paris: Hachette.
Adamson, Walter L. 1980. *Hegemony and Revolution: A Study of Antonio Gramsci's Political and Cultural Theory*. Berkeley: University of California Press.
———. 1989. "Fascism and Culture: Avant-Gardes and Secular Religion in the Italian Case." *Journal of Contemporary History* 24 (3):411–35.
———. 1993. *Avant-Garde Florence: From Fascism to Modernism*. Cambridge: Harvard University Press.
Adenauer, Konrad. 1966. *Memoirs 1945–53*. Chicago: Henry Regnery.
Adorno, Theodor W. 1967. *Prisms*. Cambridge: MIT Press.
———. 1973. *The Jargon of Authenticity*. Translated by Knut Tarnowski and Frederic Will. Evanston, Ill.: Northwestern University Press.
Agger, Ben. 1989. *Fast Capitalism: A Critical Theory of Significance*. Urbana: University of Illinois Press.
Alter, Peter. 1994. *Nationalism*. London: Edward Arnold.
Amato, Joseph. 1975. *Mounier and Maritain: A French Catholic Understanding of the Modern World*. Birmingham: University of Alabama Press.
Anderson, Benedict. 1991. *Imagined Communities: Reflections on the Origin and Spread of Nationalism*. New York: Verso.
Anderson, Perry. 1992. "The Pluralism of Isaiah Berlin." In *Zones of Engagement*, pp. 230–50. London: Verso.
———. 1996. "Under the Sign of the Interim." *London Review of Books*, January 4, 1996, p. 17.
Annual Report. 1993–94. *Communities or Resistance*. Newham: Newham Monitoring Project.
Appadurai, Arjun. 1996. *Modernity at Large: Cultural Dimensions of Globalization*. Minneapolis: University of Minnesota Press.
Arendt, Hannah. 1951. *The Origins of Totalitarianism*. New York: Harcourt Brace.

Arendt, Hannah. 1964. *Eichmann in Jerusalem: A Report on the Banality of Evil.* New York: Viking.

Aron, Raymond. 1990. *Memoirs: Fifty Years of Political Reflection.* Translated by George Holoch. New York: Holmes and Meier.

Asad, Talal. 1993. *Genealogies of Religion: Discipline and Reasons of Power in Christianity and Islam.* Baltimore: Johns Hopkins University Press.

Asad, Talal, James Fernandez, Michael Herzfeld, Andrew Lass, Susan Carol Rogers, Jane Schneider, and Katherine Verdery. 1997. "Provocations of European Ethnology." *American Anthropologist* 99:713–30.

Atkinson, Graeme. 1999. "Ten Days That Shook the Front." *Searchlight,* no. 284: 17–19.

Baker, David L. 1985. "A. K. Chesterton, the Strasser Brothers and the Politics of the National Front." *Patterns and Prejudice* 19:23–33.

Balibar, Étienne. 1991. "La Communauté europée vue du dessous: Du racisme archaique à l'état de bib-droit." *Le Monde Diplomatique,* no. 443, February, pp. 22–23.

———. 1995. "Ambiguous Universality." *Differences* 7:48–74.

———. 1996. "Is European Citizenship Possible?" *Public Culture* 8. (2):355–76.

Barzanti, Roberto, *rapporteur.* 1990. "On Subsidiarity." Opinion of the Committee on Youth, Culture, Education, the Media and Sport for the Committee on Institutional Affairs of the European Parliament. Luxemburg: European Parliament.

Bauman, Zygmunt. 1997a. "No Way Back to Bliss: How to Cope with the Restless Chaos of Modernity." *Times Literary Supplement,* no. 4895, January 24, p. 5.

———. 1997b. "The Making and Unmaking of Strangers." In *Debating Cultural Hybridity: Multi-Cultural Identities and the Politics of Anti-Racism,* edited by Pnina Werbner and Tariq Modood, pp. 46–57. London: Zed Books.

Baumann, Gerd. 1995. "Managing a Polyethnic Milieu: Kinship and Interaction in a London Suburb," *Journal of the Royal Anthropological Institute* 1 (4):725–42.

———. 1996. *Contesting Culture: Discourses of Identity in Multi-Ethnic London.* Cambridge: Cambridge University Press.

Beck, Ulrich, Anthony Giddens, and Scott Lash. 1994. *Reflexive Modernization: Politics, Tradition and Aesthetics in the Modern Social Order.* Stanford, Calif.: Stanford University Press.

Beer, Samuel. 1998. "The Roots of New Labour: Liberalism Rediscovered." *Economist,* February 7–13, pp. 23–25.

Bellier, Irène. 1994. "La Commission européenne: Hauts fonctionnaries et 'culture du management.'" *Revue française d'administration publique,* 70:253–62.

———. 1997. "The Commission as an Actor: An Anthropologist's View." In *Participation and Policy-Making in the European Union,* edited by Helen Wallace and Alasdair R. Young, pp. 91–115. Oxford: Clarendon Press.

Benoist, Alain. 1977. *Vu du Droite.* Paris: Copernic.

———. 1980. *Les idées à l'endroit.* Paris: Albin Michel.

Berlin, Isaiah. 1976. *Vico and Herder: Two Studies in the History of Ideas*. London: Hogarth Press.

———. 1979. *Against the Current: Essays in the History of Ideas*. London: Hogarth Press.

———. 1990. "Joseph de Maistre and the Origins of Fascism, I–III," *New York Review of Books*, September 27, pp. 57–64; October 11, pp. 54–58; October 25, 1990, pp. 61–65.

———. 1997. *The Crooked Timber of Humanity*. Edited by Henry Hardy. Princeton: Princeton University Press.

Berman, Marshall. 1982. *All That is Solid Melts into Air*. New York: Penguin.

———. 1989. *Modern Culture and Cultural Theory: Art, Politics, and the Legacy of the Frankfurt School*. Madison: University of Wisconson Press.

Berstein, Serge, Jean-Marie Mayeur, and Pierre Milza, eds. 1993. *Le MRP et la construction européenne*. Brussels: Editions Complexe.

Blair, Tony. 1997. Speech by the Prime Minister, The Rt Hon Tony Blair MP, at Aylesbury Estate, Southwark, June 2.

———. 1999. *The Third Way: New Politics of a New Century*. Fabian Pamphlet 588. London: Fabian Society.

Bloch-Lainé, François, and Jean Bouview. 1986. *La France Restaurée 1944–54*. Paris: Fayard.

Blot, Yvot. 1992. *Baroque et politique: Le Pen est-il néo-baroque?* Paris: Editions Nationales.

Borchardt, Klaus-Dieter. 1989. *European Unification: The Origins and Growth of the European Community*. Luxembourg: Office for Official Publications of the European Communities.

Borneman, John. 1992. *Belonging in the Two Berlins: Kin, State, Nation*. Cambridge: Cambridge University Press.

———. 1998. *Subversions of International Order*. Albany, N.Y.: SUNY Press.

Borneman, John and Nick Fowler. 1997. "Europeanization." *Annual Reviews of Anthropology*. 26:487–514.

Bouvet, Laurent, and Michel Frédéric. 1999. "Pluralism and the New French Left." In *The New European Left*, edited by Gavin Kelly, pp. 35–46. London: Fabian Society.

Bredin, Jean-Denis. 1986. *The Affair: The Case of Alfred Dreyfus*. Translated by Jeffrey Mehlman. New York: Braziller.

Bromberger, Merry and Serge Bromberger. 1969. *Jean Monnet and the United States of Europe*. New York: Coward-McCann.

Brubaker, Roger. 1992. *Citizenship and Nationhood in France and Germany*. Cambridge: Harvard University Press.

Buford, Bill. 1992. *Among the Thugs*. New York: Random House.

Caciagli, Mario, and David Kertzer, eds. 1996. *Italian Politics: The Stalled Transition*. A Publication of the Istituto Cattaneo. Boulder, Colo.: Westview.

Campbell, John. 1964. *Honour, Family, and Patronage: A Study of Institutions and Moral Values in a Greek Mountain Community*. Oxford: Clarendon Press.

*CARF: Campaign against Racism and Fascism*. 1993. "Who's the Most Racist of Them All?" no. 17, November–December, pp. 8–9.

Carter, Donald Martin. 1997. *States of Grace: Senegalese in Italy and the New European Immigration.* Minneapolis: University of Minnesota Press.

Chesterton, Arthur K. 1965. *The New Unhappy Lords.* London: Candour.

Clifford, James. 1997. *Routes: Travel and Translation in the Late Twentieth Century.* Cambridge: Harvard University Press.

Club de l'horloge. 1985. *L'identité de la France.* Paris: Albin Michel.

Cohen, Abner. 1980. "Drama and Politics in the Development of a London Carnival." *Man* 15:66–85.

———. 1982. "A Polyethnic London Carnival as a Contested Cultural Performance." *Ethnic and Racial Studies* 5:23–38.

———. 1993. *Masquerade Politics: Explorations in the Structure of Urban Cultural Movement.* Berkeley: University of California Press.

Cohen-Tangui, Laurent. 1992. *L'Europe en danger.* Paris: Fayard.

Cole, Jeffrey. 1997. *The New Racism in Europe: A Sicilian Ethnography.* Cambridge: Cambridge University Press.

Colombo, Emilio, *rapporteur.* 1990a. "On the European Parliament's Guidelines for a Draft Constitution for the European Union" (Part A). Report on behalf of the Committee on Institutional Affairs for the European Parliament. Luxemburg: European Parliament.

———. 1990b. "Explanatory Statement. On the European Parliament's Guidelines for a Draft Constitution for the European Union" (Part B). Report on behalf of the Committee on Institutional Affairs for the European Parliament. Luxemburg: European Parliament.

Connolly, Bernard. 1995. *The Rotten Heart of Europe: The Dirty War for Europe's Money.* London: Faber & Faber.

Copsey, Nigel. 1996. "Contemporary Fascism in the Local Arena: The British National Party and 'Rights for Whites.'" In *The Failure of British Fascism: The Far Right and the Fight for Political Recognition,* edited by Mike Cronin, pp. 118–40. New York: St. Martin's.

Cowan, Jane. 1997. "Idioms of Belonging: Polyglot Articulations of Local Identity in a Greek Macedonian Town." In *Ourselves and Others: The Development of a Greek Macedonian Cultural Identity since 1912,* edited by Peter Mackridge and Eleni Yannakakis, pp. 153–71. Oxford: Berg.

Craig, Gordon A. 1989. "The Rising Star of the German Right." *New York Review of Books.* June 15, pp. 22–24.

Dahrendorf, Ralph. 1997. *After 1989: Morals, Revolution and Civil Society.* New York: St. Martin's.

Delors, Jacques. 1989. *Delors Report on the Economic and Monetary Union of the European Community.* Committee for the Study of Economic and Monetary Union. Luxembourg: Office for Official Publications of the European Communities.

———. 1991. "Subsidiarity: The Challenge of Change." *Proceedings of the Jacques Delors Colloquium* (March 21–22). Maastricht: European Institute of Public Administration.

———. 1992. *Our Europe: The Community and National Development.* Translated by Brian Pearce. London: Verso.

Diebold, William. 1959. *The Schuman Plan.* New York: Praeger.

Dominquez, Virginia. 1997. "Implications: A Commentary on Stoler." *Political Power and Social Theory* 11:207–15.

Duchêne, François. 1991. "Jean Monnet's Method." In *Jean Monnet: The Path to European Unity*, edited by Douglas Brinkley and Clifford Hackett, pp. 86–113. London: Macmillan.

———. 1995. *Jean Monnet: The First Statesman of Interdependence*. New York: Norton.

Durham, Martin. 1991. "Women in the National Front." In *Neo-Fascism in Europe*, edited by Luciano Cheles, Ronnie Ferguson, and Michalina Vaughan, pp. 264–83. London: Longman.

Durkheim, Emile. 1933. *The Division of Labor in Society*. Glencoe, Ill.: Free Press.

———. 1951. *Suicide: A Study in Sociology*. Glencoe, Ill.: Free Press.

Eade, John. 1989. *The Politics of Community: The Bangladeshi Community in East London*. Aldershot: Avebury.

———. 1990. "Bangladeshi Community Organisation and Leadership in Tower Hamlets, East London." In *South Asians Overseas: Migration and Ethnicity*, edited by Colin Clarke, Ceri Peach, and Steven Vertovec, pp. 317–29. Cambridge: Cambridge University Press.

———. 1991. "The Political Construction of Class and Community: Bangladeshi Political Leadership in Tower Hamlets, East London." In *Black and Ethnic Leadership in Britain: The Cultural Dimension of Political Action*, edited by Pnina Werbner and Muhammad Anwar, pp. 84–109. London: Routledge.

Eatwell, Roger. 1991. "Holocaust Denial: A Study in Propaganda Technique." In *Neo-Fascism in Europe*, edited by Luciano Cheles, Ronnie Ferguson, and Michalina Vaughan, pp. 120–46. London: Longman.

———. 1992. "Towards a New Model of Generic Fascism." *Journal of Theoretical Politics* 4:161–94.

———. 1995. "The New Synthesis." In *Fascism*, edited by Roger Griffin, pp. 306–307. Oxford: Oxford University Press.

———. 1996. *Fascism: A History*. New York: Penguin.

Eley, Geoff. 1984. "Reading Gramsci in English: Observations on the Reception of Antonio Gramsci in the English-Speaking World, 1957–82." *European History Quarterly* 14:441–77.

———. 1994. "Nations, Publics, and Political Cultures: Placing Habermas in the Nineteenth Century." In *Culture/Power/History: Reader in Contemporary Social Theory*, edited by Nicholas B. Dirks, Geoff Eley, and Sherry B. Ortner, pp. 297–335. Princeton: Princeton University Press.

Emiliou, Nicholas. 1992. "Subsidiarity: An Effective Barrier against 'The Enterprises of Ambition?'" *European Law Review* 17 (5):383–405.

European Commission. 1992. "The Principle of Subsidiarity: Communication of the Commission to the Council and the European Parliament (27 October 1992)." Brussels: Commission of the European Communities.

Evans, Joseph W. and Leo R. Ward. 1955. *The Social and Political Philosophy of Jacques Maritain: Selected Readings*. New York: Scribner.

Evola, Julius. 1978. *Imperialismo pagano: Il fascismo dinanzi al pericolo euro-cristiano*. Padova: Edizioni di Ar.

Faubion, James E. 1993. *Modern Greek Lessons: A Primer in Historical Constructivism*. Princeton: Princeton University Press.

———. 1996. "Kinship is Dead. Long Live Kinship. A Review Article." *Comparative Studies in Society and History*, 38(1): 67–91.

Faux, Emmanuel, Thomas Legrand and Gilles Perez. 1994. *La main droite de Dieu: Enquête sur François Mitterrand et l'extrême droite*. Paris: Seuil.

Feldman, Allen. 1991. *Formations of Violence: The Narrative of the Body and Political Terror in Northern Ireland*. Chicago: University of Chicago Press.

Fischer, Claus P. 1995. *Nazi Germany: A New History*. New York: Continuum.

Fogarty, Michael P. 1957. *Christian Democracy in Western Europe, 1820–1953*. Notre Dame, Ind.: University of Notre Dame Press.

Fontaine, Pascal. 1990. *Europe—A Fresh Start: The Schuman Declaration, 1950–90*. Luxembourg: Office for Official Publications of the European Communities.

Ford, Glyn, ed. 1992. *Fascist Europe: The Rise of Racism and Xenophobia*. London: Pluto Press.

Foucault, Michel. 1978. *The History of Sexuality: An Introduction*. Vol. 1. Translated by Robert Hurley. New York: Vintage Books.

Friedländer, Saul. 1984. *Reflections of Nazism*. Translated by Thomas Weyr. New York: Avon.

Fysh, Peter, and Jim Wolfreys. 1992. "Le Pen, the National Front and the Extreme Right in France." *Parliamentary Affairs* 45:309–26.

Gable, Gerry. 1991. "The Far Right in Contemporary Britain." In *Neo-Fascism in Europe*, edited by Luciano Cheles, Ronnie Ferguson and Michalina Vaughan, pp. 245–63. London: Longman.

Gaffney, John. 1989. *The French Left and the 5th Republic: Discourses of Communism and Socialism in Contemporary France*. London: Macmillan.

Gaspard, François. 1995. *A Small City in France*. Cambridge: Harvard University Press.

Gay, Peter. 1993. *The Cultivation of Hatred: Bourgeois Experience, Victoria to Freud*. New York: Norton.

Gellner, Ernest. 1997. *Nationalism*. London: Weidenfeld and Nicolson.

Giddens, Anthony. 1992. *Modernity and Self-Identity*. Oxford: Blackwell.

Gilroy, Paul. 1991. *There Ain't No Black in the Union Jack*. Chicago: University of Chicago Press.

———. 1993. *Black Atlantic: Modernity and Double Consciousness*. Cambridge: Harvard University Press.

Ginzburg, Carlo 1983. *The Night Battles: Witchcraft and Agrarian Cults in the Sixteenth and Seventeenth Centuries*. Translated by John and Anne Tedeschi. Baltimore: Johns Hopkins University Press.

Giscard d'Estaing, Valery. *rapporteur*. 1990. "On the Principle of Subsidiarity." Report on behalf of the Committee on Institutional Affairs for the European Parliament. Luxemburg: European Parliament.

Gourevitch, Philip. 1997. "The Unthinkable: How Dangerous Is Le Pen's National Front?" *New Yorker*, April 28 and May 5, 1997, pp. 110–49.

Gray, John. 1996. *Isaiah Berlin*. Princeton: Princeton University Press.

Greenfeld, Liah. 1992. *Nationalism: Five Roads to Modernity*. Cambridge: Harvard University Press.

Griffin, Roger. 1992. "Europe for the Europeans: Fascist Myths of the European New Order, 1922–1992." Humanities Research Centre, Occasional Papers no. 1. Oxford: Brookes University.

———. 1993. *The Nature of Fascism*. London: Routledge.

———. 1995. *Fascism*. Oxford: Oxford University Press.

———. 1996a. "British Fascism: The Ugly Duckling." In *The Failure of British Fascism: The Far Right and the Fight for Political Recognition*, edited by Michael Cronin, pp. 144–65. New York: St. Martin's.

———. 1996b. "The 'Post-Fascism' of the *Alleanza Nazionale*: A Case-Study in Ideological Morphology." *Journal of Political Ideologies* 1 (2):123–45.

Haas, Ernst B. 1964. "Technocracy, Pluralism and the New Europe." In *A New Europe?*, edited by Stephen R. Graubard, pp. 62–88.

———. 1968. *The Uniting of Europe: Political, Social, and Economic Forces, 1950–1957*. Stanford, Calif.: Stanford University Press.

Habermas, Jürgen. 1987. *The Theory of Communicative Action*. Vol. 1, *Reason and the Rationalization of Society*. Vol. 2, *Lifeworld and System: A Critique of Functionalist Reason*. Translated by Thomas McCarthy. Boston: Beacon.

———. 1991. *The Structural Transformation of the Public Sphere: An Inquiry into a Category of Bourgeois Society*. Translated by Thomas Burger. Cambridge: MIT Press.

Hall, Stuart. 1980. "Race, Articulation and Societies Structured in Dominance." In *Sociological Theories: Race and Colonialism*. Paris: UNESCO.

———. 1988. *The Hard Road to Renewal: Thatcherism and the Crisis of the Left*. London: Verso.

———. 1993. "Culture, Community, Nation." *Cultural Studies* 7:349–63.

Handler, Richard. 1988. *Nationalism and the Politics of Culture in Quebec*. Madison: University of Wisconsin Press.

Harding, Susan. 1991. "Representing Fundamentalism: The Problem of the Repugnant Cultural Order." *Social Research* 58:373–93.

Harte, T. J. 1967. "*Mater et Magistra*." In *New Catholic Encyclopedia*, 9:441. New York: McGraw Hill.

Harvey, David. 1989. *The Condition of Postmodernity: An Enquiry into the Origins of Cultural Change*. Oxford: Blackwell.

Hastings, M. 1988. "La Rhétorique hygiéniste de Jean-Marie Le Pen." *Revue politique et parlementaire* 93:55–58.

Hellman, John. 1981. *Emmanuel Mounier and the New Catholic Left, 1930–1959*. Toronto: University of Toronto Press.

Herbert, Christopher. 1991. *Culture and Anomie: Ethnographic Imagination in the Nineteenth Century*. Chicago: University of Chicago Press.

Herf, Jeff. 1986. *Reactionary Moderns*. Cambridge: Cambridge University Press.

Herzfeld, Michael. 1987. *Anthropology through the Looking-Glass: Critical Ethnography in the Margins of Europe*. Cambridge: Cambridge University Press.

———. 1993. *The Social Production of Indifference: Exploring the Symbolic Roots of Western Bureaucracy*. Chicago: University of Chicago Press.

Herzfeld, Michael. 1997. *Cultural Intimacy: Social Poetics in the Nation-State.* London: Routledge.

Hiro, Dilip. 1992. *Black British, White British: A History of Race Relations in Britain.* London: Paladin.

Hoffman, Stanley. 1956. *Le mouvement Poujade.* Paris: André Colin.

———. 1995. *The European Sisyphus: Essays on Europe, 1964–1994.* Boulder, Colo.: Westview.

———. 1997. "Look Back in Anger." *New York Review of Books,* July 17, pp. 45–50.

Holmes, Douglas R. 1989. *Cultural Disenchantments: Worker Peasantries in Northeast Italy.* Princeton: Princeton University Press.

———. 1993. "Illicit Discourse," In *Perilous States: Conversations on Culture, Politics and Nation,* edited by George Marcus, Late Edition 1, pp. 255–81. Chicago: University of Chicago Press.

———. 1999. "Tactical Thuggery: National Socialism in the East End of London." In *Paranoia within Reason,* edited by George Marcus, Late Edition 6, pp. 319–41. Chicago: University of Chicago Press.

Horkheimer, Max. 1995. "The Iron Heel." In *Fascism,* edited by Roger Griffin, pp. 272–73. Oxford: Oxford University Press.

Huntington, Samuel. 1996. *The Clash of Civilizations and the Remaking of World Order.* New York: Simon and Schuster.

Husbands, Christopher T. 1982. "East End Racism, 1900–1980: Geographical Continuities in Vigilantist and Extreme Right-Wing Political Behavior." *London Journal* 8:3–26.

———. 1983. *Racial Exclusion and the City: The Urban Support of the National Front.* London: Allen & Unwin.

Jacobs, Francis, Richard Corbett, and Michael Skackelton. 1995. *The European Parliament.* New York: Cartermill International.

Jacovissi, Robert. 1980. *Movimento Friuli "il Movimento Friuli per l'alternativa friulana" ("pe autonomie dal Friûl unît une alternative furlane nazionalitarie").* Udine: Grafiche Fulvio spa.

John XXIII. 1981a. *Mater et magistra.* Encyclical of Pope John XXIII on Christianity and Social Progress. May 15, 1961. In *Papal Encyclicals, 1958–81,* edited by Claudia Carlen, pp. 59–90. Raleigh, N.C.: McGrath.

———. 1981b. *Pacem in terris.* On Establishing Universal Peace in Truth, Justice, Charity, and Liberty. April 11, 1963. In *Papal Encyclicals, 1958–81,* edited by Claudia Carlen, pp. 107–29. Raleigh, N.C.: McGrath.

Johnson, Douglas. 1991. "The New Right in France." *In Neo-Fascism in Europe,* edited by Luciano Cheles, Ronnie Ferguson, and Michalina Vaughan, pp. 234–44. London: Longman.

Jospin, Lionel. 1999. *Modern Socialism.* Fabian Pamphlet 592. London: Fabian Society.

Judt, Tony. 1992. *Past Imperfect: French Intellectuals, 1944–1956.* Berkeley: University of California Press.

———. 1996. *A Grand Illusion? An Essay on Europe.* New York: Hill and Wang.

Kalb, Donald. 1997. *Expanding Class: Power and Everyday Politics in Industrial Communities, the Netherlands, 1850–1950.* Durham, N.C.: Duke University Press.

Kaplan, Alice Yaeger. 1986. *Reproductions of Banality: Fascism, Literature, and French Intellectual Life.* Minneapolis: University of Minnesota Press.

Kertzer, David I. 1980. *Comrades and Christians: Religion and Political Struggle in Communist Italy.* Cambridge: Cambridge University Press.

———. 1996. *Politics and Symbols: The Italian Communist Party and the Fall of Communism.* New Haven: Yale University Press.

King, Sam. 1999. "Griffin Heads for Victory." *Searchlight*, no. 292: 4–7.

King, Sam and Jean Raymond. 1999. "Searchlight Essay: The French Connection." *Searchlight*, no. 286:28–29.

Knowlton, James, and Truett Cates, eds. 1993. *Forever in the Shadow of Hitler?* Atlantic Highlands, N.J.: Humanities Press.

Lash, Scott and John Urry. 1989. *The End of Organized Capitalism.* Madison: University of Wisconsin Press.

Leggevie, Claus. 1990. *Die Republikaner: Ein Phantom nimmt Gestalt an.* Berlin: Rotbouch.

Lemke, Christine and Gary Marks. 1992. *The Crisis of Socialism in Europe.* Durham, N.C.: Duke University Press.

Leo XIII. 1981. *Rerum novarum.* Encyclical of Pope Leo XIII on Capital and Labor. May 15, 1891. In *Papal Encyclicals, 1878–1903*, edited by Claudia Carlen, pp. 242–61. Raleigh, N.C.: McGrath.

Le Pen, Jean-Marie. 1985. *Les français d'abord.* Paris: Carrere/Lafon.

———. 1989. *Europe: Discours et interventions 1984–1989.* Paris: Groupes droites européennes.

———. 1997. Closing Speech of Jean-Marie Le Pen delivered at the Xth Conference of the National Front. Strasbourg, March 29–31. (http://front-nat.fr/).

Lifton, Robert J. 1986. *The Nazi Doctors: Medical Killing and the Psychology of Genocide.* New York: Basic.

Lipgens, Walter, ed. 1985. *Documents on the History of European Integration.* Vol. 1, *Continental Plans for European Union, 1939–1945.* Vol. 2, *Plans for European Union in Great Britain and in Exile, 1939–1945.* Vol. 3, *The Struggle for European Union by Political Parties and Pressure Groups in Western European Countries, 1945–1950.* Vol. 4, *Transnational Organizations of Political Parties and Pressure Groups in the Struggle for European Union, 1945–1950.* Translated by Paula Falla. Berlin: Walter de Gruyter.

Lipset, Seymour. 1960. *Political Man: The Social Basis of Politics.* New York: Doubleday.

Lipstadt, Deborah E. 1993. *Denying the Holocaust: The Growing Assault on Truth and Memory.* New York: Free Press.

Lowles, Nick. 2000. "Airbrushing Out the Past." *Searchlight*, no. 295: 7.

MacDonald, M. 1996. " 'Unity in Diversity': Some Tensions in the Construction of Europe." *Social Anthropology* 4:47–60.

Maier, Charles. 1988. *The Unmasterable Past: History, Holocaust, and German National Identity.* Cambridge: Harvard University Press.

Marcus, George. 1999. *Ethnography through Thick and Thin*. Princeton: Princeton University Press.

Marcus, Jonathan. 1995. *The Front National in French Politics: The Resistible Rise of Jean-Marie Le Pen*. New York: New York University Press.

Maritain, Jacques. 1950. *Man and the State*. Chicago: University of Chicago Press.

Martin, Emily. 1994. *Flexible Bodies: Tracing Immunity in American Culture from the Days of Polio to the Age of Aids*. Boston: Beacon.

Martin, J.-C. 1990. *Blancs et bleus dans la vendée déchirée*. Paris: Découvertes-Gallimard.

Massé, Pierre. 1991. *Le plan ou l'anti-hasard*. Paris: Hermann.

Mayhew, Henry. 1985. *London Labour and the London Poor*. 1851–61. New York: Penguin.

Mayne, Richard. 1991. "Grey Eminence." In *Jean Monnet: The Path to European Unity*, edited by Douglas Brinkley and Clifford Hackett, pp. 114–28. London: Macmillan.

Mayne, Richard, and John Pinder with John Roberts. 1990. *Federal Union: The Pioneers*. New York: St. Martin's Press.

McCormick, John. 1996. *The European Union: Politics and Policies*. Boulder, Colo.: Westview.

McLellan, David. 1974. *Karl Marx: His Life and Thought*. New York: Harper and Row.

Meinecke, Friedrich. 1970. *Cosmopolitanism and the National State*. Princeton: Princeton University Press.

Melucci, Alberto. 1989. *Nomads of the Present: Social Movements and Individual Needs in Contemporary Society*. Edited by John Keane and Paul Mier. Philadelphia: Temple University Press.

Mehta, Uday Singh. 1997. "The Essential Ambiguities of Race and Racism." *Political Power and Social Theory* 11: 234–46.

Merriman, Nick. 1993. *The Peopling of London: Fifteen Thousand Years of Settlement from Overseas*. London: Museum of London.

Meyer, Thomas. 1999. "From Godesberg to the *Neue Mitte*: The New Social Democracy in Germany." In *The New European Left*, edited by Gavin Kelly, pp. 20–46. London: Fabian Society.

Miles, Robert. 1989. *Racism*. London: Routledge.

Miller, R. J. 1967. "*Quadragesimo anno*." In *The New Catholic Encyclopedia*, 12:1. New York: McGraw Hill.

Millon-Delsol, Chantal. 1992. *L'état subsidiaire: Ingérence et non-ingérence de l'État: Le principe de subsidiarité aux fondements de l'histoire européenne*. Paris: Presses Universitaires de France.

Milward, Alan S. 1992. *The European Rescue of the Nation-State*. London: Routledge.

Milza, Pierre. 1987. *Fascisme français, passé et présent*. Paris: Flammarion.

Mintz, Jerome. 1982. *The Anarchist of Casas Viejas*. Chicago: University of Chicago Press.

Mioche, Phillipe. 1985. *Le Plan Monnet: Genèse et élaboration, 1941–1947*. Paris: Publications de la Sorbonne.

Mitrany, David. 1966. *A Working Peace System*. Chicago: Quadrangle.

Modood, Tariq and Pnina Werbner. 1997. *The Politics of Multiculturalism: Racism, Identity and Community in the New Europe*. London: Zed Books.

Moeller, Robert. 1996. "War Stories: The Search for a Usable Past in the Federal Republic of Germany." *American Historical Review*. 101(4):1008–48.

Monnet, Jean. 1978. *Jean Monnet: Memoirs*. London: Collins.

Moravcsik, Andrew. 1998. *The Choices for Europe: Social Purpose and State Power from Messina to Maastricht*. Ithaca, N.Y.: Cornell University Press.

Mosse, George L. 1978. *Toward the Final Solution: A History of European Racism*. Madison: University of Wisconsin Press.

———. 1980. "Toward a General Theory of Fascism." In *Masses and the Man*, edited by George L. Mosse, pp. 194–6. New York: Howard Fertig.

———. 1999. *The Fascist Revolution: Toward a General Theory of Fascism*. New York: Fertig.

Mosley, Nicholas. 1991. *Rules of the Game/Beyond the Pale: Memoirs of Sir Oswald Mosley and Family*. Elmwood Park, Ill.: Dalkey Archive Press.

Mühlberger, Detlef. 1991. *Hitler's Followers: Studies in the Sociology of the Nazi Movement*. London: Routledge.

Mulcahy, R. E. 1967. "Subsidiarity." *The New Catholic Encyclopedia*, 13:762–63. New York: McGraw Hill.

Nairn, Tom. 1988. *The Enchanted Glass: Britain and Its Monarchy*. London: Radius.

Nathan, Robert. 1991. "An Unsung Hero of World War II." In *Jean Monnet: The Path to European Unity*, edited by Douglas Brinkley and Clifford Hackett, pp. 67–85. London: Macmillan.

Nelde, Peter, Miquell Strubell, and Glyn Williams. 1996. *Euromosaic: The Production and Reproduction of the Minority Language Groups in the European Union*. Luxembourg: Office of Official Publications.

Newby, Howard. 1991. *Times*, March 26.

Newman, J. 1967. "*Rerum novarum*." In *The New Catholic Encyclopedia*, 12:387. New York: McGraw Hill.

Nietzsche, Friedrich. 1993. *Philosophy and Truth: Selections from Nietzsche's Notebooks of the early 1870s*. Translated by Daniel Breazeale. London: Humanities Press.

Noiriel, Gérard. 1996. *The French Melting Pot: Immigration, Citizenship, and National Identity*. Translated by Geoffroy de Laforcade. Minneapolis: University of Minnesota Press.

Paul, Kathleen. 1997. *Whitewashing Britain: Race and Citizenship in the Postwar Era*. Ithaca, N.Y.: Cornell University Press.

Payne, Stanley. 1995. *A History of Fascism, 1914–1945*. Madison: University of Wisconson Press.

Péan, Pierre. 1994. *Une jeunesse française: François Mitterrand, 1934–1947*. Paris: Fayard.

Péguy, Charles. 1950. *The Mystery of the Charity of Joan of Arc*. Translated by Julian Green. New York: Pantheon.

Pinder, John. 1991. *European Community: The Building of a Union*. Oxford: Oxford University Press.

Pitt-Rivers, Julian. 1961. *The People of the Sierra*. Chicago: University of Chicago Press.

Pius XI. 1981. *Quadregesimo anno*. Encyclical of Pope Pius XI on Reconstruction of the Social Order. May 15, 1931. In *Papal Encyclicals, 1903–1939*, edited by Claudia Carlen, pp. 415–43. Raleigh, N.C.: McGrath.

Polanyi, Karl. 1957. *The Great Transformation*. Boston: Beacon.

Poliakov, Leon. 1974. *The Aryan Myth: A History of Racist and Nationalist Ideas in Europe*. London: Heineman.

Powell, Enoch. 1969. *Freedom and Reality*. Kingswood: Paperfront.

———. 1978. *A Nation or No Nation?* London: Batsford.

Power, Susan M. 1992. *Jacques Maritain, 1882–1973: Christian Democrat, and the Quest for a New Commonwealth*. Lewiston, N.Y.: Edwin Mellen.

Rabinow, Paul. 1989. *French Modern: Norms and Forms of the Social Environment*. Cambridge: MIT Press.

———. 1997. *Essays on the Anthropology of Reason*. Princeton: Princeton University Press.

———. 1999. *French DNA: Trouble in Purgatory*. Chicago: University of Chicago Press.

Raymond, Jean. 1999. "France: Front National Split." *Searchlight*, no. 285:32–33.

Rémond, Réné. 1982. *Le droites en France de 1815 à nos jours*. Paris: Aubier-Montaigne.

Roediger, David. 1997. "A Response to Stoler." *Political Power and Social Theory*. 11:217–20.

Rogers, Susan Carol. 1991. *Shaping Modern Times in Rural France*. Princeton: Princeton University Press.

Rommen, Heinrich A. 1955. *The State in Catholic Thought: A Treatise in Political Philosophy*. London: Herder Books.

Ross, George. 1995. *Jacques Delors and European Integration*. New York: Oxford University Press.

Ross, George, Stanley Hoffmann, and S. Malzacher, eds. 1987. *The Mitterrand Experiment*. Cambridge: Polity Press.

Rousso, Henry. 1991. *Vichy Syndrome*. Cambridge: Harvard University Press.

Samual, Raphael, ed. 1989. *Patriotism—The Making and Unmaking of British National Identity*. London: Routledge.

Sassen, Saskia. 1996. "Whose City Is It? Globalization and the Formation of New Claims." *Public Culture* 8:205–23.

Sassoon, Donald. 1999. "Introduction: Convergence, Continuity, and Change on the European Left." In *The New European Left*, edited by Gavin Kelly, pp. 7–19. London: Fabian Society.

Schama, Simon. 1995. *Lanscape and Memory*. New York: Knopf.

Schneider, Jane, ed. 1998. *Italy's "Southern Question": Orientalism in One Country*. Oxford: Berg.

Schönhuber, Franz. 1981. *Ich war Dabei*. Munich: Langen Müller.

———. 1983. *Freunde in der Not*. Munich: Langen Müller.

———. 1987. *Trotz allem Deutschland*. Munich: Langen Müller.

Schumpeter, Joseph. 1987. *Capitalism, Socialism, and Democracy*. With an introduction by Tom Bottomore. London: Unwin Paperback.

Schutz, Alfred and Thomas Luckmann. 1973. *The Structure of Lifeworld.* Evanston, Ill.: Northwestern University Press.

*Searchlight.* 1993. "Councillor Beat'em Takes His Seat." No. 222:3–5.

———. 1994a. Editorial. "A Deadly Spring." No. 225:1.

———. 1994b. "When Nazi Criminals Fall Out." No. 225:4, 6.

———. 1994c. "Race War Kicks Off." No. 225:2–5.

———. 1994d. "BNP Stirs Up Violence to Boost Local Election Campaign." No. 226:3–7.

———. 1994e. "It's Civil War between Nazis as Local Elections Draw Near." No. 227:3–7.

———. 1994f. "Beyond Beackon." No. 228:2.

———. 1998a "Blood and Tears." No. 280:15.

———. 1998b. "White Noise." No. 280:9–13.

Shore, Cris. 1990. *Italian Communism: The Escape from Leninism.* London: Pluto Press.

———. 1993a. "The Inventing of the 'People's Europe': Critical Approaches to European Community 'Culture Policy.'" *Man* n.s., 28 (4):779–800.

———. 1993b. "Ethnicity as Revolutionary Strategy: Communist Identity Construction in Italy." In *Inside European Identities*, edited by Sharon Macdonald, pp. 27–53. Providence: Berg.

Shore, Cris and Annabel Black. 1992. "The European Communities and the Construction of Europe." *Anthropology Today* 8:10–11.

Sibley, David. 1995. *Geographies of Exclusion: Society and Difference in the West.* London: Routledge.

Sigmund, Paul E. 1988. *St. Thomas Aquinas: On Politics and Ethics.* Translated by Paul Sigmund. New York: Norton.

Simmons, Harvey G. 1996. *The French National Front: The Extremist Challenge to Democracy.* Boulder, Colo.: Westview.

Skocpol, Theda. 1985. "Cultural Idioms and Political Ideologies in the Revolutionary Reconstruction of State Power: A Rejoinder to Sewell." *Journal of Modern History* 57:86–96.

Small, Stephen. 1994. *Racialised Barriers: The Black Experience in the United States and England in the 1980s.* London: Routledge.

Smart, Pamela G. 1997. "Sacred Modern: An Ethnography of an Art Museum." Ph.D. dissertation, Rice University.

Smith, Anthony. 1992. "National Identity and the Idea of European Unity." *International Affairs* 68:55–76.

Smith, Christian. 1991. *The Emergence of Liberation Theology: Radical Religion and Social Movement Theory.* Chicago: University of Chicago Press.

Smith, Gavin. 1999. *Confronting the Present: Towards a Politically Engaged Anthropology.* Oxford: Berg.

Sorel, Georges. 1950. *Reflections on Violence.* Glencoe, Ill.: Free Press.

Spinelli, Altiero. 1982. "Reform of Treaties and Achievement of European Union." Resolution adopted by the European Parliament. Luxemburg: European Parliament.

———. 1983. "Content of the Draft Treaty Establishing European Union." In *Altiero Spinelli: Speeches in the European Parliament, 1976–1986*, edited by Pier Virgilio Dastoli. Rome: C.S.F.

Spinelli, Altiero. *rapporteur*. 1984. "Draft Treaty Establishing European Union." Resolution adopted by the European Parliament. Luxemburg: European Parliament.

———. 1986. *Altiero Spinelli: Speeches in European Parliament, 1976–1986*, edited by Pier Virgilio Dastoli. Rome: C.S.F.

Sternhell, Zeev. 1983. *Ni droite, ni gauche: L'idéologie fasciste en France*. Paris: Seuil.

———. 1985. *Maurice Barrès et le nationalisme français*. Brussels: Editions Complexe.

———. 1987. "Fascism." In *The Blackwell Encyclopedia of Political Thought*, edited by David Miller, p. 148. Oxford: Blackwell.

———. 1996. *Neither Right nor Left: Fascist Ideology in France*. Translated by David Maisel. Princeton: Princeton University Press.

Sternhell, Zeev, with Mario Sznajder and Maia Asheri. 1994. *The Birth of Fascist Ideology: From Cultural Rebellion to Political Revolution*. Translated by David Maisel. Princeton: Princeton University Press.

Stolcke, Verena. 1995. "Talking Culture: New Boundaries, New Rhetorics of Exclusion in Europe." *Current Anthropology* 36:1–24.

Stoler, Ann Laura. 1995. *Race and the Education of Desire: Foucault's History of Sexuality and the Colonial Order of Things*. Durham, N.C.: Duke University Press.

———. 1997a. "Racial Histories and Their Regimes of Truth." *Political Power and Social Theory* 11:183–206.

———. 1997b. "On the Politics of Epistemologies." *Political Power and Social Theory* 11:247–55.

Strathern, Marilyn. 1992. *After Nature: English Kinship in the Late Twentieth Century*. Cambridge: Cambridge University Press.

Taguieff, Pierre-André. 1988. *La force du préjugé*. Paris: La Découverte.

———. 1989. "La metaphysique de Jean-Marie Le Pen." In *Le Front national à découvert*, edited by Nonna Mayer and Pascal Perrineau, pp. 173–94. Paris: Presses de la Fondation Nationale des Sciences Politiques.

———. 1991a. "The Doctrine of the National Front in France (1972–1989): A 'Revolutionary' Programme? Ideological Aspects of a National-Populist Mobilization." *New Political Science* 16–17: 29–70.

———. 1991b. *Face au racisme. Analyses, hypothèses, perspectives*. Vol. 2. Edited by Pierre-André Taguieff. Paris: La Découverte.

———. 1994. *Sur la Nouvelle Droite*. Paris: Descartes & Cie.

Taylor, Charles. 1994. *Multiculturalism: Examining the Politics of Recognition*. Princeton: Princeton University Press.

Taylor, Paul. 1991. "The European Community and the State: Assumptions, Theories and Propositions." *Review of International Studies* 17:109–25.

———. 1997. "Prospects for the European Union." In *New Challenges to the European Union: Policies and Policy-Making*, edited by Stelios Stavridis et al., pp. 13–41. Aldershot: Dartmouth.

Taylor, Stan. 1993. "The Radical Right in Britain." In *Encounters with the Contemporary Radical Right*, edited by Peter H. Merkl and Leonard Weinberg., pp. 165–84. Boulder, Colo.: Westview.

Thompson, E. P. 1966. *The Making of the English Working Class*. New York: Vintage.

———. 1977. *William Morris: Romantic to Revolutionary*. New York: Pantheon.

Thurlow, Richard C. 1974. "Ideology of Obsession on the Model of A. K. Chesterton." *Patterns of Prejudice* 8:23–29.

———. 1987. *Fascism in Britain: A History, 1918–1985*. Oxford: Blackwell.

Tindemans, Leo. 1972. *Regionalized Belgium: Transition from Nation-State to Multi-National State*. Unpublished document.

———. 1977. "European Union." In *European Yearbook*, edited by A. H. Robertson, pp. 23:1–93. The Hague: Martinus Nijhoff.

Toderov, Tzvetan. 1993. *On Human Diversity: Nationalism, Racism, and Exoticism in French Thought*. Cambridge: Harvard University Press.

Touraine, Alain. 1988. *Return of the Actor: Social Theory in Postindustrial Society*. Translated by Myrna Godzich. Minneapolis: University of Minnesota Press.

Townshed, Charles. 1993. *Making the Peace: Public Order and Public Security in Britain*. Oxford: Oxford University Press.

Tyndall, John. 1988. *The Eleventh Hour: A Call for British Rebirth*. Welling, Kent: Albion Press.

Vaughan, Michalina. 1991. "The Extreme Right in France: 'Lepénisme' or the Politics of Fear." In *Neo-Fascism in Europe*, edited by Luciano Cheles, Ronnie Ferguson and Michalina Vaughan, pp. 211–33. London: Longman.

Verdery, Katherine. 1996. *What Was Socialism, and What Comes Next?* Princeton: Princeton University Press.

Wacquant, Loïc. 1997. "For an Analytic of Racial Domination." *Political Power and Social Theory*. 11:221–34.

Webber, Francis. 1992. "From Eurocentrism to Euro-Racism," *Race and Class* 32:11–17.

Weber, Eugen. 1962. *L'Action française*. Paris: Stock.

———. 1964. *Varieties of Fascism*. New York: Van Nordstrand.

———. 1986. *France: Fin de Siècle*. Cambridge: Belknap Press at Harvard University Press.

———. 1991. "Nationalism, Socialism, and National Socialism." In *My France: Politics, Culture, Myth*, pp. 261–84. Cambridge: Harvard University Press.

Weidenfield, Werner, and Wolfgang Wessel. 1998. *Europe from A to Z: Guide to European Integration*. Brussels: Institut für Europäische Politik. European Commission.

Weiler, Joseph 1999. *The Constitution of Europe: "Do the New Clothes Have an Emperor?" and Other Essays on European Integration*. Cambridge: Cambridge University Press.

Werbner, Pnina. 1985. "The Organization of Giving and Ethnic Elites: Voluntary Associations amongst Manchester Pakistanis." *Ethnic and Racial Studies* 8:368–88.

———. 1990a. *The Migration Process*. Oxford: Berg.

———. 1990b. "Economic Rationality and Hierarchical Gift Economies: Value and Ranking among British Pakistanis." *Man* 25: 266–85.

Werbner, Pnina and Tariq Modood, eds. 1997. *Debating Cultural Hybridity: Multi-Cultural Identities and the Politics of Anti-Racism*. London: Zed Books.

Whitney, Craig R. 1997. "French Far-Rightist Guilty of Holocaust Slight." *New York Times*, December 27, 1997.

———. 1998. "Le Pen May be Charged for a Remark about the Holocaust." *New York Times* on the Web. October 7, 1998. (http://archives.nytimes.com/archives/).

Wieviorka, Michel. 1993. *Racisme et modernité*. Paris: La Découverte.

———. 1994. *Racisme et xénophobie en Europe*. Paris: La Découverte.

———. 1996. "Violence, Culture and Democracy: A European Perspective." *Public Culture* 8:329–54.

———. 1997. "Is It So Difficult to Be an Anti-Racist?" In *Debating Cultural Hybridity: Multi-Cultural Identities and the Politics of Anti-Racism*, edited by Pnina Werbner and Tariq Modood, pp. 139–53. London: Zed Books.

Williams, Raymond. 1977. *Marxism and Literature*. Oxford: Oxford University Press.

Willis, Paul. 1981. *Learning to Labour: How Working Class Kids Get Working Class Jobs*. New York: Columbia University Press.

Wilson, Thomas M., and M. Estellie Smith, eds. 1993. *Cultural Change and the New Europe: Perspectives on the European Community*. Boulder, Colo.: Westview.

Wolf, Eric R. 1999. *Envisioning Power: Ideologies of Dominance and Crisis*. Berkeley: University of California Press.

Wolfreys, Jim. 1993. "An Iron Hand in a Velvet Glove: The Programme of the French National Front." *Parliamentary Affairs* 46:415–29.

Wright, Susan. 1998. "The Politicization of Culture." *Anthropology Today* 14: 7–15.

Young, Michael, and Peter Willmott. 1957. *Family and Kinship in East London*. Harmondsworth: Penguin Books.

Zabusky, Stacia. 1995. *Launching Europe: An Ethnography on European Cooperation in Space Science*. Princeton: Princeton University Press.

Zorgbibe, Charles. 1993. *Histoire de la construction européenne*. Paris: Presses Universitaires de France.

# INDEX

Made in the USA
Monee, IL
12 February 2021